Grains for Every Season

Rethinking Our Way with Grains

JOSHUA McFADDEN

with Martha Holmberg

PHOTOGRAPHY BY AJ MEEKER,
ASHLEY MARTI, AND DAVID ALVARADO

ARTISAN BOOKS
New York, NY

Library of Congress Cataloging-in-Publication Data.

Names: McFadden, Joshua, author. | Holmberg, Martha, author.
Title: Grains for every season : rethinking our way with grains / Joshua McFadden
   with Martha Holmberg.
Description: New York, NY : Artisan, a division of Workman Publishing
   Company, Inc., [2021] | Includes index.
Identifiers: LCCN 2021004797 | ISBN 9781579659561 (hardcover)
Subjects: LCSH: Cooking (Cereals) | Cooking (Natural foods) | Grain. | LCGFT: Cookbooks.
Classification: LCC TX808 .M24 2021 | DDC 641.3/31—dc23
LC record available at https://lccn.loc.gov/2021004797

Design by Toni Tajima
Cover illustrations by Michael Hoeweler
Jacket photographs by AJ Meeker (front) and David Alvarado (inside)

Artisan books are available at special discounts when purchased in bulk for premiums and sales promotions as well as for fund-raising or educational use. Special editions or book excerpts also can be created to specification. For details, contact the Special Sales Director at the address below, or send an e-mail to specialmarkets@workman.com.

For speaking engagements, contact speakersbureau@workman.com.
Published by Artisan
A division of Workman Publishing Co., Inc.
225 Varick Street
New York, NY 10014-4381
artisanbooks.com

Artisan is a registered trademark of Workman Publishing Co., Inc.

Published simultaneously in Canada by Thomas Allen & Son, Limited

Printed in China

First printing, October 2021

10 9 8 7 6 5 4 3 2 1

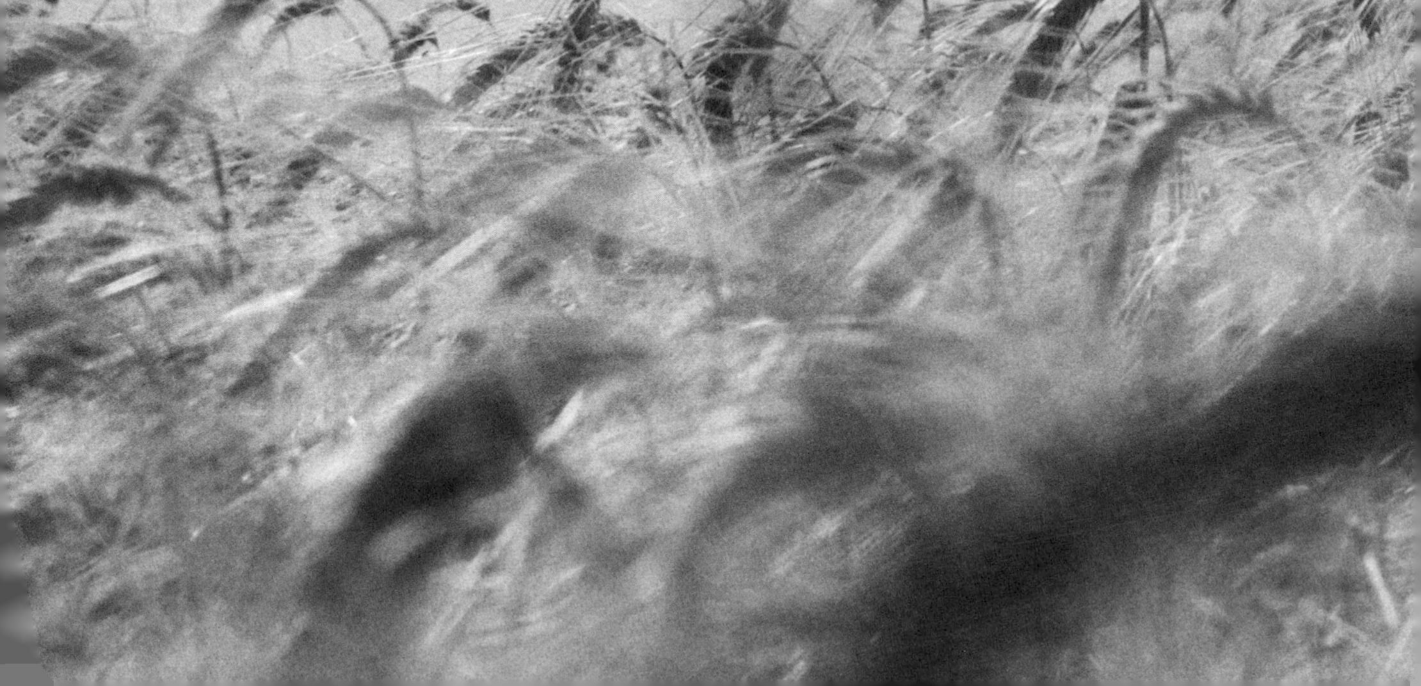

contents

Why I'm Excited about Cooking with Whole Grains and Hope You Are, Too

Like many good things in life, my appreciation of whole grains began in Italy. Farro was my first love. I was introduced to it when I cooked at the American Academy in Rome, a project started by Alice Waters. We would feature farro on our menus in a variety of ways, but especially as farrotto: toasted in oil and butter with aromatic vegetables and herbs, then slowly stirred with just enough broth to plump up the grains. In other words, risotto . . . but better. Chewier, denser texture, deeper flavor, starchy enough to be creamy but not mushy. I loved it.

Since those days in Rome, I have evolved into an eager whole-grain cook. As I write this book, I own three restaurants in Portland, Oregon—my flagship Italian restaurant Ava Gene's, its next-door-neighbor pizza place Cicoria, and Tusk, which features Middle Eastern flavors. I now incorporate not only farro into the dishes I cook at work and at home, but also its wheat-family cousins—spelt, freekeh, bulgur, wheat berries—along with other whole grains like barley, buckwheat, millet, quinoa, and more.

I wrote this cookbook because I want you to love whole grains as much as I do, and I want you to realize that it doesn't take a lot of effort to incorporate them into your cooking life. Even if you're not yet familiar with whole grains, you likely already crave their flavors and textures—nutty, toasty, chewy, all easy to love.

The world of grains is vast, and in this book I'm not attempting to be encyclopedic, just useful and inspirational, so I've limited the information and recipes to the grains that I cook with the most frequently . . . which is a lot! And for any whole grains that I didn't include, for example, amaranth or sorghum, it's only because I haven't yet had the pleasure of getting to know them well enough.

I've organized the book into chapters by individual grain, arranged in alphabetical order from barley to wild rice. In each section, you'll find recipes that use the grain itself and sometimes recipes using flour milled from that grain as well. So unlike some cookbooks, in which appetizers are at the front and desserts are at the back, this book distributes all types of dishes throughout the chapters. If you'd like to see a complete list of the recipes by their role in a meal, however, check out the list on page 347. Throughout the book, you'll find special foldout features showing you how to create some of the easiest seasonal meals using whole grains: grain bowls, stir-fries, pilafs, and pizzas. These special sections share additional recipes, teach you how to assemble the dishes, and give you six seasonal ingredient combinations to get you on your way to deliciousness.

The first pages of the book cover basic techniques for whole grains and flours, from storing to cooking to ideas for keeping prepared grains handy in your fridge or freezer, ready to transform into a meal in minutes. I also give detailed cooking instructions in each recipe, so no need to flip back and forth, but I'm hoping the basics section will be a useful reference for cooking beyond the covers of this book.

My recipes feature whole grains as you would expect, in salads and grain bowls, but also in unexpected ways—buckwheat in place of ground pork in a Thai-influenced larb-style salad (see Buckwheat, Lime, and Herb Salad, Larb Style, page 75), quinoa as a crunchy pop in tempura-style batter for fried veggies, and millet for more texture in a buttery, crumbly streusel topping on Roasted Butternut Squash Maple Millet Bread (page 122).

The recipes in this book also span the seasons. While the grains themselves are appropriate any time of year, the recipes run the range from bright and refreshing to cozy and comforting. Quinoa and Watermelon Salad with Pistachios and Spicy Pickled Peppers (page 147) is a perfect midsummer dinner on the deck (don't forget the pink wine), while Quinoa and Chicken Soup with French Lentils and Herbs (page 151) will warm you after a chilly afternoon of raking autumn leaves, or just an afternoon on the couch with a book and a blanket.

Flavor First, but Dang, Whole Grains Are Nutritious

I am driven by flavor in everything I do, so I use whole grains and whole-grain flours in my recipes first and foremost because they are delicious.

But the fact that whole grains are incredibly nutritious is a huge bonus. Most people know that whole-grain foods contain more fiber because they include the bran, which is of course important in our diets, but grains are so much more than bran delivery vehicles. They contain significant amounts of vitamins and minerals and good things like antioxidants and other phytochemicals, about which science is learning more and liking more. I've outlined the key nutrients for each grain in the profile at the beginning of each section, so take a look. I also indicate which grains are gluten-free.

You Already Know How to Cook with Whole Grains

The cooking techniques you'll use in grain dishes are simple—you'll basically just cook the grains in a liquid until they are plump and tender. The details make the difference: whether you toast first, add aromatics such as garlic and rosemary, or cook in water, broth, or even luxurious coconut milk, as in Millet Morning Porridge with Coconut Milk and Quick Mango "Jam" (page 117).

You can't mess them up; most whole grains are highly adaptable. Their mild flavors partner happily with pretty much any ingredient, as is plainly shown by the fact that in one chapter I've got a recipe for farro with squid and another for a brown-butter honey cake made with farro flour. That's range! Whole grains can play a center-of-the-plate role, as in Shrimp Fried Freekeh with Spring Vegetables (page 213), because they are nicely filling and substantial. Or they can be a smaller player, just bringing a special textural note perhaps, as in the barley that gives body to Super Grain and Veggie Burgers (page 43). Just about every recipe in this book calls for kosher salt, but please note that not all kosher salts are the same. We used Diamond Crystal brand (in the red box, widely available at many grocery stores), which has less salt per tablespoon than most other brands, so if you use a different brand, you'll want to adjust the quantities a bit. Learn more on page 324.

A Little "Refinement" Is Okay

You'll notice that many of the baked goods and pastas use whole-grain flour but also incorporate some white flour, mostly unbleached all-purpose but also tipo "00" (a finely milled Italian flour perfect for pasta) and white bread flour. White flour comes from wheat that has been refined—the bran and germ polished off, leaving just the starchy endosperm. White flour can be used to create wonderful things, but it doesn't offer much nutrition, and of course it has a much more neutral flavor than flours from whole grains.

I add white flour in many of these recipes nonetheless, because 100 percent whole-grain flour can be tricky for the uninitiated, especially when making food that needs a specific texture. The main challenge comes from gluten (a combination of two proteins, glutenin and gliadin), which is the substance that makes bread crusty on the outside and tender on the inside, produces the satisfying crunch of a cracker, gives pasta its seductive chewy texture . . . all the good things. (No, I'm not talking about whether gluten is good for your health; that's a different discussion.) But some whole-grain flours (such as buckwheat flour) don't contain any gluten, so it's difficult to create the structure that will allow bread to rise and pizza to stretch and tagliatelle to bounce. Other whole-grain flours, such as your basic whole wheat, contain gluten but also bran and germ, which change the texture and provide challenges as well.

Many cooks create excellent baked goods with 100 percent whole-grain flours. At my restaurants, for example, we use 100 percent whole wheat flour for our pastas. But good results come with experience and experimentation. For the purposes of this book, and for much of the food that I cook and serve at my restaurants, I use whatever combination of whole-grain and white flour gives me the best flavor and texture.

As you become more familiar with the recipes in this book, you should feel free to experiment with the ratios of whole-grain to white flour and nudge things closer to all whole-grain, if you like.

Help Nurture the Local Grain Economy

No matter what grain or flour you're using, what's most important is that it be good. Good as in sustainably grown, carefully harvested, milled with craft and care, and freshly cooked up into something delicious as soon as possible.

There's a whole-grain revolution taking place in this country, and if you haven't yet noticed it, you will soon, as grain farmers move away from the commodity model, in which the priorities are a high yield per acre and selling on the global market.

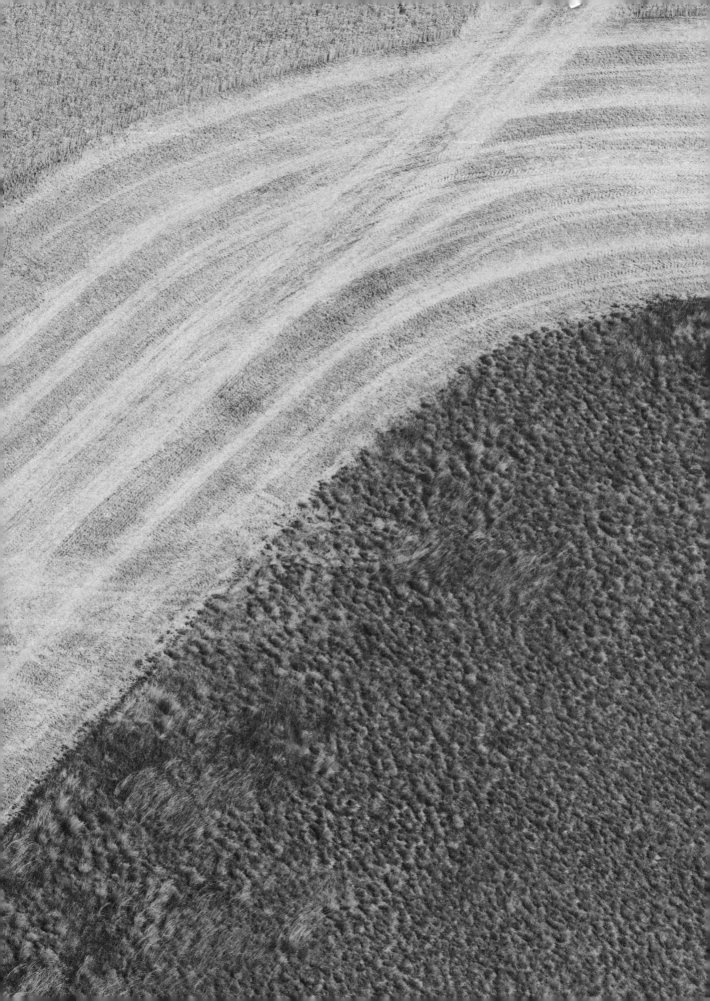

Much like the farm-to-table movement that has blossomed over the last few decades, grain farmers are trying to keep things local, too, selling to local businesses and directly to consumers through farmers' markets and online outlets. These passionate farmers are making planting choices with a lot more in mind than just the price of wheat on the Chicago Board of Trade exchange this season.

Along with looking for ways to preserve and nourish their soils, this new breed of grain farmer keeps the end user in mind, learning what bakers, chefs, and consumers want to cook. They are discovering heritage varieties—sometimes called "landrace" grains—that are way more delicious and full of character than a mass-market grain, and often more nutritious.

But producing amazing food like this is hard work! We need to support the farmers who are devoting their lives to our culinary happiness, so I encourage you to explore your own local grain economy. Look for vendors at your farmers' market. Ask your favorite bakeries where their flours come from. Many of these producers will ship their products, if you can't find anyone in your own community. Farm-to-table grains can become as common as locally grown peaches and tomatoes if we, as consumers, will support the effort.

I've created a list of producers that I use and admire (see page 332), to serve as a resource for you and to give them a shout-out.

My Ongoing Whole-Grain Journey

I'd like to acknowledge some individuals who have been along with me on my whole-grain adventure ride over the past few years. They have fueled my excitement for whole grains, taught me so much, and helped me push the boundaries with whole grains and whole-grain flours. JoMarie Pitino changed the entire pasta program at Ava Gene's, and it was fun to be a part of that passion. Nora Mace has always found a perfect balance of whole-grain flours in pastries, baked goods, and bread at Tusk and Ava Gene's. Nora helped with several of the recipes in this book and supported the idea throughout development. Daniel Green, with whom I worked at Cicoria and Ava Gene's, also has a positive obsession with whole grains and whole-grain flours. Our pizza at Cicoria and several recipes in this book would not exist if not for him.

In addition to hanging out with interesting food people, one of the privileges of being a restaurant chef is having access to innovations in farming. I get to taste new—or more likely old, as in heirloom—vegetables that a farmer may be experimenting with this season, and I can play with them in my own kitchen and then see how my customers like them. Sometimes I even visit these passionate growers at their farms, where I can stand among the crops growing in the fields. In the past, that usually meant rows of gorgeous emerald kale or rainbow-colored chard, or even groves of elegant olive trees at Albert Katz's olive oil operation in California (see Sources, page 332). But now, in addition to vegetables, I'm seeing those proverbial amber waves of grain in my local farm region, and I'm finding local grain products not just from my restaurant vendors but at grocery stores, too. The world is rediscovering whole-grain cooking, looking to the past and around the world for interesting varieties, updating those traditions with the exciting flavors and dishes that we love to eat nowadays. I find it all inspiring, which is why I've shared it with you in this book. I hope it provides plenty of delicious inspiration to launch you on your own whole-grain adventure.

What *Is* a Grain, Anyway?

A whole grain is one of nature's many ingenious creations: compact, sturdy, self-sufficient, and—fortunately for us animals—delicious and nutritious.

The word "grain" is often defined as a seed from a cereal crop . . . and a cereal is one of several types of grasses that are cultivated by humans in order to get those seeds. (Here's a fun fact: The word "cereal" comes from Ceres, the Roman goddess of the harvest. She's so pretty! And nice! No lightning bolts or punishments, just abundance. Her Greek name is Demeter, which is the name of one of the main certifying bodies for biodynamic agriculture.)

True cereal grains are members of the Poaceae botanical family and include barley, corn, millet, oats, rice, rye, sorghum, and wheat. Within each of those are subvarieties, especially within the wheat family, which includes einkorn, farro (also called emmer), freekeh, Kamut, and spelt.

But there are also things called pseudo-grains, which include amaranth, buckwheat, and—the biggie these days—quinoa. These pseudo-grains belong to different botanical families, but for our purposes of being wholesome and delicious, we will consider them grains. And don't forget wild rice! Not in the same family as rice, and with the wonderful Latin name *Zizania aquatica* (among a few others). All this to say that the world of whole grains is wide and has grown even wider in recent years, as growers and eaters rediscover ancient grain varieties.

In this book, I'm not taking a comprehensive approach; I'm including recipes for the grains that I think are the most versatile (and delicious) in the kitchen, which means you won't see a teff or sorghum recipe. But that doesn't mean you couldn't use those or other grains in some of my recipes. My goal is to get you as a home cook so comfortable with and excited by whole grains that you learn to incorporate them into all kinds of daily cooking, from a breakfast muesli to fresh seasonal salads for lunch to a chicken and grain dish for dinner to a pan of brownies to take to a school event.

In order to understand both the nutritional benefits and cooking challenges of whole grains, it's helpful to look at a single grain. The specific components and quantities of vitamins and minerals, fiber, and other compounds vary among grains, but all grains have the same structure.

What's not pictured here is the **hull**, the tough outer coating that protects the grain when it's out in the fields living a plant's life. The hull isn't edible and needs to be removed, either during harvesting or by some sort of abrasion process after harvest. This is where we get to bring in the old-timey terms "threshing" and "winnowing."

Threshing is where the grains are whomped somehow to crack and loosen the hulls. Winnowing is the process that blows away the loosened hulls (now known as the chaff), leaving just the edible grain behind. Some grains are bred to have hulls that are light and papery, and that loosen and fall off easily, so no actual threshing is required. These are (rather poetically) called "naked" grains. Others have hulls that cling to the grain and need more convincing before releasing; these are "covered" grains.

The **bran** layer envelops the entire grain and provides protection for the grain, and lots of healthy fiber, plus some B vitamins and antioxidants, for us.

The **endosperm** is the largest part of the grain, and it's the energy source for the grain, were it to grow into an actual plant. The endosperm contains some proteins, vitamins, and minerals, but it's mostly carbohydrates—starch.

The **germ** is essentially the embryo of the plant (think of the word "germinate"), the part that would grow into another plant, being fed by the endosperm. The germ contains proteins, B vitamins, minerals, and healthy fats. These fats, however, are what can cause a whole grain to go rancid easily, so they are a benefit but one that must be managed.

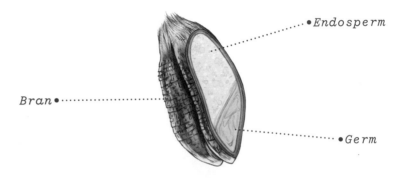

When all these components are intact, that grain is a "whole" grain. When any of them are removed, the grain becomes "refined," which isn't always a terrible thing, but any sort of refinement does impact the nutritional value of the grain, along with its flavor and cooking characteristics.

One way a grain gets refined is by removing all or part of the bran. Some varieties of grains, such as barley and farro, have hard hulls that need heavy abrasion to remove them, and unfortunately that action can remove some of the bran as well. This brings us to the terminology related to hulls, which needs some sorting out: The term "hulled" means the hulls have been removed by a process that leaves all of the bran, and "hulless" means the grain was grown with a hull that falls off easily. (Could we come up with better terms? This reminds me of the "boned" vs. "boneless" chicken dilemma.)

"Pearled" means the bran has been polished off; "semipearled" means some bran is left intact. A pearled grain therefore contains fewer nutrients but takes less time to cook and will cook up a bit more tender and fluffy than one with the bran intact.

le Grain Foods for Every Meal of the Day®

HOLE GRAINS

Whole-Grain Basics and Techniques

Depending on what dish you're making, your grain may need slightly customized treatment, but the following general information and techniques apply to all the grains in this book.

▷▷ *Storage*

The fats in the germ of a whole grain can go rancid fairly easily at room temperature—especially if the grain has been cracked, flaked, rolled, or milled into a flour or meal—so you want your grains to stay as cool and dry as possible, and definitely out of direct sunlight. While it would be ideal to keep everything in the fridge or freezer, that's not practical . . . unless you don't have many grains and/or have massive appliances!

A good compromise is to store whole grains in a jar or other sealed container (as opposed to just leaving them in their bag) in the pantry for no longer than six months.

If you live in a hot or humid climate, or if you're only reaching for those grains every couple of months, go ahead and freeze them from the start, either in a freezer container or in their original packaging sealed inside a freezer bag. If you have a vacuum sealer, now is the time to deploy it; freeze the grains in portion sizes that you're likely to use in one recipe.

However you contain your grains, be sure to label with the grain type and the date you freeze it (masking tape and a Sharpie work well for this). Farro and barley can look maddeningly similar without any clues.

When well frozen, all uncooked whole grains will be fine for a year, possibly more.

▷▷ *Rinsing*

To me, rinsing grains is a bit like scalding milk—you'll see it in some recipes, but it feels like a step left over from an older time. Nowadays, almost all grains, whether produced domestically or elsewhere, are clean and well sorted, so it's not like you're rinsing off the dust from a long wagon-train transport. But rinsing won't hurt anything, so feel free to do it, unless you plan to toast the grains. In that case, the moisture will interfere with proper toasting, especially if you're toasting in oil (wet grains + hot oil = not a safe situation).

▷▷ *Soaking*

Many cooks like to soak their grains for a few hours or overnight as a way to speed cooking, but I'm not one of them. While a soak of at least eight and up to twenty-four hours helps the bran layer soften so that liquid and flavorings can penetrate more easily during cooking, I've found that the cooking time is only cut by ten minutes or so, not enough time savings for me to go through the (slight) hassle of soaking. I *do* soak brown rice for the Slow-Roasted Chicken Buried in Gingery Brown Rice (page 66), however, because I've found that it helps the rice and chicken cook at the right rate. But just because I don't soak doesn't mean you shouldn't try it for yourself. I encourage anything that gets you to cook whole grains more often!

▷▷ *Toasting*

I love to toast my grains before I cook them when I want to deepen the flavor. Toasting can also help keep the individual grains nice and separate once they're cooked. The term "toasting" is a catchall, because sometimes I toast with oil, sometimes without, either in the oven on a sheet pan or on the stovetop in a skillet. Here are my basic methods.

DRY-TOAST IN THE OVEN: Heat the oven to 350°F (175°C). Spread the grain on a sheet pan and bake until lightly golden and nutty smelling, about 10 minutes. Transfer to a plate or tray so it stops cooking and cools quickly.

DRY-TOAST IN A SKILLET: Heat a large skillet over medium-high heat, pour in the raw grains, and cook, stirring and shaking the pan frequently to move the grains around so they cook evenly. Toast until the grains are slightly darker and smell nutty and toasty; this usually takes 3 to 5 minutes. Transfer to a plate or tray so the grains stop cooking and cool quickly.

SKILLET-TOAST WITH OIL: Pour a small glug of olive oil into a heavy medium skillet over medium heat, add the grain, and cook, stirring frequently, until slightly darker and

smelling toasty. Take your time, because you don't want it to get too dark, but you do want it thoroughly toasted. It should take 5 to 7 minutes, but start tasting around 4 minutes. Transfer to a plate or tray so they stop cooking and cool quickly.

SKILLET-TOAST WITH OIL AND AROMATICS: Pour a small glug of olive oil into a large skillet over medium heat and add a clove or two of smashed garlic and a pinch of dried chile flakes.

Cook slowly until the garlic is getting soft, fragrant, and nicely golden brown, about 3 minutes. Add the grain and cook over medium heat, stirring constantly so the grains toast evenly, until they have darkened slightly and are fragrant, 5 to 7 minutes. Watch the garlic—if it looks or smells at risk of burning, scoop it out and then return to the grains as you assemble your recipe. And if it has in fact burned, discard it and the cooking oil.

▸▸ *Cooking*

Grains may be cooked a number of ways, all of which involve hydrating the hard kernels into something nicely chewy-tender. The method you use may depend on what your recipe recommends or simply what you feel like doing. I use all of the following methods, mostly based on my mood of the moment or what else is happening in the kitchen. For certain grains, however, I prefer the boil-like-pasta method (see page 28); I have indicated this in each relevant grain section.

ABSORPTION METHOD: This is the method that you most likely use to cook white rice: You combine a measured amount of grain with a measured amount of liquid, bring to a boil, cover, and simmer until all the liquid is absorbed and the rice is properly cooked, fluffy, and tender. The method works well for most whole grains, though it requires a bit of finessing. Unlike mass-produced refined rice, whole grains can vary from producer to producer, even batch to batch, in the amount of liquid they need to become tender and fully cooked, so you'll need to pay attention as you cook, adding a splash more here or

draining off a bit of excess liquid there.

I give ratios of grain to liquid in individual grain sections, but those are just guidelines. Once you dial in a good ratio for the batch of grains currently in your pantry, be sure to mark it on the bag or tape it to the inside of your cupboard door.

Here are the steps for the absorption method: Put your measured grain (toasted or untoasted) and water or broth in a heavy-bottomed pot with the measured salt (and butter, if using). Cover and bring to a boil—keep a vigilant eye so the water doesn't boil over. Once boiling,

immediately adjust the heat so it simmers nicely when covered again. Simmer like this until the grains are tender and cooked through but not mushy (unless you're making porridge); start checking about 5 minutes before the beginning of the suggested time range. (Note that you don't want to stir the grains after the first few seconds of simmering, or you'll bring out the starch and make the grains stickier or more porridge-y. Which is great for a porridge, but not for fluffy, separate grains.)

If the grains seem hard or chalky in the middle but you don't see any more liquid, add a couple of tablespoons and resume; repeat as needed. Conversely, if the grains are cooked to your liking but you can still see liquid around the bottom of the pan, dump everything into a big sieve and tap to remove excess liquid.

In either case, once the grains are cooked and any liquid has been drained off, cover the pot again and let it sit off the heat for about 5 minutes, which will let everything equilibrate. Fluff with a fork, and away you go.

An advantage to the absorption method over the "boil like pasta" method (see below) is that you can use a flavored liquid, such as broth, instead of just water.

PILAF METHOD: A step beyond simple absorption is what's sometimes called the "pilaf" method. This is where you start by sautéing some finely chopped onion, shallot, carrot, or other aromatic vegetables (called a mirepoix, pronounced MEER-pwah) in oil or butter, then add the grain and sauté for a few minutes, as with the "skillet-toast with oil" method (see page 26). Once the grains are shiny and just slightly darker, add your measured liquid, cover, and continue with the absorption method.

BOIL-LIKE-PASTA METHOD: Bring a large amount of water to a boil in a large saucepan (use at least four times as much water as grain, with plenty more room in the saucepan to allow for boiling up), add salt, and add the grains. Adjust the heat so the water boils but isn't

exploding over the rim of the pan. Boil, uncovered, until the grains are cooked to your liking; again, start checking about 5 minutes before the lower end of the time range, just so you don't miss your target. When the grains are cooked to your liking, drain well, return the grains to the pan, cover, and let rest for 5 minutes, then fluff with a fork.

You won't want to use broth in the boil-like-pasta method because you'll pour some off, which would be wasteful.

For all these methods, remember that the grains will continue to cook a bit until you've taken them out of the pan, so think "just past al dente."

▷▶ *Popping Grains*

While dried corn is the popping standout among grains, most other grains can be popped to transform them from hard, dense kernels into something lighter, crunchier, and toastier in flavor. The idea is to subject the grain to a blast of heat so that the moisture held within expands instantly, puffing the kernel as the starchy interior swells and bursts. Sorghum pops the way corn does, displaying a white puffy interior, though the kernels themselves are tiny compared to popped corn. Other grains with which I have had popping success are brown rice, wild rice, barley, and buckwheat. The final result isn't light and fluffy-puffy like popcorn, but I love the texture and sometimes use the same grain two ways in a dish—cooked in liquid and popped—with the popped version as a final textural accent.

Here's how I pop grains: Heat a (dry) heavy-bottomed pot or deep heavy skillet over high heat until just about smoking. Pour in enough grains to lightly cover the surface of the pan in a single layer and immediately shake the pan to move the grains around. You should hear some cracking and popping and you'll see the grains become slightly larger. Unlike popcorn, most other grains won't actually hop out of the pan, but if yours seem lively, go ahead and cover the pan to avoid any surprises. Tip the grains onto a plate or tray as soon as most have popped to let them cool. You can use as is or season with some salt and any popcorn seasonings (see page 99).

A plain whole grain is so crazy nutritious, it's hard to imagine making it even more so, but the simple technique of sprouting can do just that. Sprouting means creating conditions that send a message to the grain kernel that it's time to produce a sprout so it can plant itself in the soil and get started making more rye or farro. We cleverly interrupt that process as soon as the kernel cracks open and a tiny sprout appears, and then we eat the sprouted grain much as we would an unsprouted one.

So why go through this process? Nutrition is a big reason. Sprouting breaks down some of the grain's starch, and also breaks down phytate, a form of phytic acid that can impede absorption by our bodies of some vitamins and minerals. I also like the flavor and texture of sprouted grains. To me, they taste just a bit sweeter and richer.

Here's how I sprout grains:
First, make sure your grains are totally whole—not rolled, pearled, or hulled, please. Rinse the grains in cool water, then transfer to a bowl, cover with cool water, and soak overnight.

Drain, rinse again, and drain thoroughly. Transfer to a sterilized jar that is spacious enough for the grains to swell up; ½ cup (about 100 g) grains in a quart jar gives you plenty of room. Cover the mouth of the jar with a double layer of cheesecloth secured by a rubber band (or use a nifty perforated sprouting lid). Tip the jar so it's upside down at an angle and place in a bowl or other position so that it stays secure. You want air to enter the jar through the cheesecloth and the moisture to drip out (that's why a bowl is a good idea). Set the jar in a cool place; between 68° and 75°F (24° and 20°C) is perfect.

Every 12 hours, rinse and drain the grains again. You can keep them in the jar and just pour the water through the cheesecloth or perforated lid. Check the grains after 24 hours to look for little "tails" emerging; it may take a few days before sprouting begins.

Once the sprouts are about as long as the grain itself, they are ready. You're not trying to make bean sprouts here; the grain kernel is still the main player. Rinse the sprouted grains, drain really well, and store in the refrigerator up to three days. I use them in all types of dishes, and you should, too. I don't list sprouting as a separate step in the recipes in this book—that's a bit too much advance planning!— but know that just about any of these dishes would be excellent with sprouted grains. To be perfectly safe, however, you should only eat the sprouted grains after cooking, to reduce any risk of foodborne illness.

AIM FOR ACCURACY, WHICHEVER MEASURING METHOD YOU USE

A digital scale is one of the best investments a home cook can make. Not only does weighing ingredients give more accurate and consistent results, particularly when it comes to baking, but it's actually easier and less messy, too.

To get an accurate measure of dry ingredients for baking, put a mixing bowl on the scale and set the scale to zero (tare), then add flour, tare the scale again, and add the next ingredient. You eliminate the need for measuring cups and cut down on the number of dishes to wash. This does require your recipe to offer weight measurements, not just volume, such as cups or tablespoons. In this book, we're using both systems—volume and weight. The weights will often be in metric, but kitchen scales allow you to toggle between US and metric, so even if you're not familiar with the metric system you can easily use it. Once you get comfortable with metric, I think you'll love it—the units of measure are so much more logical and easy to scale up or down than our arcane US system!

So what's wrong with a measuring cup? For liquid ingredients, measuring cups work brilliantly. Liquids flow into a cup measure pretty much the same way every time. Your measure of chicken broth will be close enough to my measure of chicken broth

(though even in this case, measuring cups can be marked slightly inaccurately, unless you're using scientific equipment). But because dry ingredients like flour are so easily compressed and things such as chopped nuts can settle differently in a measuring cup, volume measures can vary dramatically, which makes getting a consistent, accurate measure using measuring cups a challenge.

If you don't have a scale (really, you should get one), how you measure can make all the difference. For best results with measuring flour by volume, I recommend the spoon-and-sweep method. First, stir the flour with a spoon to aerate it, spoon it into a measuring cup until it's overflowing, and level off the top with a knife. A cup of flour measured this way should weigh about 4¼ ounces or 120 grams. On the other hand, if you were to dip that same measuring cup into the bag of flour and drag it through the flour like a scoop, *then* sweep off the top, you would end up with a much heavier cup (and more flour than intended). Also, though I use this spoon-and-sweep method of volume measurement for all the flours in this book, there may still be slight weight differences between flours, depending on the mill, the amount of humidity in your environment, and other factors that can't be controlled in a cookbook!

Cooked grain can be refrigerated for up to five days, and nothing is more convenient than having a batch of cooked quinoa, millet, or barley ready to transform into dinner in an instant.

IN THE FRIDGE: Store the cooked grains tightly covered. Most grains get a little stiff when they're cold, because their starches tighten up, so to use them in a dish where they won't be cooked again, loosen them up by zapping them for a few seconds in a microwave or steaming in a covered pot with a splash of water. For something like a salad, just let the grains come to room temperature.

IN THE FREEZER: To freeze, make sure your cooked grains are completely cool. Measure out portions (1 cup, 2 cups, or more if you cook large batches); put into freezer bags; and label with the grain type, amount, how it was cooked (in water or with flavorings such as broth or bay leaf), and the date you cooked and froze it. Flatten out the grains to make a slim package, which will help the grains freeze faster. Freezing the grains this way also makes it easy to just break off a portion if you don't want to use the whole amount at one time.

To use, thaw overnight in the fridge, or steam or microwave the frozen grain until thawed. If adding to a hot dish such as a soup or stew, go ahead and drop in the frozen grains, then proceed with the recipe.

WILD RICE

HOSHIGAKI

WILD + BROWN
rice

SUPER GRAIN MIX

BUCKWHEA

Barley

Barley

Hordeum vulgare

▸ CONTAINS GLUTEN ◂

•▷ **Why I love it:** Barley was my gateway grain. I first ate it as a kid as I slurped down a hot bowl of Campbell's Beef with Vegetables and Barley soup. What's in those cans does not compare to the nutritious locally grown barley I eat now, but my ten-year-old self thought it was delicious.

•▷ **What it tastes like:** Maybe thanks to Campbell's, barley is fairly familiar to most of us. It's on the sweet side of nutty with a texture that's pleasantly firm and chewy and the tiniest bit slippery, with no trace of chalkiness. The flavor is fairly neutral, making barley extremely versatile.

•▷ **Common forms:** Hulled, also called hulless, has had the tough outer hull removed (with some varieties, the hull falls off during harvest: with others, it's abraded off mechanically), but the bran is still (mostly) intact. Pearled (or pearl) barley is most common. It's not technically a whole grain, as some or all of the bran has been "pearled" or polished off, so it isn't as nutritious as hulled, but it still is plenty healthful, and it cooks much more quickly. Quick-cooking barley is pearl barley that has been partially cooked, rolled into flakes (sort of the way oatmeal is), and dried.

•▷ **Favorite ways to prepare it:** Because barley holds its shape so nicely, it's excellent in soups and stews as well as in salads, where it drinks up the dressing without turning mushy. Hulled is a good choice for salads and other dishes in which you want the barley grains to stay separate and be chewy, while pearled barley absorbs more water and swells more, releasing a bit of starch, providing creaminess to your dish, meaning it's a good choice for barley "risotto."

•▷ **How it's good for you:** Barley is super nutritious and boasts one of the highest amounts of fiber of all whole cereal grains, including a special type of fiber (a soluble fiber called beta-glucan, also found in oats) that helps control blood sugar and reduces the risk of heart disease. Barley has also been shown to reduce blood pressure and significantly lower total cholesterol. Even better: That beta-glucan fiber is found within the entire barley grain, not just the bran layer, as with some other grains. So even refined barley contains some of this good stuff.

Details

→ 1 cup uncooked barley weighs 7 ounces (200 g).

→ Use 3 parts liquid to 1 part barley, as a rule of thumb, for the absorption method (page 27).

→ Cook quick-cooking barley for 10 to 20 minutes; pearled for 20 to 30 minutes; hulled for 45 to 60 minutes.

→ 1 cup (200 g) uncooked barley yields 3½ cups (600 g) cooked.

→ 1 cup barley flour weighs 4¼ ounces (120 g).

Barley Salad with Beets, Plums, and Pistachios

1 cup (200 g) uncooked barley, pearled or hulled

3 cups (720 ml) water

1 bay leaf

1 dried red chile, such as chile de árbol

Kosher salt

Extra-virgin olive oil

8 ounces (225 g) red or yellow beets

3 tablespoons red wine vinegar or sherry vinegar

Freshly ground black pepper

8 ounces (225 g) red or yellow plums, pitted

4 scallions, trimmed (including ½ inch/1.5 cm off the green tops), sliced on a sharp angle, soaked in ice water for 20 minutes, and well drained

½ cup (60 g) roasted pistachios, roughly chopped

Dried chile flakes

Small handful torn fresh mint and/or flat-leaf parsley leaves

This is a simple and perfect grain salad that we make every year at my restaurant when we have luscious local plums. It's an example of why you'll be smart to have cooked barley in your fridge. Salads like this can be made with any combination of vegetables you have on hand (and any cooked grain, for that matter), so use this one as a template for your seasonal favorites. Don't be shy with the pistachios, which add not only incredible flavor and crunch but a nice pop of color contrast, too. —**Serves 4**

Heat the oven to 375°F (190°C).

Put the barley, water, bay leaf, dried chile, and 1 teaspoon salt in a small saucepan with a lid. Bring to a boil, then quickly reduce the heat to a simmer. Cover and cook until the barley is tender and all the water has been absorbed, 45 to 60 minutes for hulled barley, about 30 minutes for pearled barley. If the barley is tender but there's liquid left, just drain it off; if the water has been absorbed but the barley isn't fully tender, add a few tablespoons more water and keep cooking until tender.

When the barley is ready, drain well and discard the bay leaf and chile. Toss the barley with a nice glug of olive oil and spread onto a tray so the grains are separate. Cool completely at room temperature.

Meanwhile, arrange the beets in a baking dish in a single layer. Season with salt and pour ¼ cup (60 ml) water into the dish. Cover tightly with foil, transfer to the oven, and steam-roast until the beets are tender when pierced with a knife. Depending on the size and density of the beets, this could take between 30 minutes and 1 hour.

When the beets are tender, let them cool until you can handle them, then rub or pare away the skins. Cut the beets into bite-size chunks, pile into a bowl, and toss with the vinegar, ½ teaspoon salt, and many twists of black pepper. Let the beets sit a minute to absorb the vinegar, then drizzle on some olive oil and toss again.

Cut the plums into the same size chunks as the beets and add to the bowl, along with the scallions, pistachios, barley, and a pinch of chile flakes.

Toss everything again gently, so you don't smash the plums. Taste and season with more vinegar, salt, black pepper, chile flakes, or olive oil—you want to get a nice sweet/salty/spicy thing going. Shower with the fresh herbs and serve right away, at cool room temperature.

Variation

Skip the beets, double the plums, and use about 1 cup (150 g) fresh red currants. Use shiso instead of mint or parsley.

Lightly Curried Lamb, Cabbage, and Barley Soup

Extra-virgin olive oil

3 pounds (1.35 kg) meaty lamb
shanks

Kosher salt and freshly
ground black pepper

1 cup (240 ml) dry white wine

2 quarts (2 liters) chicken
broth, homemade
(page 311) or low-sodium
store-bought

1 large leek, white and light-
green parts only, thinly
sliced and well rinsed

One 5-inch (12.5 cm) sprig
rosemary, or ½ teaspoon
dried

Three or four 4-inch (10 cm)
sprigs thyme, or ½ teaspoon
dried

5 garlic cloves, smashed and
peeled

2 tablespoons mild or hot
curry powder

1 cup (200 g) pearled barley

4 cups very thinly sliced white
or savoy cabbage (about
225 g)

1 large potato (I like Yukon
Gold), cut into 1-inch
(2.5 cm) cubes

I love the way the barley absorbs the warm spices of curry powder. I prefer a mild, sweet curry, but if you like more spicy heat, use a hot curry mix. The barley also absorbs liquid as it sits, so when serving leftovers (which will be even better than the soup is on the first day), you may need to add more broth or water. The soup freezes nicely, so think about stashing a few cups for later. —**Makes 3 quarts (3 liters), serves 8**

Heat a glug of olive oil over medium-high heat in a pot that's large enough to hold the lamb shanks. Season the lamb shanks with salt and pepper, add them to the pot, and brown them on all sides, taking your time to get a nice bit of color, about 10 minutes total. Reduce the heat if the lamb seems to be getting too brown too fast.

Pour in the wine and simmer until the wine has reduced to about ½ cup (120 ml), then add the broth. Adjust the heat to a lively simmer, cover, and cook, until the lamb is very tender and literally falling off the bone. Make sure you're not actually boiling the shanks, which could toughen the meat. Depending on the size and density of your lamb shanks, this could take 1 to 3 hours. When the lamb is cooked, remove it from the broth, let cool, then pull the meat from the bones. Cut or pull the meat into bite-size pieces. Skim any visible fat off the broth.

Heat 2 tablespoons olive oil in a large pot or Dutch oven over medium heat. Add the leek, a pinch of salt, a few twists of pepper, and the sprigs of rosemary and thyme. Cook, stirring frequently, until the leek starts to soften and become fragrant—but not at all browned— about 3 minutes. Add the garlic and curry powder and cook for another minute or so, until the garlic is soft but not browned.

Add the skimmed lamb broth and the barley to the leeks and simmer for 10 minutes. Add the cabbage and potato and cook until the cabbage is very tender and sweet and the potato and barley are fully tender when you take a bite, another 30 minutes or so.

Add the lamb and simmer for about 5 minutes, then taste and adjust the seasoning with more salt or black pepper (if you've used canned chicken broth, the soup may already be fairly salty).

Serve hot on a cold day.

Super Grain and Veggie Burgers

⅓ cup (70 g) uncooked barley or farro

Kosher salt and freshly ground black pepper

⅓ cup (60 g) uncooked quinoa

⅔ cup (80 g) raw cashews

Extra-virgin olive oil

4 ounces (115 g) shiitake or cremini mushrooms, stemmed and finely chopped

1 cup (160 g) finely chopped carrots

1⅓ cups (200 g) finely chopped onion

6 garlic cloves, finely chopped

One 15.5-ounce (439 g) can chickpeas, rinsed and drained well

½ cup (50 g) uncooked rolled oats

2½ cups (125 g) panko breadcrumbs (whole-grain, if possible)

½ cup (120 ml) soy sauce

2 tablespoons hot sauce, such as sriracha

2 tablespoons sherry vinegar

1½ tablespoons potato starch

Yes, this recipe does have a long list of ingredients and several steps . . . don't start making these burgers 20 minutes before you want to eat. The good news is that the recipe makes a dozen burgers and they freeze beautifully, so an hour spent prepping yields future meals for days. I wrap each burger individually—uncooked—so that I can just pull out as many as I want to cook. Thaw the frozen burgers before cooking; ideally, leave them in the fridge overnight, but you can thaw them on the counter to speed things up if need be. —**Makes twelve 4-ounce (115 g) burgers**

Put the barley, 1 cup (240 ml) water, and ½ teaspoon salt in a small saucepan with a lid. Bring to a boil, then quickly reduce the heat to a simmer. Cover and cook until the barley is tender and the water has been absorbed, 45 to 60 minutes for hulled barley, about 30 minutes for pearled barley. If the barley is tender but there's liquid left, just drain it off; if the water has been absorbed but the barley isn't fully tender, add a few tablespoons more water and keep cooking until tender. Cool completely.

Meanwhile, combine the quinoa, ½ cup plus 2 tablespoons water (135 ml), and ½ teaspoon salt in a separate small saucepan with a lid. Bring to a boil, then quickly reduce the heat to a simmer. Cover and cook until the quinoa is tender and the water has been absorbed, 15 to 18 minutes. Cool completely.

Meanwhile, put the cashews in a small bowl, cover with warm water, and soak until they have softened a bit, at least 1 hour. (They won't be mushy, they'll just get less crunchy.)

Heat a glug of olive oil in a large skillet over medium-high heat. Add the mushrooms, season lightly with salt and pepper, and sauté until they have released their liquids, the liquid has been cooked off, and the mushrooms are fully tender and browning a bit, about 5 minutes. Scrape into a large bowl and let cool.

Add a bit more oil to the pan, then add the carrots and sauté until they start to soften, 3 to 4 minutes. Add the onion and season lightly with salt and pepper. Continue cooking until the vegetables are quite soft and fragrant and starting to turn golden. Don't let the onions actually brown or the burgers will be bitter. Add the garlic, cook another minute, and then transfer the vegetables to the bowl with the mushrooms and let everything cool completely.

Meanwhile, drain the cashews well and finely chop. Mash the chickpeas with a fork or potato masher until about half are mashed and the rest are slightly broken up. (Whole chickpeas will make the burgers too chunky and crumbly.)

continues

When the sautéed vegetables are cool, add them to the chickpeas, cashews, quinoa, barley, oats, and panko ●. Toss with clean hands to integrate all of the ingredients.

In a small bowl, whisk together the soy sauce, hot sauce, vinegar, and potato starch. Add this to the other ingredients ● and work the mixture with your hands so everything is blended nicely ●. Taste, either as is or by frying up a small lump, and adjust the seasoning with more salt, black pepper, hot sauce, soy sauce, and/or vinegar.

Shape the mixture into 12 patties (about ½ cup or 115 g each) ●. Set the patties on a rack and leave at room temperature for 30 minutes or so to dry the surface. For burgers that you're not going to

eat right away, arrange them on a tray in a single layer ●, freeze until firm, then pile the frozen burgers into a zip-top freezer bag or other container and freeze completely. You can remove the number of burgers that you need, leaving the rest frozen for later. For freezing longer than 1 month, wrap the burgers individually and then put in a freezer bag to prevent freezer burn.

To cook, heat a glug of olive oil in a heavy-bottomed skillet over medium-high heat. Add the burgers, leaving enough room for a spatula to scoot in and flip them. Cook until nicely browned and heated through, about 5 minutes on each side.

Serve right away, with your favorite burger fixings.

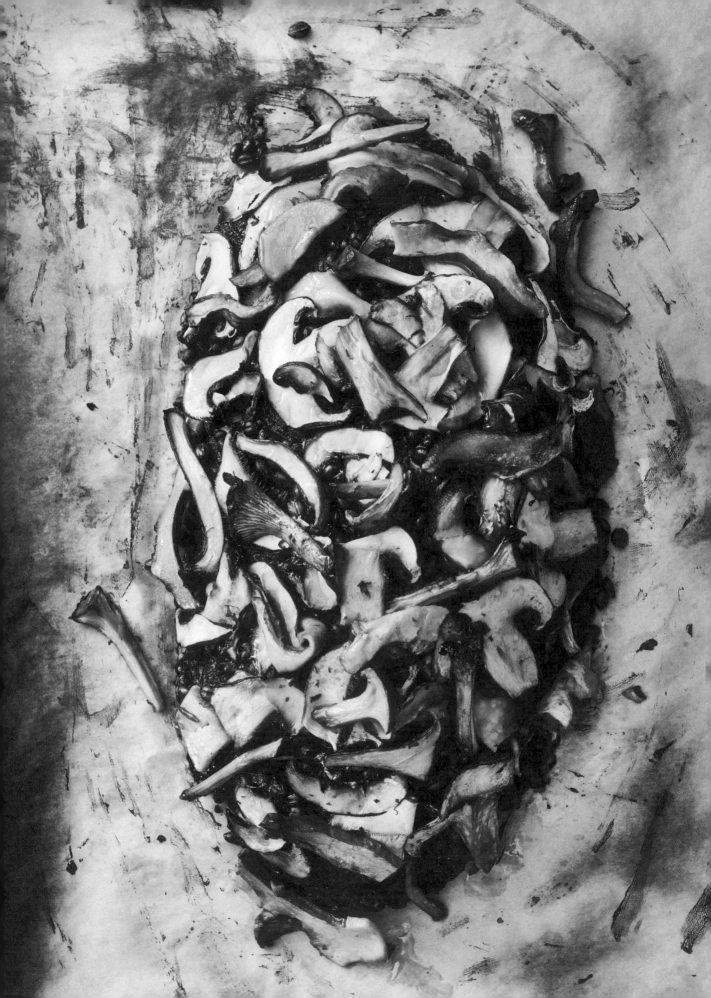

Meat Loaf with Barley and Mushrooms

MEAT LOAVES

½ cup (100 g) uncooked barley

Kosher salt

Extra-virgin olive oil

1 cup (150 g) finely chopped onion

¾ cup (120 g) finely diced carrot

6 garlic cloves, chopped

5 tablespoons (75 g) tomato paste

2 tablespoons Dijon mustard

2 tablespoons barley malt syrup or pure maple syrup (optional)

1 tablespoon fish sauce (I like Red Boat brand)

1½ teaspoons chopped fresh thyme

1½ teaspoons chopped fresh rosemary

1 teaspoon soy sauce

1 large egg

1 large egg yolk

Freshly ground black pepper

2½ pounds (1.125 kg) ground beef, preferably grass-fed

1½ cups (180 g) finely grated pecorino cheese

3 cups (150 g) panko breadcrumbs

TOPPING

Extra-virgin olive oil

1 garlic clove, smashed and peeled

1 pound (450 g) mixed fresh mushrooms (half cremini and half a wild variety is nice), thinly sliced

Kosher salt and freshly ground black pepper

½ cup (120 g) tomato paste

Note: If you're only cooking one meat loaf and freezing the other one, cut the topping ingredients in half. Cook your toppings fresh when it's time to bake your frozen meat loaf.

Meat loaf made with a grain of some kind isn't anything new; thrifty cooks have long added oatmeal to meat loaf as a way to "extend" the more expensive meat. But adding a grain does more than save money—it helps to lighten the texture, so your meat loaf isn't a brick of solid meat. Plus, it brings a whole different level of nutrition to the dish. I use cooked barley here, but you could make the recipe with cooked farro, and you might think about playing with quinoa as well.

Even though meat loaf is a classic "family" dish, I serve it at dinner parties, dressing it up by smothering it with sautéed mushrooms and more barley—for texture and because it looks fantastic.

The recipe makes two loaves, so unless you're serving a crowd, only bake one and freeze the other one for later (raw, really well wrapped). —**Makes two 8 × 4-inch (20 × 10 cm) loaves, each one serves 3 or 4**

MAKE THE MEAT LOAVES: Put the barley, 1½ cups (360 ml) water, and ½ teaspoon salt in a small saucepan with a lid. Bring to a boil, then quickly reduce the heat to a simmer. Cover and cook until the barley is tender and all the water has been absorbed, 45 to 60 minutes for hulled barley, about 30 minutes for pearled barley. If the barley is tender but there's liquid left, just drain it off; if the water has been absorbed but the barley isn't fully tender, add a few tablespoons more water and keep cooking until tender. Cool completely. Measure out ½ cup (85 g) and set aside for the topping.

Heat a small glug of olive oil in a large skillet over medium heat. Add the onion, carrot, and 1 teaspoon salt and cook, stirring frequently, until the vegetables are quite soft and fragrant but not browned, about 10 minutes. Add most of the garlic (save about one-quarter

for the mushroom topping) and cook another minute or so. Transfer the vegetables to a plate or tray to cool completely (pop them into the fridge to speed things up).

In a small bowl, whisk together the tomato paste, mustard, barley malt syrup (if using), fish sauce, thyme, rosemary, soy sauce, egg, egg yolk, 1 teaspoon salt, and several twists of black pepper.

With your hands or a fork, break up the beef into smallish chunks and put into a large bowl. Add the sautéed vegetables and shower with the pecorino, barley, and breadcrumbs. Knead gently to incorporate the ingredients into the beef (the lighter your touch, the more tender the meat loaf). Now pour on the tomato paste mixture and knead some more to thoroughly blend everything.

continues

Do a quick taste test by frying up a tablespoon of the mixture. If needed, add more salt or pepper.

Heat the oven to 350°F (175°C). Line a sheet pan or other shallow-sided baking dish with parchment.

Shape the beef mixture into two 8 × 4-inch (20 × 10 cm) loaves each about 2 inches (5 cm) high. (If you're going to freeze one, wrap it well and freeze now.)

Set the meat loaves on the sheet pan and bake until just cooked through and the internal temperature reaches 160°F (71°C), about 35 minutes.

MEANWHILE, MAKE THE TOPPING: Heat a small glug of olive oil in a skillet over medium heat. Add the garlic and cook slowly to toast the garlic so it's soft, fragrant, and nicely golden brown but not burnt, about 5 minutes.

Add the mushrooms, increase the heat a bit, season generously with salt and black pepper, and sauté the mushrooms until their liquids have been released and then been cooked off, 5 to 8 minutes, depending on the mushrooms. Cook another few minutes, until they're nicely browned and starting to crisp around the edges. They will cook more in the oven, so don't go too far. Set aside.

When the meat loaves are ready, remove from the oven and increase the oven temperature to 450°F (230°C). Spread an even layer of tomato paste over each loaf and then pat the reserved ½ cup (85 g) barley and the mushrooms over the surface, pressing so they stick.

Return to the oven for about 10 more minutes to nicely crisp the coating. Remove the meat loaves from the oven and let sit for 5 to 10 minutes so the juices redistribute, then cut into thick slices. It's okay if some of the mushroom-barley topping falls off; just scoop it up and spoon it over the slices.

Peanut Butter–Barley Cookies with Add-Ins

Pictured on pages 50–51

4 ounces (115 g) unsalted
    butter, at room
    temperature

½ cup (100 g) granulated sugar

½ cup lightly packed (105 g)
    light or dark brown sugar

½ cup (120 g) peanut butter,
    smooth or crunchy (you
    decide)

1 large egg, at room
    temperature

1 teaspoon pure vanilla extract

1¼ cups plus 2 tablespoons
    (165 g) barley flour

½ teaspoon baking soda

½ teaspoon kosher salt

ADD-INS (OPTIONAL; SEE NOTE)

2 cups (270 g) crumbled
    Peanut Brittle (recipe
    follows)

1 cup (50 g) crushed potato
    chips

1 cup (180 g) Reese's Pieces
    candy

Note: If you're using more than
one add-in, the total amount
should not exceed 2 cups, so
adjust as necessary.

The subtle nuttiness of barley flour harmonizes really nicely with the peanut flavor in these crisp-chewy cookies. We're giving you three options for add-ins here—potato chips, peanut brittle, and Reese's Pieces candies—but the basic cookie is so satisfying, you can skip the add-ins and enjoy the simplicity. —**Makes about 2 dozen cookies**

Heat the oven to 375°F (190°C).

In a stand mixer fitted with the paddle, cream the butter, granulated sugar, and brown sugar on medium speed until light and fluffy, about 5 minutes. Add the peanut butter and mix just to combine.

In a small bowl, whisk the egg and vanilla a bit with a fork. Add to the butter and sugars and mix until incorporated.

In a medium bowl, whisk together the barley flour, baking soda, and salt. Add to the dough and mix on low speed until the flour is about halfway incorporated. If you're going for an add-in, stop the mixer, add the add-in, and finish mixing in the flour. Otherwise, just keep mixing the flour until it's incorporated. Don't overmix, or your cookies could be tough.

Line a couple of baking sheets with parchment. Scoop up 2-tablespoon balls of cookie dough and arrange them a few inches apart on the baking sheets. The cookies will ooze a little if they include brittle or candies, so leave plenty of space between them.

Bake until the cookies just start to puff and crack and turn golden, 8 to 10 minutes. Cool for about 15 minutes on the baking sheet (they'll be really fragile at first) before transferring to a rack to finish cooling completely.

Store in an airtight container at room temperature for up to 1 week.

Variation

For the best ice cream sandwich cookies: Replace 2 tablespoons of the brown sugar in the dough with 2 tablespoons honey and bake as directed. Sandwich a big scoop of chocolate, strawberry, or salted caramel ice cream between 2 cookies, freeze for a few hours, and enjoy. The cookies will be soft and perfectly chewy.

continues

Peanut Brittle

This makes just the right amount of brittle for the peanut butter–barley cookies, so double the recipe if you feel a craving for a snack.

Makes 2 cups (270 g)

Cooking spray (optional)

1 cup (140 g) roughly chopped salted roasted peanuts

½ cup plus 2 tablespoons (125 g) sugar

4 tablespoons (60 g) unsalted butter, cut into 4 pieces

1 tablespoon water

½ teaspoon kosher salt

⅛ teaspoon baking soda

Line a sheet pan with a silicone baking mat or mist the pan with cooking spray. Spread the peanuts on the lined pan.

In a heavy-bottomed saucepan, combine the sugar, butter, water, and salt. Set the pan over medium-low heat and cook without stirring until the butter is melted.

Give the pan a swirl and increase the heat a little ⬤. Cook without stirring at all until the mixture starts to develop some color. Give the toffee a quick and gentle stir with a wooden spoon or heatproof spatula. Cook until the toffee is dark caramel brown ⬤.

Remove from the heat and stir in the baking soda; the mixture will bubble up a bit—don't be surprised. Quickly pour it over the peanuts and spread with a spatula ⬤. Let cool completely and then break or chop into pieces (see Note).

Note: If you're using the brittle in the cookies, smaller pieces will spread less and give you a tidier cookie. Big pieces will ooze out and give you a lacier, amoeba-shaped cookie. We like the oozier, messier route!

Crispy Brown Rice with Deeply Roasted Broccoli, Carrots, and Turnips 58

Chicken Soup with Brown Rice, Radishes, and Lots of Lemon 61

Spiced Brown Rice with Chickpeas 63

Super Grain Mix 65

Slow-Roasted Chicken Buried in Gingery Brown Rice 66

Toasted Brown Rice Horchata 69

Brown Rice

Brown Rice

Oryza sativa

▶ GLUTEN-FREE ◀

•▷ *Why I love it:* As an early 1970s hippie health food, brown rice became shorthand for a lifestyle that likely included Grateful Dead LPs, Dr. Bronner's soap, ample cannabis, and the whiff of patchouli. That's me today—minus the, ahem, patchouli, of course. Brown rice may not be as fluffy as white rice can be, but I'm a fan of its nutritional content and its mellow flavor.

•▷ *What it tastes like:* Given all its varieties (see Common Forms, below), brown rice ranges in flavor, too. All brown rices are chewier than their white, more refined forms, and the flavors are generally nutty and sweet; jasmine and basmati are quite fragrant. Short-grain will be a little stickier and clumpier, while long-grain rices will retain separate grains.

•▷ *Common forms:* There are many: short-, medium-, and long-grain (including basmati and jasmine) varieties; there is even sweet brown rice, which becomes very sticky when cooked and can be used for dishes such as Thai rice balls. There are proprietary types of whole-grain rice as well, grown by producers who breed them for special characteristics and give them brand names, an indicator of the growing popularity of whole-grain rice. And brown isn't the only "color"—rices such as Chinese black rice and purple Thai rice are also whole-grain with the color coming from their bran layer.

•▷ *Favorite ways to prepare it:* Any way you like white rice. For this book, I'm sticking to just short- and long-grain brown rices (with one exception— the sweet brown rice in Super Grain Mix, page 65). Rices do well with any cooking method— absorption, boil-like-pasta, or pilaf—and they cook well in soups and stews. Just remember brown rice takes quite a while to cook, so you need to coordinate with the cooking times of your other ingredients.

•▷ *How it's good for you:* Brown rice has more than twice as much of just about every nutrient as white rice. The exception is protein, but that's only because much of the brown rice kernel is fiber and not just protein and starch, as with white rice, so it's not a fair fight.

Details

→ 1 cup uncooked short- or medium-grain weighs 7 ounces (200 g).

→ 1 cup uncooked long-grain weighs 6½ ounces (180 g).

→ As a rule of thumb for the absorption method, use 2 parts liquid to 1 part rice.

→ Cook most brown rice for 40 to 50 minutes, but different varieties cook at slightly different rates, so always check the package instructions.

→ 1 cup uncooked rice yields 3 cups (525 g) cooked.

→ 1 cup uncooked short- or medium-grain rice yields 3 cups (525 g) cooked.

Crispy Brown Rice with Deeply Roasted Broccoli, Carrots, and Turnips

1 cup (200 g) uncooked short-grain brown rice

Kosher salt

Vegetable oil, for frying

12 ounces (335 g) broccoli, stems trimmed and peeled, cut into long florets

Extra-virgin olive oil

Freshly ground black pepper

8 ounces (225 g) carrots, cut into long spears (if the carrots are small, just halve or quarter lengthwise)

8 ounces (225 g) turnips, halved, quartered, or cut in chunks, depending on their size

3 tablespoons red wine vinegar or sherry vinegar

Dried chile flakes

½ cup (60 g) salted roasted cashews, roughly chopped

5 or 6 scallions, trimmed (including ½ inch/1.5 cm off the green tops), sliced on a sharp angle, soaked in ice water for 20 minutes, and drained well

Small handful fresh flat-leaf parsley leaves

Small handful fresh cilantro leaves and tender stems

Fresh Orange and Garlic Confit Vinaigrette (page 319; see Note)

Note: I hope you'll have a batch of the dressing already in your refrigerator, but if not and you're in a hurry, you can dress the dish by squeezing an orange and maybe half a lemon over everything, then tossing with some good olive oil.

The popped rice that's the base for this salad is fun, crunchy, and quite unexpected—all good things. You can simmer the rice a couple of days ahead (or use what you have stashed in the fridge or freezer) and fry it the next day. Make the salad right away, or even the following day, as the fried rice stays crunchy for at least 24 hours in an airtight container. The overall flavor goal in this salad is to balance the earthiness of the broccoli and root vegetables—which I cook right up to the edge of burnt—with the sweet, bright citrus dressing. —**Serves 4 to 6**

Up to 24 hours ahead, rinse the rice and soak in a bowl of cool water for 2 hours. Drain.

Bring a large pot of water to a boil, salt it lightly (about 1 teaspoon per quart), add the rice, and boil until the rice is fully tender but not too "exploded," 45 to 60 minutes. Drain thoroughly, tapping the sieve to shake out as much water as possible. Spread the rice on a large tray and let it dry completely at room temperature. If you won't be using it in the next 2 hours, cover and refrigerate.

Line a sheet pan with paper towels and put it near the stove. Pour a couple of inches of vegetable oil into a large heavy-bottomed pan that is deep enough to not worry about spillovers during frying. Heat the oil over medium-high heat until it's about 365°F (185°C).

Working in batches, carefully add some cooked rice to the oil and fry until the rice grains puff slightly and get a bit darker.

Scoop the rice out of the oil with a slotted spoon and transfer to the lined sheet pan ●. Season lightly with salt and set aside. Continue to puff the remaining rice.

Heat the oven to 450°F (230°C).

Put the broccoli in a large bowl, drizzle with olive oil, season lightly with salt and pepper, and toss to coat. Spread onto a sheet pan. Repeat with the carrots and turnips, but try to keep them separate on the baking sheet in case one cooks more quickly than the other and you have to scoot it off.

Roast the vegetables until they are tender and nicely browned—charred is even better—around the edges, about 30 minutes. The broccoli will probably finish first, but it all depends on the vegetables. You may need to switch the pans from one oven rack to the other. Remove from the oven, sprinkle with the vinegar, and let cool to room temperature.

When ready to serve, pile all the vegetables in a large bowl and season lightly with a generous pinch of dried chile flakes and more salt and pepper. Add the cashews, scallions, parsley, and cilantro and toss to mix. Add about ⅓ cup (80 ml) vinaigrette. Toss, taste, and adjust the seasoning with more salt, pepper, chile flakes, or vinegar. Add the crispy rice, toss once more, and serve right away.

Variation

Instead of using broccoli, carrots, and turnips, use chunks of raw tomato (or cherry tomatoes)—don't cook them—along with roasted or grilled summer squash. Use mint and basil instead of parsley and cilantro, and add a few thin slices of red onion instead of the scallions. Dress with Cilantro-Raisin Vinaigrette (page 314).

Chicken Soup with Brown Rice, Radishes, and Lots of Lemon

1 teaspoon vegetable or extra-virgin olive oil

1 cup (200 g) uncooked long-grain brown rice, rinsed and shaken until mostly dry

½ lemon

Kosher salt

1 bunch radishes, with their greens if they look fresh

2 quarts (2 liters) Best Chicken Broth (page 311)

2 to 3 cups (280 to 420 g) chopped cooked chicken (from making the broth)

Tabasco or other hot sauce

Freshly cracked black pepper

Extra-virgin olive oil, for drizzling

4 to 6 lemon wedges, for squeezing

In this twist on chicken and rice soup, I use brown rice to bring more nutrition to the table than the usual white rice, and radishes bring an earthy flavor that's way more interesting than your basic chicken soup flavor profile. But to make this soup as delicious as it can be, it's important to dial in the final flavorings of hot sauce, salt, lemon juice, and black pepper, especially the interplay of salt and lemon. —Serves 4 to 6

Heat the oil in a medium saucepan over medium-high heat. Add the rice and toast it, stirring constantly, until it starts to smell nutty, about 3 minutes.

Add 2 cups (480 ml) water, the lemon half, and 1 teaspoon salt. Bring to a boil, reduce to a simmer, cover, and simmer gently until all the water has been absorbed, about 45 minutes (unless your package specifies different timing).

When the rice is cooked, uncover and let it steam in the pan for a few minutes. Fish out and discard the lemon.

Meanwhile, prepare the radishes by trimming off the tops and tails and cutting them into halves or quarters, depending on their size (you want about 2 cups/250 g). If you're using the radish tops—and I hope you are—rinse them really well so there's not a speck of grit left, then tear them once or twice (you should have about 1 cup lightly packed/100 g).

In a soup pot, heat up the chicken broth. Add the chicken, cooked rice, radishes, and radish tops (if using). Simmer for about 5 minutes to soften the radishes just a touch and nicely wilt the greens.

Add a few shots of hot sauce and some twists of black pepper. Taste and add more hot sauce, salt, black pepper, or lemon until the soup is both zesty and comforting at the same time.

Serve in big bowls with a drizzle of olive oil and let the diners squeeze in more lemon as they like.

Pilafs for Every Season

A grain pilaf can be a simple side dish, or you can turn a pilaf into a main dish with tender meat cradled within the grain. I'm including amounts and cooking times for grains and liquids as a guideline. Each batch of grain absorbs liquid differently, so pay attention as you get to the end of the cooking time. You may need to add a splash more or, if excess liquid remains once the grain is tender, cook the pilaf with the lid off for a few minutes to evaporate the extra moisture.

How to assemble your pilaf:

Refer to the foldout chart for ingredients by season.
Heat the oven to 375°F (190°C).

1. Heat a glug of extra-virgin olive oil in an ovenproof skillet or small Dutch oven over medium heat, add the **GRAIN** and **AROMATICS**, and gently toast until fragrant.

2. Add the **HERBS/SPICES** and cook for a few seconds.

3. Nestle in the **PROTEIN** and **VEGETABLES** so they're evenly distributed. Some ingredients might need to be partially cooked ahead (see **TIPS** in the chart).

4. Add the **LIQUID**, bring to a boil, reduce to a simmer, and cover.

5. Transfer to the oven and bake until the liquid has been absorbed, the grains are tender, and the other ingredients are cooked (check meats/poultry with a thermometer). Cooking time will vary with each grain; see **TIMING**.

6. Remove from the oven, let sit undisturbed for 5 minutes, then uncover, fluff gently, and fold in the **FINISHING**. Serve hot.

Spiced Brown Rice with Chickpeas

2 tablespoons virgin coconut oil or extra-virgin olive oil

1 medium yellow onion, finely chopped

One 3-inch (7.5 cm) chunk fresh ginger, peeled and finely chopped

5 garlic cloves, minced

2 teaspoons ground turmeric

1 teaspoon ground cardamom

1 teaspoon ground coriander

1 teaspoon cumin seeds

1 teaspoon brown mustard seeds

1 cup (200 g) uncooked brown basmati or other long-grain rice

1 tablespoon kosher salt

Pinch of dried chile flakes

2 cups (480 ml) chicken broth, homemade (page 311) or low-sodium store-bought, or water

One 15.5-ounce (439 g) can chickpeas, rinsed and drained well

Small handful fresh mint, parsley, and/or cilantro leaves, for garnish

Yogo Ranch Dressing (page 313) or plain yogurt, for serving

Lime wedges, for squeezing

This quick-to-prep dish is simple, comforting, and nutritious enough to be a main dish, though it's lovely as a side partner to a pork chop or chicken breast, or as a filling for stuffed peppers. I like to use brown basmati for this, but any brown rice will work fine; just pay attention to the cooking time and the amount of liquid, as short-grain rice can take longer than long-grain and is a touch thirstier. —Serves 4 to 6

Heat the oil in a large heavy-bottomed saucepan or medium Dutch oven over medium heat. Add the onion, ginger, and garlic and sauté slowly until soft and fragrant, about 8 minutes. Increase the heat to medium-high and add the turmeric, cardamom, coriander, cumin seeds, and mustard seeds. Cook, scraping the pan so the spices toast but don't burn, until the onion starts to brown a touch around the edges; this will give the broth a nice, deep flavor.

Add the rice and cook another minute or so, stirring constantly, so the rice toasts a bit, then add the salt and chile flakes. Add the chicken broth, bring to a boil, then adjust the heat so the rice simmers gently. Cover and cook until the broth is absorbed and the rice is tender, 40 to 50 minutes, checking to make sure the pan isn't getting dry. If the liquid has all absorbed but the rice isn't quite tender, add a bit more liquid and keep cooking until tender; if the rice has gotten tender but there's still a bit of liquid, spoon some off and then increase the heat, uncover, and cook rapidly to boil off the remaining excess.

Fold in the chickpeas, cover the pot, and remove from the heat. Leave to steam and warm the chickpeas for about 5 minutes. Taste and adjust with more salt or chile flakes. Top with the fresh herbs. Serve with a dollop of ranch dressing and a squeeze of lime.

Super Grain Mix

1 cup (200 g) uncooked short-grain brown rice

½ cup (100 g) uncooked pearled farro

½ cup (90 g) uncooked millet

½ cup (100 g) uncooked sweet brown rice (optional)

¾ cup (125 g) uncooked buckwheat

¾ cup (130 g) uncooked quinoa

Unsalted butter

Kosher salt

Chopped fresh herbs (such as dill, parsley, cilantro, or basil), for serving (optional)

Having a batch of this mix in your pantry makes side dishes easy. Just scoop out a cupful and away you go. I mostly cook these grains with water, but chicken broth or mushroom broth is delicious, and you can finish with chopped fresh herbs, chopped nuts, or a spoonful of Garlic-Chile Crunch (page 306).
—**Makes 4 cups (12 to 16 servings)**

In an airtight container, combine the short-grain brown rice, farro, millet, sweet brown rice (if using), buckwheat, and quinoa.

When ready to cook, measure out 1 cup (200 g) of the grain mixture and place in a medium saucepan with a lid. Add a scant 2 cups (450 ml) water, 1 tablespoon butter, and 1 teaspoon salt. Bring to a boil, then reduce the heat, adjusting so that the grains simmer nicely. Cover and cook until all the water has been absorbed and the grains are fully tender, about 30 minutes.

Pay attention to the water level toward the end of cooking. If the water runs out before the grains are tender, add a few spoonfuls and continue cooking. If the grains are fully tender but there's still a lot of moisture, drain off the excess water through a strainer.

Put the grains back into the saucepan (or keep them there), fluff with a fork, cover, and let stand to steam for about 5 minutes.

Serve plain or with a handful of chopped herbs.

Slow-Roasted Chicken Buried in Gingery Brown Rice

2 cups (400 g) uncooked long-grain brown rice

1¾ cups (420 ml) chicken broth, homemade (page 311) or low-sodium store-bought

2 tablespoons soy sauce

1 tablespoon fish sauce (I like Red Boat brand)

A few dashes hot sauce

Extra-virgin olive oil

2 cups (300 g) finely chopped onion

6 tablespoons (30 g) finely chopped fresh ginger

3 tablespoons finely chopped garlic

One 3- to 4-pound (1.3 to 1.8 kg) chicken

Kosher salt and freshly ground black pepper

2 tablespoons unsalted butter

Small handful fresh cilantro leaves, roughly chopped

Lime wedges, for squeezing (optional)

This recipe was inspired by a Middle Eastern dish in which the rice is perfumed by spices and everything is cooked overnight in a really slow oven. I've speeded up the cooking a bit and I'm using Asian-inflected aromatics instead. Don't expect roast chicken like you know it—you won't be getting a golden bird with crisp skin—this one is closer to a poached chicken. It is fall-apart tender and moist and the rice is soft and almost porridge-y, flavored with fragrant ginger and garlic and of course all the chicken juices, which bake right into the rice—that's where the magic happens. It's super comforting, and easy to make. Bonus: If you have any rice left over, roll it into balls, coat in flour, egg, and panko, and fry like arancini (risotto balls). —**Serves 4 to 6**

Put the rice in a bowl, cover with cool water by a couple of inches, and leave to soak for at least 2 hours and up to 24 hours (for longer than 2 hours, keep it in the fridge). Drain the rice, tapping the sieve to shake off as much water as possible.

Heat the oven to 325°F (160°C).

Mix together the chicken broth, soy sauce, fish sauce, and a couple shakes of hot sauce in a small bowl and set aside.

Heat a glug of olive oil in a large skillet over medium heat. Add the onion and cook until it's starting to get soft and fragrant but not at all browned, about 3 minutes. Add the ginger and cook for another minute. Add the garlic and cook until the garlic is fragrant but not browned, another minute or so.

Add the drained rice to the onion mixture and cook, stirring, for another minute or so, until all the rice is nicely coated with oil. Remove from the heat.

Season the chicken inside and out with salt and pepper.

Choose a Dutch oven or other heavy pot that will hold the chicken without squishing it too much but without a lot of extra room, which would change the way the rice cooks. It's ideal if the pot has a lid, but if not, you can use foil. Spread about a ½-inch (1.25 cm) layer of the rice on the bottom of the pot, set the chicken on top, and pile the rest of the rice around the chicken so it's sitting in a little nest. Wipe off any rice grains from the top of the chicken, if need be.

Pour in the seasoned chicken broth, cover the pot, and put in the oven. Roast the chicken for 1 hour.

Uncover and carefully spread the butter over the chicken breast and any other exposed parts. Continue roasting, uncovered, until the rice has absorbed all the liquid and is tender and the chicken is fully cooked, another 30 to

45 minutes. The chicken should register at least 165°F (74°C) in the breast and 175°F (80°C) in the thigh to make sure it's cooked, but that shouldn't be any problem—the chicken is likely to be very well done and falling off the bone once the rice is fully cooked, and the rice itself will be heading toward mushy.

If you like, you can heat the broiler and broil for a few minutes until the chicken skin is a bit darker and the top layer of rice is crispy. Keep an eye on things, however, because you don't want the chicken to burn.

Let the dish rest for about 10 minutes. Then scoop out some rice and pull off some chicken meat using a spoon for each serving. (You can also lift the chicken onto a cutting board and cut it up, but it's so tender that it should pull apart easily while still in the pot.)

Serve topped with the cilantro and with lime wedges on the side, if you like.

Toasted Brown Rice Horchata

1 cinnamon stick

½ cup (100 g) uncooked brown rice, short- or long-grain

1½ cups (210 g) raw almonds, skin-on or blanched

½ cup (120 ml) pure maple syrup

2 teaspoons pure vanilla extract

Large pinch of kosher salt

5 cups (750 ml) boiling water

Toasting the rice deepens the flavor, giving this Mexican-inspired drink a nice edge. Thorough straining is key to a good texture, so bring some attention to that. If you have a nut-milk bag, this is a perfect use for it. —**Makes about 1½ quarts (1.5 liters)**

Put the cinnamon stick, rice, and almonds in a large heavy-bottomed skillet. Set over medium-low heat and cook, moving the ingredients around so they don't burn, until very fragrant, about 8 minutes. The almonds will visibly darken in spots.

Transfer the toasted rice and almonds to a large heatproof bowl and add the maple syrup, vanilla, and salt. Smash or break up the cinnamon stick into small pieces and add them to the bowl. Pour in the boiling water. Let the mixture sit at room temperature for at least 4 hours and up to overnight.

Transfer everything in the bowl to a blender (you may need to do this in two batches, depending on your blender size). Starting slow, blend the mixture until it's as fine as possible. Strain through a fine-mesh sieve set over a bowl, pressing to get as much liquid as possible out of the solids. To be sure you get the maximum yield, put the pulp into some cheesecloth and squeeze out any remaining liquid. If the texture of the liquid seems a bit too gritty, strain again or strain through a double layer of cheesecloth.

Taste and adjust the seasoning with more salt or vanilla, if needed. Chill the horchata and serve over ice, with a grating of cinnamon if you like. Store in the fridge for up to 2 days.

Variation

Serve the horchata with a cooled shot of espresso or some cold-brew coffee.

Buckwheat

Buckwheat

Fagopyrum esculentum

▶ GLUTEN-FREE ◀

•▷ *Why I love it:* Buckwheat is awesome. This grain has range—whether used to make Japanese soba noodles or galettes de sarrasin, the darkly hued crepes of Brittany, France. And it's sly: Despite its name, it has nothing to do with wheat; it's actually part of the rhubarb family and isn't even technically a grain (see page 19).

•▷ *What it tastes like:* The flavor of buckwheat is vaguely nutty, like all grains, but with a slight vegetable note and even a hint of bitterness. It's chewy but tender when cooked, crunchy when toasted.

•▷ *Common forms:* Buckwheat kernels are called groats; they have an appealing pellet shape. In their natural state, they'll be called raw or green, but you'll also find them roasted, which will be labeled "kasha."

•▷ *Favorite ways to prepare it:* The buckwheat groats can be toasted in a dry skillet until crunchy and eaten just like that, or they can be cooked in liquid until tender but still slightly chewy. Buckwheat will drink up a lot of liquid, so depending on your recipe, you may need to add a touch more before serving, to keep things from getting stodgy.

•▷ *How it's good for you:* Nutritionally, buckwheat contains many vitamins and minerals, and it's a complete protein, which is rare for a grain . . . or even a pseudo-grain!

Details

→ 1 cup uncooked buckwheat weighs 6 ounces (170 g).

→ Use 2 parts liquid to 1 part buckwheat as a rule of thumb for the absorption method.

→ Cook for 15 to 25 minutes.

→ 1 cup (170 g) uncooked buckwheat yields 3 cups (490 g) cooked.

→ 1 cup buckwheat flour weighs 4¼ ounces (120 g).

Buckwheat, Lime, and Herb Salad, Larb Style

Peanut or canola oil

2 cups (360 g) uncooked buckwheat groats

Kosher salt

½ cup (75 g) chopped shallots

6 tablespoons (90 ml) fresh lime juice (from about 2 limes)

1 small fresh red Thai or serrano chile, seeded, deribbed, and thinly sliced

2 tablespoons finely grated or minced garlic

¼ cup (60 ml) fish sauce (I like Red Boat brand)

Leaves and tender stems from 1 bunch mint

Leaves and tender stems from ½ bunch cilantro

1 cup (120 g) diagonally sliced scallions, trimmed (including ½ inch/1.25 cm of the green tops), soaked in ice water for 20 minutes, and drained well

1¼ cups (175 g) roughly chopped salted roasted peanuts

Many small iceberg lettuce leaves or hearts of romaine leaves

Radishes, cucumber slices, lime wedges, and chile sauce or other hot sauce, for serving

One of my favorite Thai dishes—actually, one my favorite dishes from any cuisine—is larb, a salad usually made with seasoned pork, lots of lime juice, fresh herbs, and chiles that's served with lettuces and more herbs with which to scoop up the pork. I got inspired by the flavor and texture combinations and decided to make a vegetarian version, using buckwheat instead of the ground meat. The pairing of crunchy toasted buckwheat and tender, chewy simmered buckwheat creates a fabulous texture. So much of deliciousness comes from texture, right? This recipe makes a large amount, perfect for a party, but feel free to cut the quantities in half. —Serves 8

Heat a glug of oil in a heavy-bottomed medium skillet over medium heat. Add a little less than half the buckwheat and cook, stirring frequently, until toasted. Take your time, because you don't want it to get too dark, but you do want it thoroughly toasted. It should take 5 to 7 minutes, but start tasting around 4 minutes. The texture should be crisp but not hard and the flavor will be nutty and pleasant. When it's ready, dump the buckwheat onto a sheet pan and spread out to cool.

Bring a medium saucepan of water to a boil, and add 1 teaspoon salt and the remaining buckwheat. Reduce the heat to a simmer and cook until the buckwheat is tender, 12 to 15 minutes. Drain well and let cool.

Combine the shallots and lime juice in a medium bowl and let sit for about 20 minutes; this will remove some of the harshness of the raw shallots. Stir in the chile, garlic, fish sauce, 3 tablespoons oil, and 1 teaspoon salt.

Transfer the cooked buckwheat to a large bowl, pour on the shallot dressing, and toss thoroughly. (You can do this up to 30 minutes before you serve the salad.)

Just before serving, toss in the toasted buckwheat, mint, cilantro, scallions, and peanuts. Taste and adjust the seasoning with more lime juice, fish sauce, or salt.

Arrange the lettuce leaves and other garnishes on a platter, along with the buckwheat mix. Serve right away, inviting the diners to fill lettuce leaves with the buckwheat mixture, some radish and cucumber, and a squeeze of lime. Add hot sauce to taste!

Baked Eggs with Broccoli Rabe, Spiced Tomato, and Buckwheat

1 bunch broccoli rabe, dry ends trimmed, chopped into 1-inch (2.5 cm) pieces

Extra-virgin olive oil

Kosher salt and freshly ground black pepper

1 cup (170 g) uncooked buckwheat groats

½ cup (60 g) walnuts

5 garlic cloves, finely chopped

2 teaspoons ground cumin

1 teaspoon sweet or hot paprika (your choice)

One 14.5-ounce (410 g) can whole peeled tomatoes, undrained

One 15.5-ounce (439 g) can chickpeas, rinsed and drained well

4 tablespoons (60 g) unsalted butter

Handful fresh mint and cilantro leaves, torn

6 large eggs

Turmeric Mayo (page 315), Yogo Ranch Dressing (page 313), a few dashes hot sauce, and some crumbled ricotta salata or feta, for serving (optional)

This recipe is like shakshuka, the Middle Eastern dish of eggs baked in a skillet of spiced tomato and pepper sauce. Buckwheat creates a tender, chewy nest for the eggs, and the whole meal comes together with liberal additions of the condiments, including enough hot sauce to wake you up on a Sunday morning. —Serves 3 to 6

Heat the oven to 450°F (230°C).

Toss the broccoli rabe in a glug of olive oil, season with salt and pepper, and spread onto a baking sheet. Roast until mostly tender and lightly browned around the edges, about 15 minutes. Set aside.

Heat a glug of olive oil in a large heavy skillet over medium heat. Add the buckwheat and cook, stirring frequently, until toasted. Watch the heat level, because you don't want the buckwheat to get too dark, but you do want it thoroughly toasted. After about 4 minutes, add the walnuts and toast until all is fragrant, another 2 to 3 minutes.

Add the garlic, cumin, and paprika and cook, stirring frequently, for another couple of minutes. Add 2 cups (480 ml) water, cover, and adjust the heat so the buckwheat simmers nicely. Cook until mostly tender, about 15 minutes.

Add the tomatoes and their juices and season with ½ teaspoon salt and several twists of black pepper. Simmer, uncovered, for 4 or 5 minutes, breaking up the whole tomatoes with a spatula or wooden spoon. Add the broccoli

rabe and chickpeas and simmer until the broccoli rabe is tender and the tomato sauce is nice and thick, another 10 minutes or so.

Remove from the heat and stir in the butter, mint, and cilantro; adjust the seasoning.

Transfer the mixture to a baking dish (if your skillet is ovenproof and ready for the brunch table, you can use that) and use a spoon to create 6 little wells in the mixture for the eggs.

Crack each egg into a small bowl (to be sure no shell gets in) and then slide it into a well. Season with salt and pepper and bake until the whites are set, 8 to 10 minutes, a few minutes longer for firm yolks.

Top with the condiments, if desired, passing more at the table.

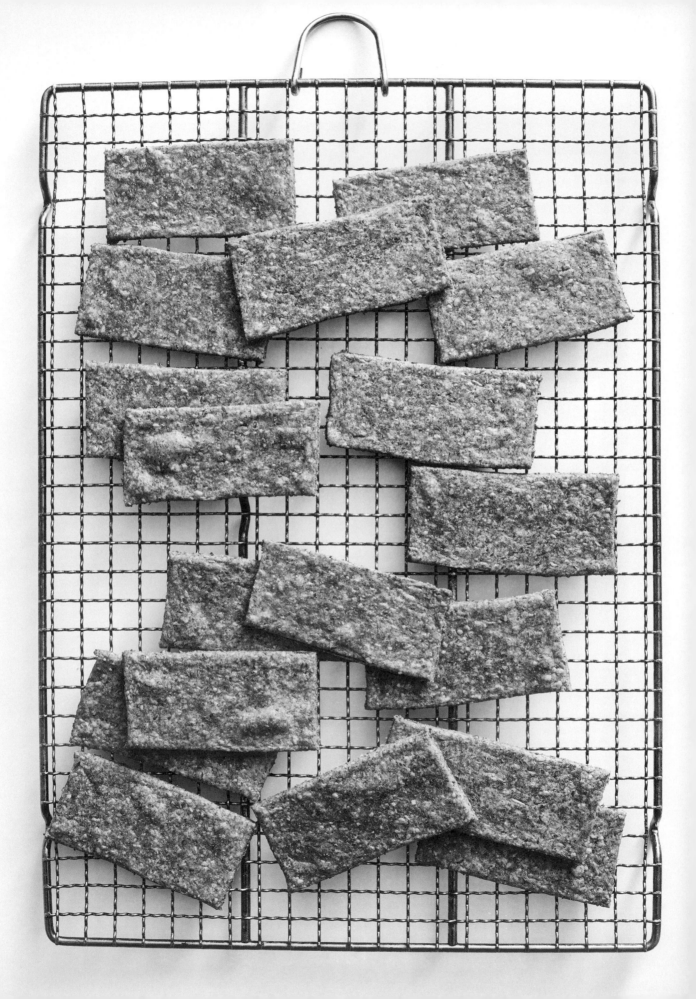

Buckwheat Crackers

¾ cup (90 g) buckwheat flour

¾ cup (90 g) unbleached all-purpose flour, plus more for dusting

¾ cup (90 g) whole wheat or spelt flour

½ cup (50 g) ground flaxseeds

¾ cup (90 g) finely grated Parmigiano-Reggiano or pecorino cheese, or a mix of the two

1 tablespoon kosher salt

¾ cup (180 ml) water

6 tablespoons (90 ml) extra-virgin olive oil

Making crackers from scratch is remarkably easy, and the results are so much nicer than store-bought, especially when your crackers are loaded with complex flavor from whole grains. Different batches of flour will absorb water differently, so use the amount of water in the recipe only as a guide. —**Makes about 5 dozen 2-inch (5 cm) crackers**

Whisk together the buckwheat flour, all-purpose flour, whole wheat flour, ground flaxseeds, cheese, and salt in a large bowl.

Stir the water and oil together in a spouted measuring cup. Pour about three-quarters of it into the flour mixture. Stir, adding the rest very gradually, until the dough starts to come together. Dump the dough onto the counter and knead a few times until you have a cohesive dough ●. You may not use all the water, or you may need to add another spoonful or two. Wrap in plastic and refrigerate for at least 30 minutes and up to overnight.

When you're ready to bake, heat the oven to 350°F (175°C).

Divide the dough into 4 pieces for easier handling. Working with one piece at a time, roll it out until it's very thin, dusting the work surface with a bit of flour as needed. Cut the dough into squares or whatever shape you like, transfer the crackers to a baking sheet (no need to grease it), and repeat with the rest of the dough.

Bake until the crackers look dry and are starting to brown around the edges, about 20 minutes. (I advise baking one or two test crackers so you can home in on the exact timing.) Transfer the crackers to a rack to cool completely; they will crisp as they cool.

Store in an airtight container at room temperature for up to 1 week. Serve with any kind of cheese, or with hummus or other dip.

David Lebovitz's Salted Honey Pie

The "Damrosch" Buckwheat Crust
   (page 83)

4 ounces (115 g) unsalted butter,
   melted

⅓ cup (65 g) sugar

2 teaspoons cornstarch

¾ teaspoon kosher salt

1 teaspoon pure vanilla extract

¾ cup (250 g) honey

3 large eggs, at room temperature

½ cup (120 g) sour cream, heavy
   cream, or crème fraîche

1 tablespoon apple cider vinegar

Flaky sea salt, such as Maldon

David adapted his version of this slightly addictive pie from Brooklyn's Four & Twenty Blackbirds pie shop. If you have single-origin honey, such as chestnut or, hey, buckwheat, this pie will make a beautiful showcase for the honey's distinctive flavor and perfume.

Assemble the crust and blind-bake as directed. Remove the crust from the oven and leave the oven at 350°F (175°C). Set the crust on a baking sheet to catch possible drips.

Whisk together the melted butter, sugar, cornstarch, salt, vanilla, and honey in a medium bowl. Whisk in the eggs one at a time, then whisk in the sour cream and vinegar. Pour the filling into the crust (don't forget to scrape the bowl). Bake until the edges of the filling are golden brown and the center is almost set, 45 to 50 minutes. It should still jiggle but not be liquidy.

Let the pie cool completely on a rack. Sprinkle with flaky sea salt before serving.

The "Damrosch" Buckwheat Crust

1 tablespoon unsalted butter, at room temperature

¾ cup (125 g) uncooked buckwheat groats

I learned to make this pie crust from Barbara Damrosch, the owner, with her husband, Eliot Coleman, of Four Season Farm in Maine. (Barbara published this recipe in their book, *The Four Season Farm Gardener's Cookbook*.) I worked at the farm for a couple of life-changing seasons earlier in my career, and Barbara and Eliot have been my heroes ever since. This crust, which is like a not-sweet, slightly crunchy graham cracker crust, couldn't be simpler; it works best with a custardy filling, such as a quiche. Or try the salted honey filling on page 82, courtesy of pastry chef and cool dude David Lebovitz. —**Makes one 9-inch (23 cm) pie crust**

Spread the butter all over the bottom and up the sides of a 9-inch (23 cm) pie plate (glass works best for this, but metal or ceramic is fine) ●.

Pour the buckwheat into the center of the pie plate and then shake and turn the plate to encourage the buckwheat to spread out into an even layer, with no holes. Use your fingertips if needed to get even coverage ●. You won't be able to fill every tiny hole with a buckwheat groat, but take your time and do your best.

Proceed with the filling for your recipe, which you can either bake in the crust or (depending on the recipe) add to a blind-baked crust.

To blind-bake, heat the oven to 350°F (175°C) and bake the unfilled crust until lightly toasted, 8 to 10 minutes. Let cool, taking care not to dislodge any buckwheat, then add the filling of your choice and continue with your recipe ●.

Buckwheat Cream Scones, Your Way

1½ cups (175 g) unbleached all-purpose flour

¾ cup (100 g) buckwheat flour

½ cup (60 g) whole wheat flour

⅓ cup (65 g) granulated sugar

1 tablespoon baking powder

1 teaspoon kosher salt

4 ounces (115 g) cold unsalted butter, cut into 8 pieces

¾ cup (180 ml) heavy cream, plus 2 tablespoons extra if needed

½ cup (120 g) sour cream

1 teaspoon pure vanilla extract

Add-ins (optional; list follows)

GLAZE

Heavy cream or 1 large egg, beaten

Turbinado sugar (see Note)

FROSTINGS—CHOOSE ONE (OPTIONAL)

Classic Vanilla Frosting (recipe follows)

Meyer Lemon Frosting (recipe follows)

Maple Frosting (recipe follows)

Chocolate Frosting (recipe follows)

Favorite Nut Glaze (recipe follows)

Note: Turbinado sugar is nice for this because it's coarse and crunchy. Look for Sugar In The Raw brand.

A freshly baked scone is a beautiful thing, though you'd never know it from the dreadful, oversize, dry pucks that show up in so many coffee shops these days. This dough produces delicate, flavorful scones that can be frozen and baked to order, and you can choose your own flavor adventure from the many add-ins and frostings, all of which are quick to make and last in the fridge for a couple of weeks. —**Makes 12 scones**

Put the all-purpose flour, buckwheat flour, whole wheat flour, granulated sugar, baking powder, and salt in a food processor and pulse a few times to blend. Add the butter ● and pulse until the butter bits are very fine. The mixture should be like a light sand with hardly any visible butter ●.

Transfer the mixture to a large bowl. In a medium bowl, whisk together the heavy cream, sour cream, and vanilla. Fold the cream mixture into the flour mixture along with any add-ins if you're using them ●.

Dump the dough onto a clean work surface and knead it a bit to bring it together ●. The dough should be fairly dry, but if it seems too dry to come together, add 1 to 2 more tablespoons of cream. Divide the dough in half and shape each into a flat disk about 6 inches (15 cm) across. Dust with a bit of flour if the dough is too sticky to work with ●.

Chill the dough disks in the freezer for 30 minutes or wrap and refrigerate for up to 1 day. (To freeze unbaked scones, cut and wrap individually before you freeze them.)

Heat the oven to 375°F (190°C). Line a large baking sheet with parchment.

Cut each disk of dough into 6 wedges, like a pie ●. If you're planning on using a frosting, brush the scones with heavy cream. If you're not using a frosting, brush the scones with either the beaten egg or heavy cream and sprinkle with turbinado sugar.

Arrange the scones on the baking sheet with a couple of inches between them ● and bake until slightly golden and cooked through, 18 to 20 minutes. Let the scones cool on the baking sheet for a few minutes and then transfer to a rack to cool.

For frosted scones, spread or drizzle the frosting on the scones while still slightly warm. The scones are at their best if you can serve them as soon as they've cooled to just barely warm. Store leftover scones in an airtight container at room temperature for up to 2 days. Reheat for 10 minutes in a 325°F (160°C) oven before serving.

continues

+ ADD-INS:

Chop all your ingredients roughly, to provide some nice texture; keep small fruit—such as blueberries—whole. Use about 1 cup for nuts or fruit, a bit less for candied ginger and chocolate. Though you can never have too much chocolate.

Candied ginger

Dried fruit

Dark, white, or milk chocolate

Toasted nuts

Fresh fruit (frozen is easier if the fruit is super juicy, like raspberries)

Classic Vanilla Frosting

Makes ¾ cup (245 g)

1 cup (120 g) powdered sugar, sifted

⅛ teaspoon kosher salt

¼ cup (50 g) granulated sugar

¼ cup (60 ml) heavy cream

1 tablespoon unsalted butter

1 teaspoon pure vanilla extract

Whisk together the powdered sugar and salt in a small bowl. Combine the granulated sugar, cream, and butter in a small saucepan and bring to a boil. Pour over the powdered sugar, add the vanilla, and whisk until smooth.

Meyer Lemon Frosting

Makes ¾ cup (245 g)

1 cup (120 g) powdered sugar, sifted

⅛ teaspoon kosher salt

¼ cup (50 g) granulated sugar

3 tablespoons heavy cream

1 tablespoon unsalted butter

Finely grated zest of 1 Meyer lemon or 1 regular lemon

1 tablespoon fresh Meyer lemon juice or regular lemon juice

Whisk together the powdered sugar and salt in a small bowl. Combine the granulated sugar, cream, and butter in a small saucepan and bring to a boil. Pour over the powdered sugar and whisk until smooth. Add about half of the zest and all of the lemon juice. After frosting the scones, sprinkle with the remaining zest.

Maple Frosting

Makes about ¾ cup (215 g)

½ cup (60 g) powdered sugar, sifted

¼ teaspoon kosher salt

⅓ cup (80 ml) pure maple syrup

¼ cup (60 ml) heavy cream

1 tablespoon unsalted butter

1 teaspoon pure vanilla extract

Whisk together the powdered sugar and salt in a small bowl. Combine the maple syrup, cream, and butter in a small saucepan and bring to a boil.

Pour over the powdered sugar, add the vanilla, and whisk until smooth.

Chocolate Frosting

Makes about ¾ cup (210 g)

1 cup (120 g) powdered sugar, sifted

3 tablespoons (15 g) unsweetened cocoa powder

⅛ teaspoon kosher salt

¼ cup (60 ml) heavy cream

1 tablespoon unsalted butter

Whisk together the powdered sugar, cocoa powder, and salt in a small bowl. Combine the cream and butter in a small saucepan and bring to a boil. Pour over the powdered sugar mixture and whisk until smooth.

Favorite Nut Glaze

Makes about ½ cup (145 g)

1 cup (120 g) powdered sugar

1 tablespoon nut butter, such as almond, hazelnut, or peanut butter

¼ teaspoon kosher salt

2 to 3 tablespoons heavy cream or nut milk

In a stand mixer fitted with the paddle (or in a medium bowl with a wooden spoon), combine the powdered sugar, nut butter, and salt. Gradually beat in the cream and mix until the glaze is smooth and glossy.

opposite: Blueberry Scones + Meyer Lemon Frosting

Seasonal Fruit Crisp with Oat-Buckwheat Streusel Topping

Softened butter, for the
baking dish

FRUIT FILLING OF YOUR CHOICE
(recipes follow; choose one)

STREUSEL TOPPING

½ cup (50 g) uncooked
rolled oats

½ cup (60 g) unbleached all-
purpose flour

¼ cup (30 g) buckwheat flour

¼ cup packed (50 g) dark or
light brown sugar

2 tablespoons granulated
sugar

¼ teaspoon ground cinnamon

¼ teaspoon kosher salt

⅛ teaspoon freshly grated
nutmeg

6 tablespoons (85 g) unsalted
butter, cut into ½-inch
(1.25 cm) pieces

FOR SERVING

Ice cream or whipped cream

In this world, there are cobbler people and there are crisp people. I am a crisp person. Buttery, sugary nuggets of streusel glazed with bubbling fruit juices? Come on!

Buckwheat is quite assertive, so I tame it with white flour, but in this case, the bitter edge of buckwheat plays beautifully with the rest of the streusel ingredients. This streusel topping and the basic method will be good with just about any seasonal fruit, but the amounts of sugar and cornstarch in the filling will vary according to how sweet and juicy your fruit is . . . or isn't.

This crisp travels nicely through the seasons, so use whatever looks good. I'm including four favorites. —**Makes one 8 × 8-inch (20 × 20 cm) pan or pie dish (see Note)**

Heat the oven to 350°F (175°C). Butter an 8 × 8-inch (20 × 20 cm) baking dish with about 1 tablespoon soft butter.

MAKE THE FRUIT FILLING: In a large bowl, toss the fruit with the cornstarch, sugar, salt, and optional flavoring. Set aside and stir from time to time until the sugar is no longer dry looking.

MAKE THE STREUSEL TOPPING: Put the oats, all-purpose flour, buckwheat flour, brown sugar, granulated sugar, cinnamon, salt, and nutmeg in a large bowl and whisk to blend ●. Drop in the butter and, with clean hands, pinch, squeeze, and otherwise knead the butter into the dry ingredients, aiming to form small clumps. This will create the "streusel-y" texture.

Spread the fruit and any juices in the bowl into the prepared pan ●. Cover with the streusel topping ●. Bake until the juices start to bubble around the edges

and the topping is golden brown, 40 to 50 minutes. Let cool for at least 15 minutes before serving, so that the juices can thicken up.

Serve warm, with ice cream or whipped cream.

Note: Double all the ingredients and bake in a 9 × 13-inch (23 × 33 cm) baking dish.

FRUIT FILLING

Choose from one of the recipes that follow.

Rhubarb Filling

6 cups 1-inch (2.5 cm) chunks rhubarb (about 1½ lb/675 g)

1 tablespoon cornstarch

½ cup (100 g) granulated sugar, more if your fruit is tart

¼ teaspoon kosher salt

¼ teaspoon ground aniseed (optional)

Mixed Berry Filling

6 cups mixed fresh berries (about 2 lb/910 g)

1 tablespoon cornstarch

½ cup (100 g) granulated sugar, more if your fruit is tart

¼ teaspoon kosher salt

¼ teaspoon ground cinnamon (optional)

Nectarine Filling

5 cups 1-inch (2.5 cm) chunks nectarine (about 1¾ lb/850 g)

1 tablespoon cornstarch

½ cup packed (105 g) dark or light brown sugar, more if your fruit is tart

¼ teaspoon kosher salt

¼ teaspoon pure almond extract (optional)

Pear Filling

4 cups ½-inch (1.25 cm) pear slices (about 1½ lb/675 g)

1 tablespoon cornstarch

½ cup (100 g) granulated sugar, more if your fruit is tart

¼ teaspoon kosher salt

¼ teaspoon ground cardamom (optional)

Corn

Corn

Zea mays

▸ GLUTEN-FREE ◂

•▷ *Why I love it:* As someone who cooked in Rome and owns an Italian restaurant, I equate corn with polenta. You can call it grits, cornmeal mush, or whatever suits your fancy, but for me, a pot of thick, smooth, golden cornmeal is corn's highest expression.

•▷ *What it tastes like:* Dried corn tastes nothing like fresh. That's because when corn is fresh, such as corn on the cob, it's considered a vegetable, but when it's dried, as in cornmeal, masa harina, hominy, or popcorn, corn becomes a grain and tastes more earthy than sweet. Hominy has a unique flavor, slightly sour and mineral-y with an appealing chewy texture.

•▷ *Common forms:* Polenta is technically a specific kind of cornmeal made from Italian eight-row flint corn (*otto file*), but any medium or fine cornmeal will do as polenta. Grits are simply a coarsely ground cornmeal, and hominy (dried or canned) is corn kernels that have been nixtamalized (soaked in a lye or lime bath to soften the outer hulls). Hominy is ground into a flour called masa harina, which is then used to make masa, the basis of Mexican corn tortillas, tamales, and other dishes.

•▷ *Favorite ways to prepare it:* As polenta, natch. But corn fritters and corn bread are just fine, too. Hominy wants to swim in a soup or stew, where it can absorb all the surrounding flavor.

•▷ *How it's good for you:* For a while, corn was considered not super nutritious, partly because of its association with the dreaded high-fructose corn syrup that so many food manufacturers were dosing their products with. And with the recent focus on healthy fats, corn was suspect because of its quantity of omega-6 fatty acids, which are not as nutritious as omega-3s. But the overall view is that corn is plenty healthy and is loaded with lots of antioxidants and carotenoids, including lutein and zeaxantin, which are good for eye health, and when it's nixtamalized (soaked in an alkaline solution), as is the case with corn used for tortillas, tamales, posole, and other Mexican, Central American, and South American dishes, the calcium and niacin contents increase.

Details

→ 1 cup uncooked cornmeal weighs 5¾ ounces (160 g).

→ 1 cup uncooked hominy weighs 6 ounces (170 g).

→ Use 4 parts liquid to 1 part cornmeal to cook a cornmeal mush like polenta by the absorption method. Use the boil-like-pasta method for hominy.

→ Cook cornmeal as polenta for 25 to 45 minutes, though I often cook mine for much longer, adding liquid as needed to keep it creamy. For hominy, soak it overnight, then cook for about 1 hour.

→ 1 cup (160 g) uncooked cornmeal yields 4 cups (1 kg) cooked.

→ 1 cup (170 g) uncooked hominy yields 3 cups (720 g) cooked.

Popcorn and Friends

3 tablespoons coconut oil

⅓ cup (75 g) unpopped organic popcorn kernels

Kosher salt or Popcorn Seasoning (recipes follow)

Popcorn is underrated. Compared to many crunchy snacks, it's inexpensive and easy to make, and the unpopped popcorn itself lasts in your cupboard for ages. Especially when you dress it up with one of the seasonings on page 99, popcorn can be downright exciting. —**Makes about 10 cups (110 g)**

Heat the oil in a large saucepan with a lid over medium-high heat.

Carefully add 5 or 6 kernels to the oil and cover the pan. Listen for the pop. When at least 3 or 4 have popped, remove the pan from the heat, carefully remove the lid (keep your face away, to avoid surprises), and add the rest of the kernels.

Cover the pot again, return it to the heat, and cook, shaking the pan gently. Once you're hearing only one pop every 2 or 3 seconds, take the pan off the heat and immediately pour the popcorn into a large bowl. Watch out, because one or two kernels may still pop at this point.

While the popcorn is still slightly warm but not hot, sprinkle with salt or a seasoning of your choice.

continues

POPCORN SEASONINGS

Choose one or several of these popcorn seasonings, pair it with some nice organic popcorn kernels, and you have yourself a fine gift, for thank-yous, housewarmings, or any time you want to bring a treat that feels handmade (and is economical).

"Cool Ranch" Seasoning

Makes about 1½ cups (165 g)

½ cup (30 g) nutritional yeast
¼ cup (30 g) buttermilk powder
3 tablespoons kosher salt
2 tablespoons sugar
2 tablespoons garlic powder
2 tablespoons onion powder
1 tablespoon Aleppo pepper flakes or other fruity, mild chile flakes
2 tablespoons dried parsley
2 tablespoons dried basil
1 tablespoon dried dill
1 teaspoon ground celery seed
½ teaspoon freshly ground black pepper

Stir all the ingredients together and store in a tightly sealed glass jar for up to 2 months. Sprinkle onto cooked popcorn while it's still slightly warm but not hot.

"Cracker Jack" Seasoning

Makes about 1¼ cups (180 g)

¾ cup (100 g) ground Peanut Brittle (page 53, ground in a food processor)
¼ cup (35 g) chopped honey-roasted peanuts (optional)
¼ cup (30 g) date sugar
1 tablespoon kosher salt
1 teaspoon granulated sugar

Stir all the ingredients together and store in a tightly sealed glass jar for up to 1 month; the honey-roasted peanuts might soften a bit. Sprinkle onto cooked popcorn while it's still slightly warm but not hot.

Coconut Curry Seasoning

Makes about 1½ cups (100 g)

¾ cup (30 g) unsweetened coconut flakes
½ cup (30 g) nutritional yeast
2½ tablespoons kosher salt
1½ tablespoons mild or hot curry powder
2 teaspoons finely grated lime zest
1 teaspoon sugar

Stir all the ingredients together and store in a tightly sealed glass jar for up to 2 months. Sprinkle onto cooked popcorn while it's still slightly warm but not hot.

Sesame Turmeric Seasoning

Makes about 1¼ cups (135 g)

½ cup (80 g) sesame seeds, toasted
½ cup (30 g) nutritional yeast
1 tablespoon kosher salt
2 teaspoons dried parsley
1 teaspoon garlic powder
1 teaspoon ground turmeric
1 teaspoon paprika
¾ teaspoon ground cumin
2 teaspoons finely grated lemon zest (optional)

Stir all the ingredients together and store in a tightly sealed glass jar for up to 2 months. Sprinkle onto cooked popcorn while it's still slightly warm but not hot.

French Onion Seasoning

Makes about 1 cup (180 g)

¾ cup (60 g) nutritional yeast
5 tablespoons (35 g) onion powder
5 tablespoons (35 g) dried minced onion
¼ cup (30 g) finely grated Parmigiano-Reggiano cheese
2½ tablespoons kosher salt
2 teaspoons garlic powder
1 teaspoon ground caraway
1 teaspoon buttermilk powder

Stir all the ingredients together and store in a tightly sealed glass jar for up to 2 months. Sprinkle onto cooked popcorn while it's still slightly warm but not hot.

Cornmeal Fritters

½ cup (80 g) medium-grind
cornmeal

½ cup (60 g) whole wheat flour

1 teaspoon baking powder

½ teaspoon kosher salt

¼ teaspoon baking soda

8 twists of black pepper

½ cup (120 ml) buttermilk

½ cup (75 g) finely chopped
onion

1 large egg, lightly beaten

2 tablespoons honey

3 or 4 dashes hot sauce

Add-ins (optional; list follows)

Vegetable oil, for frying

+ ADD-INS:

Aim for about 1 cup (240 ml)
total add-ins, in whatever
combination sounds good
to you.

Fresh, frozen, or
canned corn kernels

Chopped scallions or
spring onions

Chopped jalapeños or
other fresh hot chile

Grated sharp cheddar cheese

Pinch of ground cumin

1 tablespoon chopped
fresh thyme or rosemary

Sautéed "succotash vegetables":
small-diced green beans,
zucchini, red bell pepper,
sweet onion

Chopped pickles, especially
pickled green tomatoes and
spicy green beans

Chopped cooked shrimp,
picked crab, or chopped
smoked oysters

Deep-frying at home isn't something most of us do very often, but these corn fritters are definitely a good reason to heat up a pot of oil. You actually don't need a large quantity of oil, as you can fry just a few at a time, which keeps things manageable. Be sure your oil is fresh; I like to start with a new bottle just to be sure. Even something we assume is "shelf stable" like vegetable oil can become rancid if it sits in the cupboard too long.

The fritters are tasty with just the basic recipe—they remind me of hush puppies—but they can be insanely good with some of the add-ins listed below. Take a look and go crazy with your ingredients. Serve your fritters with a dusting of finely grated Parmigiano-Reggiano (yes, I know that's not very Southern) or with one of these dips: Yogo Ranch Dressing (page 313), Turmeric Mayo (page 315), Spicy Creamy Green Sauce (page 314), Tzatziki (page 318), or Romesco Sauce (page 315).
—**Makes about 12 fritters**

Mix the cornmeal, whole wheat flour, baking powder, salt, baking soda, and black pepper in a small bowl. In another bowl, mix the buttermilk, onion, egg, honey (you might need to stir quite a bit to dissolve and distribute the honey), and hot sauce. Pour the cornmeal mixture into the buttermilk mixture and stir just until mixed. If you're including any of the add-ins, fold them in now.

Pour 2 inches (5 cm) of oil into a Dutch oven or heavy-bottomed pan and heat to 375°F (190°C). Arrange a double layer of paper towels on a large plate or tray.

When the oil is hot, use two tablespoons to scoop out some batter and then gently place it into the oil. It will sink and then float back up. Repeat with a few more portions of batter, pausing for a few seconds after adding each to let the oil regain temperature.

Fry the fritters until they are a rich golden brown and the interior is fully cooked, about 6 minutes total, flipping with tongs or a fork a few times for even cooking.

Scoop out with a slotted spoon or spider and drain on the paper towels. Serve right away. If you have leftovers, keep them covered in the refrigerator for up to 2 days and reheat wrapped loosely in foil in a 375°F (190°C) oven until warmed through. They won't be as crisp as when first fried, but they'll still be delicious.

Perfect Soft Polenta

1 cup (160 g) stone-ground
  cornmeal

1 teaspoon kosher salt

1 quart (1 liter) water

2 tablespoons unsalted butter

About ½ cup (60 g) grated
  Parmigiano-Reggiano or
  pecorino cheese, or other
  cheese of your choice, or
  more to taste (optional)

My heart belongs to the Italian kitchen, so what can I say about polenta other than that it is a necessity of life. I'm lucky enough to get stone-ground cornmeal from an amazing Oregon farm, Ayers Creek, that grows a couple of old varieties of corn, including Amish butter corn and Roy's Calais flint corn. Look for a cornmeal made from corn grown in your region, or try a more widely distributed but high-quality brand of polenta such as Golden Pheasant. A bowl of creamy polenta flavored with salt, butter, and Parmigiano-Reggiano is all a human soul requires, but you can use creamy polenta as a base for so many other delicacies—see the end of the recipe for some ideas for variations. —**Serves 4**

Put the cornmeal and salt in a large heavy-bottomed pot and slowly whisk in the water. Bring the mixture to a boil and then adjust the heat so the polenta just barely simmers when covered. Be careful, because the polenta will spit like lava, and it's just about as hot!

Cook over gentle heat, stirring often with a long spoon or stiff silicone spatula, and making sure to scrape the bottom of the pot and into the corners, until the cornmeal has fully expanded and doesn't feel at all crunchy when you take a bite and the polenta pulls away from the sides of the pan, anywhere from 45 minutes to 3 hours, depending on your polenta. I like to cook mine for a long time, as I think it just gets creamier and creamier.

Stir in the butter and cheese (if using), taste, and adjust with more salt if you like. For runny polenta, serve right away. For toppings, see Variations (below). For polenta that you'll cut and fry (see Fried Polenta Sticks, page 105), pour into an oiled shallow baking dish or sheet pan and let set at room temperature. Pick a pan size that will give you polenta about ½ inch (1.25 cm) thick.

Variations

→ Make an easy dinner with a bowl of soft polenta topped with wilted Swiss chard, kale, steamed broccoli, or other cooked greens and finished with a grating of Parmigiano-Reggiano.

→ Top each serving with a poached egg, a knob of salted butter, and some crispy fried bacon bits.

→ Top with sautéed mushrooms— including some wild ones, if possible. You can follow the directions for sautéing mushrooms on page 48.

→ Fold in some kimchi or sauerkraut for a crunchy, tangy contrast.

→ On the sweeter side, float some heavy cream or milk on top of an individual bowl, drizzle with molasses, and sprinkle with cinnamon and a handful of raisins. Don't worry that there's cheese in the polenta; the flavors will all meld just fine. (Though if you're making the polenta expressly for dessert, skip the cheese.)

→ Top with Honey Butter with Bee Pollen (page 307) or Maple Butter (page 307) and a handful of fresh blueberries or raspberries.

→ Top with Beef and Pork Ragù (page 320) and a shower of grated cheese.

Fried Polenta Sticks

Perfect Soft Polenta
   (page 102)

Toppings and seasonings of
   your choice (list follows)

Extra-virgin olive oil or other
   oil, for frying

Aside from a big bowl of perfect polenta by itself, or with a dollop of ragù on top, a stick of fried polenta with a tasty topping is just about the best expression cornmeal can have. Make this using leftover polenta or cook up a pot of polenta expressly for frying these sticks. It will last in the fridge for up to 4 days (before you fry it), so you can make a batch and then serve them a couple of times during the week. —**Serves 4 to 8, depending on place in the meal and toppings**

Follow the directions for the soft polenta and pour the cooked—but still fluid—polenta onto an oil-rubbed sheet pan or other shallow dish with edges. You want the polenta sticks to be about ½ inch (1.25 cm) thick, so choose a pan that suits the amount of polenta you have. (If you're ever making a soft polenta to eat for dinner, make extra and pour that into an oiled pan and you're good to go for polenta sticks later.)

Let the polenta cool and firm up, about 30 minutes. When it is completely set, flip it out onto a cutting board and cut it into strips the size of fish sticks, or whatever shape you like.

Get your toppings ready before you start to fry. Arrange a layer of paper towels on a tray or plate to drain the polenta sticks.

Pour ¼ inch (6 mm) of oil into a wide skillet and heat over medium-high heat. Working in batches, carefully arrange a single layer of polenta sticks in the pan with enough room in between so you can slip the spatula in. Fry until each side is golden brown and the polenta sticks are heated through, about 4 minutes per side. Don't try to move the sticks for the first minute of cooking, or they may stick to the pan.

Drain for a few seconds on the paper towels, then serve right away, with the topping of your choice.

Toppings

→ Ava Gene's classic: Season the frying oil first by slowly toasting a smashed clove of garlic plus a few sprigs of thyme and/or rosemary. Discard the garlic and herbs, then fry the polenta. Serve with a generous grating of Parmigiano-Reggiano and a squeeze of lemon.

→ A big dollop of Romesco Sauce (page 315) and a shower of chopped fresh cilantro.

→ A ladleful of Beef and Pork Ragù (page 320).

Seafood Stew with Hominy and Warm Spices

⅔ cup (115 g) uncooked hominy

Kosher salt

8 ounces (225 g) shell-on shrimp, preferably wild-caught

Extra-virgin olive oil

3 cups (720 ml) chicken broth or vegetable broth, homemade or low-sodium store-bought, or water

2 teaspoons smoked paprika, sweet or hot

½ teaspoon ground cumin

1 teaspoon ground turmeric

¼ teaspoon ground cinnamon

¼ teaspoon ground ginger

Pinch of saffron threads

½ cup (75 g) thinly sliced onion

1 tablespoon finely chopped fresh ginger

1 tablespoon finely chopped garlic

Big pinch of dried chile flakes

3 tablespoons tomato paste

1 cup (240 ml) dry white wine

1 pound (450 g) mussels, rinsed and debearded

8 ounces (225 g) firm but flaky white-fleshed fish, such as cod, halibut, ling cod, or hake, cut into 2-inch (5 cm) pieces

2 to 3 tablespoons fresh lemon juice

Freshly ground black pepper

½ cup (15 g) roughly chopped fresh cilantro or flat-leaf parsley

Chewy but tender, hominy adds great body to this brothy stew. The kernels contribute a tiny bit of starch, which thickens the liquid just the right amount, and they readily absorb the warm, Moroccan-inspired palette of spices. The recipe calls for cooking the hominy before adding it to the stew, so be sure to plan ahead for that, as hominy requires some soaking and long cooking to get it to just the right consistency. As for the seafood, use what looks best at your market, as long as you include the shrimp, whose shells produce a flavorful broth.

As with all fish stews, this one would love to be served with a big slice of grilled bread brushed with olive oil and rubbed with garlic or slathered with Turmeric Mayo (page 315). —**Serves 4**

The night before you want to make the stew, put the hominy in a bowl and cover with cool water by a couple of inches. Soak overnight.

Drain the hominy, put it in a medium saucepan, and add water to cover by 3 inches (7.5 cm) and ½ teaspoon salt. Bring to a simmer and cook until fully tender and the kernels are starting to "explode" a bit, about 1 hour. Drain well and set aside.

Peel and devein the shrimp, saving the shells and keeping the shrimp in the fridge (if you have the fishmonger peel them, ask them to give you the shells).

To make a quick shrimp stock, heat a medium saucepan over medium heat. Add a glug of olive oil and the shrimp shells and toast them up for a good 5 minutes, stirring frequently. Add the broth and simmer

for 30 minutes. Season with ½ teaspoon salt, then strain the stock to remove the solids and return it to the saucepan.

Combine the smoked paprika, cumin, turmeric, cinnamon, ground ginger, and saffron in a little bowl and set aside.

Heat a generous glug of olive oil in a large pot, such as a Dutch oven, over medium-high heat. Add the onion and fresh ginger. Cook, stirring and scraping, until the onion is soft and fragrant but not at all browned, about 2 minutes. Add the garlic and chile flakes and cook another minute or so, making sure nothing browns.

Add the tomato paste and the smoked paprika mixture and cook, stirring and scraping, until the tomato paste starts to toast and darken a bit and the spices smell fantastic, another 1 to 2 minutes.

continues

Seafood Stew with
Hominy and Warm Spices,
continued

Add the wine and simmer until
reduced by about half, about
5 minutes. Increase the heat to
high, add the mussels, and cover
the pot. Steam the mussels,
shaking the pot every few
seconds, until they are all open;
this should take 2 to 3 minutes,
depending on the mussels.
Using a slotted spoon or tongs,
transfer all the opened mussels
to a bowl and set aside. If a few
are still closed, cook them for
another minute or so; discard
any stubborn ones that refuse
to open.

Add the shrimp stock and the
cooked hominy to the pot. Adjust
the heat to a simmer, cover, and
simmer until the hominy is plump
and tender, 6 to 8 minutes. Add
the chunks of fish and simmer for
a couple of minutes, then add the
shrimp and cook, uncovered so
you can see what's happening,
until the fish and shrimp are
opaque. It's okay if the fish starts
to flake apart a bit, that's the idea.

Add 2 tablespoons of the lemon
juice and taste the broth. Adjust
with black pepper and more salt,
chile flakes, and/or lemon juice
until the flavor is nice and bright.
Return the mussels to the pot,
shower with the cilantro, and
serve in big bowls, with an extra
bowl at the table for the empty
mussel shells.

Variation

Add the kernels cut from one or
two ears of sweet corn when you
add the shrimp.

Tender, Slightly Sweet Corn Bread

Pictured on pages 110-11

½ cup (60 g) whole wheat, spelt, or farro flour

2 cups (320 g) stone-ground cornmeal

2 tablespoons sugar

2 teaspoons baking powder

½ teaspoon baking soda

2 teaspoons kosher salt

½ cup (120 ml) boiling water

1½ cups (335 g) plain whole-milk yogurt

2 large eggs

4 tablespoons (60 g) unsalted butter

Honey Butter with Bee Pollen (page 307), for serving (optional)

Your corn bread will of course only be as good as your cornmeal, so be sure to use a good stone-ground meal, preferably one that's fresh from a local mill (see Sources, page 332). Stone-ground meals are usually coarser than the typical grocery store stuff (such as Quaker cornmeal), so here I use a neat trick that keeps the texture of the final bread from being too coarse as well: I make a mush with some of the cornmeal, which allows it to absorb some liquid before being blended into the batter.
—**Makes one 9-inch (23 cm) round corn bread**

Heat the oven to 400°F (200°C). Place a 9-inch (23 cm) cast-iron skillet (or other heavy ovenproof baking dish, such as a small Dutch oven) on the middle rack.

Whisk together the whole wheat flour, 1½ cups (240 g) of the cornmeal, the sugar, baking powder, baking soda, and salt in a large bowl.

Put the remaining ½ cup (80 g) cornmeal in a small bowl and stir in the boiling water. Stir vigorously until it becomes thick and mushy.

Whisk together the yogurt and eggs in a medium bowl, then whisk in the cornmeal mush. Pour this mixture into the dry ingredients and stir several times to blend. You don't want to overmix or the corn bread will be tough, so it's okay if a few lumps remain.

Take the skillet from the oven (use good oven mitts!), add the butter, and swirl the pan so it melts. It will probably sizzle quite a bit and even brown, which is fine. But if it looks or smells burned, pour it out and start over!

Pour about half the melted butter into the corn bread batter and stir to incorporate. Pour all the batter into the hot pan, making sure to scrape in every last bit of batter.

Return the skillet to the oven and bake the corn bread until it starts to pull away from the sides and looks a bit browned around the edges, and a skewer comes out clean when you poke the center, 20 to 30 minutes.

Let the corn bread cool for about 10 minutes in the skillet, then run a knife between the corn bread and the pan to loosen the corn bread and tip it onto a clean towel. Use the towel to invert the corn bread onto a rack. Let cool, though eating it while it's still slightly warm, with the honey butter, is an excellent idea. The corn bread will reheat nicely wrapped in foil in a 375°F (190°C) oven for about 10 minutes.

Variations

Any of these additions will bring new dimension to classic corn bread, but why stop at one?

SAVORY

Fold 2 cups (320 g) fresh corn kernels into the batter.

Fold 1 cup (120 g) grated sharp cheddar into the batter.

Fold ½ cup (120 g) drained chopped canned green chiles into the batter.

SWEET

Fold 2 cups (300 g) fresh or frozen blueberries into the batter.

Lay slices of ripe peach on top of the batter once it's in the skillet.

Millet

Millet

*Panicum miliaceum, Pennisetum glaucum,
Setaria italica, Eleusine coracana,
Digitaria exilis*

▶ GLUTEN-FREE ◀

•▷ **Why I love it:** Millet is enjoyed throughout much of the world, especially West Africa and India (where its drought tolerance and sustainability are advantages), yet in the US, millet hasn't been widely known until recently, except perhaps by cooks whose heritage connected them to millet-loving countries or some early devotees of "health food." The general interest in whole grains and in particular the search for gluten-free grains has brought millet to more American tables than ever before. I love millet for its light, fluffy texture and mild flavor, which pairs equally well with sweet and savory ingredients.

•▷ **What it tastes like:** Millet has a mild, nutty flavor and a cute little round grain shape that cooks up light and tender, a bit like couscous (which, to be clear, is not a grain, but rather a tiny pasta made from wheat flour and water).

•▷ **Common forms:** Proso millet is the most commonly consumed millet variety in the United States and Europe, though it's often just labeled "millet." Teff is a type of millet with seeds less than 1 mm in diameter (tiny), and teff flour is used for injera, the iconic flatbread from Ethiopia.

•▷ **Favorite ways to prepare it:** I love millet in breakfast dishes, with a bit of sweetness, but it's great in savory dishes also. Millet does well with the absorption method, though if I'm going to use it in a highly seasoned dish, I'll just cook it in lightly salted water using the boil-like-pasta method, which requires less tending from the cook.

•▷ **How it's good for you:** Like all whole grains, millet is powerfully nutritious. High in fiber and with a low glycemic index, millet contains fewer calories per cup than most other grains, such as brown rice or quinoa. Millet also contains significant amounts of B vitamins, iron, zinc, and magnesium, as well as antioxidant flavonoids and two amino acids—methionine and cysteine—that are lacking in all other grains.

Details

→ 1 cup uncooked millet weighs 7 ounces (200 g).

→ Use 2 parts liquid to 1 part millet; a bit less water will yield a fluffy pilaf consistency, while more liquid produces a creamy porridge.

→ Cook millet for 15 to 20 minutes.

→ 1 cup (200 g) uncooked millet yields 3½ cups (580 g) cooked.

→ 1 cup millet flour weighs 4¼ ounces (120 g).

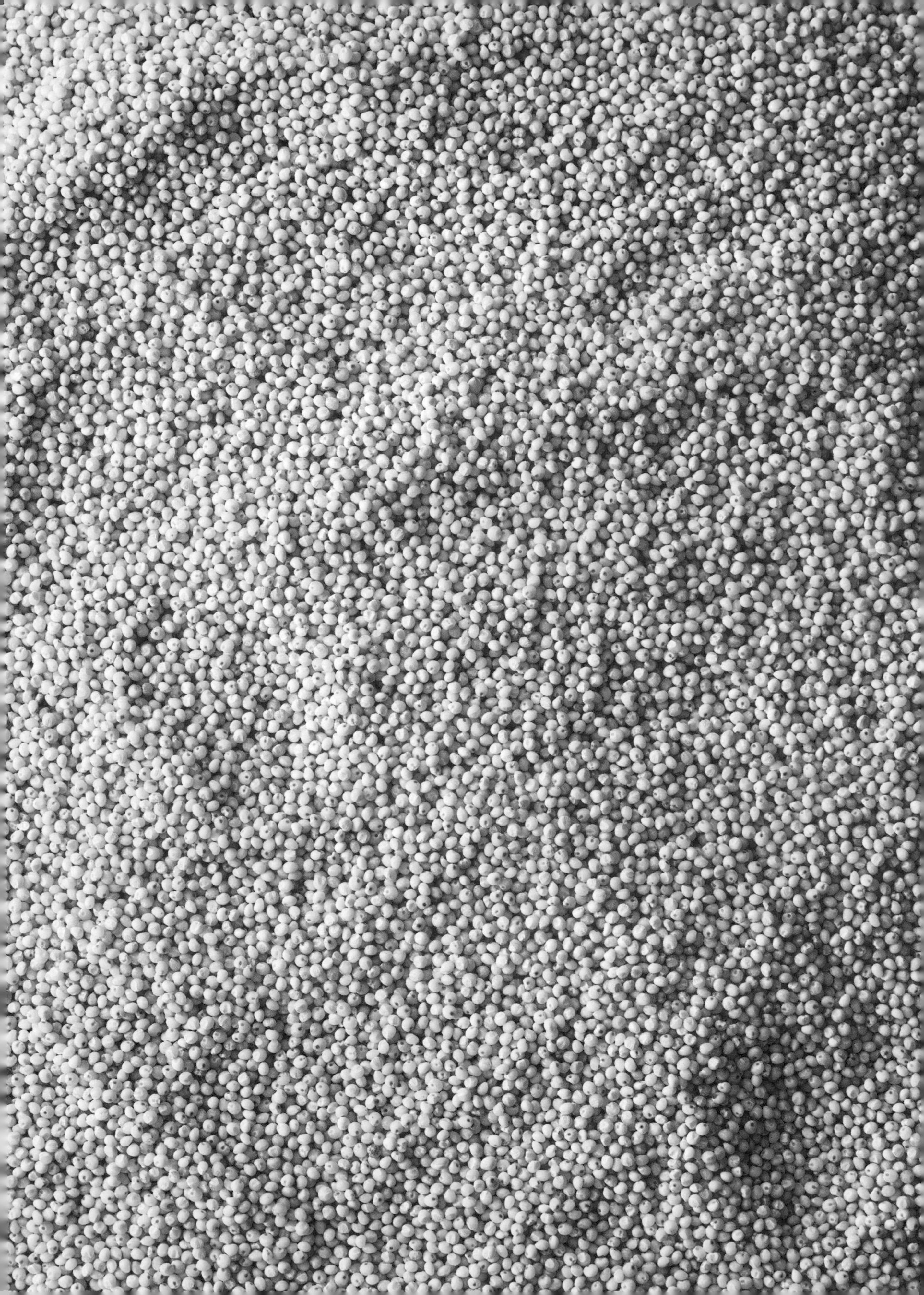

Millet Morning Porridge with Coconut Milk and Quick Mango "Jam"

Two 14.5-ounce (410 g) cans unsweetened full-fat coconut milk

1 cup (200 g) uncooked millet

½ teaspoon kosher salt

½ teaspoon pure vanilla extract

3 ounces (100 g) dried mango, cut or ripped into pieces no bigger than an inch or two

Pure maple syrup

Optional toppings: Toasted coconut, sesame seeds, and/or chopped toasted cashews

I'm calling this a "morning" porridge because I like eating it for breakfast, but it's so creamy and delicious that you could serve it as a dessert. You can do half coconut milk and half regular milk (or nut milk) to lighten things up a bit, because all coconut is indeed fairly indulgent. I like to make a larger batch of the mango topping and keep it in the refrigerator for up to about 10 days; it's excellent on the Muesli with Buckwheat, Dried Fruit, Coconut, and Turmeric (page 132) or a Whole Wheat English Muffin (page 246). —**Serves 4**

Pour the coconut milk into a large saucepan and bring to a boil. Add the millet and salt and adjust the heat to a gentle simmer. Cook very gently, stirring occasionally, until the consistency is like sloppy risotto; the millet should still have a slight bite to it but should not feel chalky, 25 to 30 minutes. If it seems to be getting dry during cooking, add a bit of water. When it's cooked, stir in the vanilla.

Meanwhile, put the mango pieces in a small pan with enough water to cover. Bring to a boil and then reduce the heat to a gentle simmer. Cook, uncovered, until the mango is very soft and almost translucent and the water has cooked down to just a bit of syrup coating the mango, about 10 minutes; add more water during cooking if the pan gets too dry before the mango is soft.

To serve, top the warm porridge with the warm mango jam and a nice glug of maple syrup. Bonus points for toasted coconut, sesame seeds, and/or chopped toasted cashews.

Crispy Millet Cakes with Shrimp, Scallions, and Old Bay

1 cup (200 g) uncooked millet

Kosher salt

4 garlic cloves, smashed and peeled

1 pound (450 g) shrimp, preferably wild-caught, peeled and deveined

1 bunch scallions (about 6), thinly sliced

2 tablespoons Old Bay seasoning

Finely grated zest of 1 lemon

2 large eggs, beaten

2 tablespoons plain whole-milk or low-fat yogurt

1 cup (120 g) millet flour, barley flour, or brown rice flour (or any wheat flour, if you are okay with gluten)

Vegetable or extra-virgin olive oil, for frying

Lemon wedges, for squeezing

Yogo Ranch Dressing (page 313), Turmeric Mayo (page 315), Tzatziki (page 318), or Ginger, Garlic, and Fish Sauce Dipping and Dunking Sauce (page 314), for serving

These tasty, golden-crusted patties are a brilliant showcase for millet. The grain's neutral flavor lets the mild shrimp shine and nicely absorbs the ever-so-spicy Old Bay flavors. Millet's texture is tender but toothy, which makes the patties substantial enough to serve on a bun as a seafood sandwich with a slice of tomato and some crispy iceberg lettuce or with an egg on top for breakfast. And millet is gluten-free, so if you use millet flour as the binder, you're good. —Serves 4 to 6

Put the millet in a medium saucepan and add water to cover by 3 inches (7.5 cm), 1 tablespoon salt, and the garlic. Bring to a boil, cover, reduce to a simmer, and cook until very tender and no longer chalky, about 20 minutes.

Drain the millet and garlic, shaking to remove excess water. Let sit for a few minutes, then spread it onto a baking sheet and let dry, raking through the grains a few times for even drying. Smash the garlic with a fork, but leave in the mix.

Cut the shrimp into small pieces, so that they distribute well in the fritter mix, but large enough that they remain succulent. Cut "large" shrimp into 10 pieces.

Transfer the millet to a bowl. Add the shrimp, scallions, Old Bay, and lemon zest. Toss to mix.

Whisk together the eggs and yogurt in a small bowl and fold into the millet mixture. Let sit for a couple of minutes, then fold in half the flour—add only enough to make a shapeable batter. To

test, shape about ¼ cup (60 ml) of batter into a little puck. If it holds together, you're good. If it's too sloppy to hold together, stir in a bit more flour and repeat the test.

To cook, arrange a double layer of paper towels on a tray. To shallow-fry, pour about ¼ inch (6 mm) of oil into a large heavy skillet. To deep-fry, pour 3 inches (7.5 cm) of oil into a deep pot (be sure the pot is deep enough that the oil can't bubble up and overflow). Heat the oil to 335°F (168°C). Add a few patties and fry until deep golden brown and fully cooked inside (including the shrimp), about 4 minutes on each side, depending on the size of your patties. (Don't overcrowd the pan, and wait a few seconds before adding more patties so the oil temperature doesn't dip.) Remove with a slotted spoon and drain on the paper towels; cook the remaining patties.

Serve hot, with lemon wedges and the condiment/sauce of your choice.

Scallion-Sesame Millet Cakes

Extra-virgin olive oil

3 garlic cloves, finely chopped

1 cup (200 g) uncooked millet

3 cups (720 ml) chicken broth, homemade (page 311) or low-sodium store-bought, or water

Kosher salt

1 cup (150 g) finely sliced scallions, white and light-green parts only

½ cup (60 g) grated Parmigiano-Reggiano cheese

½ cup (80 g) grated carrot

2 teaspoons finely grated lemon zest

Freshly ground black pepper

A few dashes hot sauce

¼ cup (40 g) sesame seeds, lightly toasted

Lemon wedges, for squeezing

Spicy Creamy Green Sauce (page 314), Yogo Ranch Dressing (page 313), Tzatziki (page 318), or Cilantro-Raisin Vinaigrette (page 314), for serving (optional)

Millet is a grain with two personalities: When uncooked, it brings little pops of crunch to a dish, as in the streusel topping on Roasted Butternut Squash Maple Millet Bread (page 122). When long-cooked, millet becomes soft and creamy, which is what happens in these savory patties, allowing them to hold together without any binder such as egg.

I like to serve these as a side dish to a simple chop or roast chicken. These patties freeze well uncooked, too, so I usually cook and eat half the day I make them and chuck the rest in the freezer for easy meals later; just let the patties thaw on the counter for about 1 hour before cooking. —**Makes eight ½-cup (100 g) patties, serves 4 as a side dish**

Heat a glug of olive oil in a medium saucepan over medium heat. Add the garlic and sauté until fragrant, about 1 minute. Add the millet and cook, stirring constantly, until lightly toasted, about 5 minutes; you'll start to smell it and will see a slight color change.

Add the broth and ½ teaspoon salt (skip the salt if using salted broth), bring to a boil, then quickly reduce the heat to a simmer. Cover and cook until the millet is very tender and the liquid has been absorbed, about 20 minutes. For this dish, you want to slightly overcook the millet so that it gets porridge-y. If the millet is very tender but there's liquid left, just drain it off; if the water has been absorbed but the millet isn't fully tender, add a few tablespoons more water and keep cooking until very tender.

Remove the millet from the heat, fluff it up a bit with a fork, and stir in the scallions, Parmigiano, carrot, and lemon zest. Season lightly with salt, a few twists of black pepper, and the hot sauce. Taste and adjust the seasoning.

Cover the pan and let the millet mixture sit for about 20 minutes; this will take the edge off the raw scallions and also let the millet starch get sticky, which you want.

Fold in the sesame seeds. Scoop about ½ cup (100 g) of the mixture and shape into a patty. Repeat with the remaining mixture. Heat a generous glug of olive oil in a large skillet over medium-high heat. Working in batches, carefully lay the cakes in the pan, taking care not to crowd them. You'll want to add more oil between batches. Cook the cakes until heated through and nicely browned and crunchy on both sides, about 6 minutes per side.

Serve hot, with a lemon wedge and sauce of your choice, if desired.

Roasted Butternut Squash Maple Millet Bread

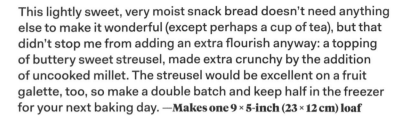

STREUSEL TOPPING

⅓ cup (40 g) whole wheat flour

¼ cup (50 g) uncooked millet

¼ cup packed (50 g) dark or light brown sugar

2 tablespoons granulated sugar

½ teaspoon kosher salt

¼ teaspoon ground cinnamon

4 tablespoons (60 g) unsalted butter, cut into small pieces

BREAD

Butter and flour, for the loaf pan

3 cups diced peeled butternut squash (about 1 lb/450 g)

1 tablespoon vegetable or olive oil

2 cups (240 g) whole wheat flour

½ cup (100 g) uncooked millet

Kosher salt

1 teaspoon baking powder

½ teaspoon baking soda

1 teaspoon ground cinnamon

1 teaspoon ground ginger

½ teaspoon ground cardamom

¼ teaspoon freshly grated nutmeg

2 large eggs

4 ounces (115 g) unsalted butter, melted

1 cup (240 g) sour cream

½ cup (120 ml) pure maple syrup

½ cup packed (100 g) light brown sugar

2 teaspoons pure vanilla extract

This lightly sweet, very moist snack bread doesn't need anything else to make it wonderful (except perhaps a cup of tea), but that didn't stop me from adding an extra flourish anyway: a topping of buttery sweet streusel, made extra crunchy by the addition of uncooked millet. The streusel would be excellent on a fruit galette, too, so make a double batch and keep half in the freezer for your next baking day. —**Makes one 9 × 5-inch (23 × 12 cm) loaf**

MAKE THE STREUSEL: Put the whole wheat flour, millet, brown sugar, granulated sugar, salt, and cinnamon in a small bowl and whisk to blend. Drop in the butter pieces and, with clean hands, pinch, squeeze, and otherwise knead the butter into the dry ingredients, aiming to form small clumps. This will give the topping its "streusel-y" texture. Set aside in a cool place.

MAKE THE BREAD: Heat the oven to 350°F (175°C). Butter and flour a 9 × 5 × 3-inch (23 × 12 × 7.5 cm) loaf pan.

Toss the squash with the oil, spread on a baking sheet, and roast until very tender and just slightly browned around the edges, about 30 to 40 minutes.

Meanwhile, whisk the whole wheat flour, the millet, 2 teaspoons salt, and the baking powder, baking soda, cinnamon, ginger, cardamom, and nutmeg in a bowl and set aside.

When the squash is done, let it cool slightly, then puree in a food processor until smooth. Transfer the puree to a mixer bowl and

beat in the eggs, melted butter, sour cream, maple syrup, brown sugar, and vanilla until smooth. Fold in the dry ingredients, mixing only until blended.

Spread the batter into the prepared pan. Distribute the streusel over the top of the batter, and put the pan on a baking sheet to catch any streusel that might fall off as the cake rises. Bake until a cake tester comes out clean, 45 to 55 minutes. Let the loaf cool in the pan on a rack.

Variations

Apple Maple Millet Bread: Omit the butternut squash. Sauté 4 cups (450 g) diced apple in 1 tablespoon unsalted butter until very soft, then mash with a fork to make a chunky puree. Use instead of the butternut squash puree.

Strawberry-Rhubarb Maple Millet Bread: Omit the butternut squash. Put 2 cups (225 g) sliced rhubarb and 1 cup (150 g) sliced strawberries in a bowl, sprinkle with ¼ cup (50 g) sugar, and leave to macerate for 1 hour. Mash together to form a chunky puree. Use instead of the butternut squash puree.

Oats

Oats

Avena sativa

▶ GLUTEN-FREE (BUT OFTEN CONTAMINATED WITH WHEAT DURING
GROWING AND PROCESSING. IF YOU ABSOLUTELY REQUIRE GLUTEN-FREE,
BE SURE TO CHECK, AS MANY BRANDS NOW SPECIFY) ◀

•▷ ***Why I love it:*** Most people like oats thanks to their familiarity with oatmeal, in either a breakfast bowl or a favorite bake-sale cookie. I often start my day with a filling bowl of oatmeal. I also drink my oats in the form of Oat Milk (page 128). Oats are quick-cooking, mild, and comforting.

•▷ ***What it tastes like:*** I think oats are one of the sweetest grains, with no bitterness at all. They play well with others and take on the flavors of whatever seasonings you add.

•▷ ***Common forms:*** Rolled oats, also called old-fashioned oats, are oat groats that have been steamed, rolled, flattened, and dried. Steel-cut oats are oat groats that have been cut into smaller pieces. Quick-cooking/instant oats are steamed for longer and rolled into thinner pieces than rolled oats. Don't use quick-cooking in recipes unless specifically called for.

•▷ ***How to prepare it:*** Oatmeal is the quintessential dish starring oats, and I especially like them in the form of "overnight oats" (see page 129), meaning no cooking involved. While I try to incorporate oats into my life in as many ways as possible, I do find myself thinking of oats mainly for sweet dishes rather than savory, which may be due to their slightly pasty texture. I've tried using oats in savory dishes, but it just doesn't work for me . . . the word "gruel" comes to mind.

•▷ ***How it's good for you:*** Oats are almost always whole grain, even in "instant" form, so you know you're getting a full measure of nutrition, including beta-glucan, the type of fiber (also found in barley) that has been shown to reduce cholesterol and improve heart health. For real.

Details

→ 1 cup uncooked rolled oats weighs 3½ ounces (100 g)

→ 1 cup uncooked steel-cut oats weighs 6 ounces (170 g)

→ Use 2 parts liquid to 1 part rolled oats; use 3 parts liquid to 1 part steel-cut oats.

→ Cook rolled oats for 5 to 10 minutes; cook steel-cut oats for 25 to 40 minutes.

→ 1 cup (100 g) uncooked rolled oats yields 2 cups (500 g) cooked.

→ 1 cup (170 g) uncooked steel-cut oats yields 3 cups (160 g) cooked.

→ 1 cup oat flour weighs 4¼ ounces (120 g).

Oat Milk

1½ cups (150 g) uncooked
  rolled oats
1 quart (1 liter) cool water
Pinch of kosher salt
2 pitted dates (optional)

You can make a fine oat milk without adding the optional dates, but I love the sweet toffee notes they contribute. You definitely want to strain this through cheesecloth, and not simply a mesh strainer, in order to get the best texture. Use oat milk as you would any milk—in your morning coffee, splashed on cereal, or poured into a tall frosty glass and set beside a slice of Super Fudgy Chocolate Oat Layer Cake with Chocolate Oat Milk Frosting (page 139). —**Makes 1 quart**

Line a sieve with a double layer of cheesecloth. Put the oats, water, salt, and dates (if using) into a blender and blend for 1 minute. Let the mixture sit in the blender for about 10 minutes to absorb more flavor, then pulse a few times more.

Strain the oat milk through the lined sieve into a container with a lid. Store in the refrigerator for up to 1 week. Shake before using.

Variations

Berry Oat Milk: Add 1 pint (300 g) strawberries, raspberries, blueberries—whatever you fancy—to the oats and water when you blend. The oat milk will have a slightly thicker texture; stir well before serving.

Horchata-Style Oat Milk: Add 1½ teaspoons pure vanilla extract, ½ teaspoon ground cinnamon, and 2 more pitted dates.

Overnight Oat Parfaits

Oat parfaits are my favorite brunch dish; they're easy to throw together once your dry base mix is made, so don't hesitate to make them for a weekday breakfast. Use regular rolled oats, not quick-cooking ones, which would get too mushy, or steel-cut, which take longer to soften. —**Makes about 20 parfaits**

DRY BASE MIX

7¼ cups (720 g) uncooked rolled oats

5 tablespoons (50 g) flaxseeds

2 tablespoons chia seeds

2 tablespoons poppy seeds

1⅔ cups (150 g) unsweetened cocoa powder (optional)

½ teaspoon kosher salt

OVERNIGHT ADD-INS

Dried strawberries

Dried blueberries

Chopped dried banana (the sticky kind, not banana chips)

Chopped dried figs

Chopped dried dates

LIQUID

Dairy milk

Nut, grain, or seed milk

Coconut water mixed with a splash of coconut milk, sweetened with honey, if you like

MAKE THE DRY BASE MIX: Mix the oats, flaxseeds, chia seeds, poppy seeds, cocoa powder (if using), and salt together in a big bowl. Store in an airtight container for up to 1 month.

TO ASSEMBLE OVERNIGHT PARFAITS: Assemble the parfaits in single-portion jars or lidded containers in this order (amounts below are all per parfait):

▷ **DRY BASE MIX:** ½ cup (50 g)—place in the bottom of the jar

▷ **ADD-INS:** 1 or 2 tablespoons of one or more—stir in

▷ **LIQUID:** slightly less than ½ cup—stir in

Cover and refrigerate for up to 24 hours.

TO SERVE: Dress each parfait with a spoonful or two of a creamy topping and a spoonful of a crunchy topping.

Creamy toppings

Jam, any flavor

Nut butter, any flavor

Maple syrup

Honey

Yogurt

Fresh fruit, any type

Crunchy toppings

Nuts, any type, lightly toasted and roughly chopped

Ground flaxseeds

Maple sugar

Bee pollen

Granola, store-bought or homemade (page 131)

Coconut chips

Freeze-dried fruits, crushed into powder

Sesame seeds

Poppy seeds

Puffed grains

Truly Irresistible Granola

5 cups (500 g) uncooked
   rolled oats

1¼ cups (50 g) unsweetened
   coconut flakes

1¼ cups (175 g) pumpkin seeds

1¼ cups (170 g) sunflower seeds

¾ cup packed (160 g) dark or
   light brown sugar

½ cup plus 1 tablespoon (135 g)
   pure maple syrup

¾ cup (180 ml) extra-virgin
   olive oil (use something
   mellow, not an aggressive
   Tuscan-type oil)

2¼ teaspoons kosher salt

This granola is fairly minimalist as far as granolas go—no nuts or raisins or other dried fruit—and yet the flavor and crunch factor are so fantastic, it's hard to stop eating. The other benefit of this recipe's simplicity is the cost: With no expensive nuts and using oats as the anchor ingredient, the price per pound is way less than anything you could buy. —**Makes about 2½ pounds (1 kg)**

Heat the oven to 300°F (150°C). Line two sheet pans with parchment.

Put all the ingredients in a big bowl ● and toss with clean hands or a big spoon until everything is completely and evenly distributed ●.

Divide the granola between the two sheet pans and spread into an even layer. Toast in the oven for 10 minutes, then rake through the granola to get the bottom bits on the top. Return the pans to the oven, swapping racks. Repeat this every 10 minutes until the granola is evenly toasted to a rich golden brown; this will take between 30 and 40 minutes in most ovens.

Let the granola cool completely. Store in an airtight container at room temperature for up to 2 weeks, possibly longer.

Muesli with Buckwheat, Dried Fruit, Coconut, and Turmeric

5 cups (500 g) uncooked
 rolled oats

1 cup (170 g) uncooked
 buckwheat groats, toasted
 (see Toasting, page 26)

1¼ cups (150 g) cashews,
 toasted and chopped

1 cup (140 g) Toasted Pumpkin
 Seeds (page 306)

1 cup (80 g) dried banana
 chips, crushed into small
 bits

1 cup (140 g) chewy dried
 banana pieces, cut into
 small bits

1 cup (120 g) dried pineapple
 chunks, chopped

½ cup (100 g) ground flaxseeds

½ cup (100 g) chia seeds

½ cup (80 g) sesame seeds

½ cup (20 g) unsweetened
 coconut flakes

2 tablespoons bee pollen
 (optional)

½ cup (65 g) date sugar

½ cup (65 g) maple sugar

2 tablespoons ground
 turmeric

1½ teaspoons kosher salt

¾ cup (180 ml) coconut oil

I'm naming this one of the "sleeper" recipes in this book, meaning at first glance, it might not seem too exciting—it's muesli, after all!—but once you've tasted it, you will be hooked. Not too sweet, but with just enough to keep you going in for the next bite, and so full of good and nutritious stuff, this is likely to become your new house cereal. I love the way the milk turns golden because of the turmeric, too.

The recipe makes a big batch, so if it's just for you or a couple of people, cut it in half. If you can't find date or maple sugar, use light brown sugar. —**Makes about 14 cups (1.9 kg), 14 to 20 servings**

Put the oats, buckwheat, cashews, pumpkin seeds, crushed banana chips, chopped chewy banana, pineapple, ground flaxseeds, chia, sesame, coconut flakes, and bee pollen (if using) in a large bowl and toss to mix.

Combine the date sugar, maple sugar, turmeric, salt, and coconut oil in a small saucepan and heat to melt the coconut oil. Stir to blend completely.

Pour this sugar-oil mixture over the grain mixture and toss, toss, toss until totally blended. Store in an airtight container in the cupboard for up to 1 month.

Note: Serve with milk or alt-milk as a breakfast cereal or use the "overnight oats" method (see page 129). You can add more good stuff when you serve, if you like: Fresh or frozen fruits, chocolate bits, nut butters, jams, and toasted pecans are all good places to start.

Chocolate-Coated Oat, Date, and Cashew Bars

1½ cups (150 g) uncooked rolled oats

1¼ cups (150 g) raw cashews (pieces are fine)

1 cup (140 g) raw hazelnuts, skin-on or blanched

2 cups (350 g) pitted dates, lightly packed into the measuring cup

½ cup plus 2 tablespoons (150 g) cashew butter

½ cup (45 g) unsweetened cocoa powder, either natural or Dutch process

¼ cup (60 ml) pure maple syrup

1 teaspoon kosher salt

1 tablespoon extra-virgin olive oil, plus more for oiling the pan

3 ounces (85 g) semisweet or bittersweet chocolate, chopped

Slightly chewier than most granola bars, these power treats get their appealing texture and deep toffee-like flavor from dates. Look for Medjool dates, which are usually very moist and sticky. You can use store-bought roasted cashews and hazelnuts, if you have them; simply skip the toasting step (but do toast the oats). —**Makes thirty-six 1 × 3-inch (2.5 × 7.5 cm) bars**

Heat the oven to 350°F (175°C).

Spread the oats, cashews, and hazelnuts on a sheet pan and bake for about 10 minutes, then stir everything around on the pan to promote even toasting. Continue baking until the mixture is nicely toasted and fragrant, another 5 to 10 minutes. Let everything cool. (If you're worried about overbrowning, slide everything off the hot sheet pan onto another tray or plate to cool.)

Put the cooled oats, cashews, and hazelnuts and the dates into a food processor and pulse until it all comes together. Add the cashew butter, cocoa powder, maple syrup, and salt and pulse again a few times. You're not trying to make a smooth puree, you simply want to distribute the ingredients more or less evenly. Finish the job by transferring to a bowl and mixing with your hands to really get it together.

Spread a thin layer of olive oil on the sides and bottom of a 9 × 13-inch (23 × 33 cm) baking dish, transfer the mixture to the dish, and press it out until it's all the same thickness and nice and flat, like granola bars. Refrigerate for 30 minutes.

Melt the chocolate and the olive oil in a small pan over very low heat. Pour over the chilled granola mixture and spread with a spatula into an even layer; it helps to drop the pan on the counter a few times from a height of a few inches to distribute the chocolate evenly. (It may seem like there's not enough chocolate, but once it has set up and the bars are cut, the chocolate layer will be appropriate.)

Refrigerate again for at least 1 hour before cutting into bars. Store in an airtight container in the refrigerator for up to 1 month.

Better Than Fig Newtons

DOUGH

1¼ cups (125 g) uncooked rolled oats or a blend of rolled grains (see Note)

1¼ cups (150 g) unbleached all-purpose flour

½ teaspoon kosher salt

¼ teaspoon baking soda

4 ounces (115 g) unsalted butter, at room temperature

¼ cup firmly packed (50 g) dark or light brown sugar

2 tablespoons honey

1 large egg, at room temperature

1 tablespoon whole milk

FILLING

2 cups (300 g) dried figs or pitted dates (if your fruit seems very dry or hard, soak in hot water for 30 minutes, then drain)

1 cup (120 g) walnuts, toasted

½ teaspoon kosher salt

¼ teaspoon ground cinnamon

½ cup (120 ml) water or fruit juice (apple, orange, cherry)

Egg wash: 1 large egg beaten with a splash of water

3 tablespoons turbinado sugar, for topping

Note: Rolled oats alone will work well in this recipe, but try a multi-grain hot cereal with a blend of different grains for added flavor and nuttiness.

This recipe is a strong upgrade from the store-bought cookie, which was my mother's idea of a "healthy" snack but never excited me much. Here the cookie pastry is tender and buttery and the filling has a chewy texture and toffee notes from real figs. Check that your dried figs are fairly moist, as some can be really leathery. —**Makes about 30 cookies**

MAKE THE DOUGH: Process the grains in a food processor until they form a light flour, with some small bits of grain visible. Add the all-purpose flour, salt, and baking soda and pulse a few times to blend; set aside.

In a stand mixer fitted with the paddle, cream the butter, brown sugar, and honey until light, about 3 minutes. Add the egg and mix to combine. Add the milk and mix. The mixture may look curdled, but that's okay!

Add the flour mixture and mix just until the dough starts to come together. With a large flexible spatula, stir to bring the dough together until no floury bits are left.

Dump the dough onto a work surface and shape into a square block. Wrap in plastic and refrigerate for at least 1 hour or up to 1 day.

MEANWHILE, MAKE THE FILLING: Pulse the figs in a food processor until they are mostly broken up. Add the walnuts, salt, and cinnamon and pulse until the mixture forms a coarse crumble. Gradually add the water or juice and pulse until the mixture is the consistency of a thick paste.

Heat the oven to 350°F (175°C). Line a sheet pan with parchment.

Divide the cold dough into 3 equal portions ●. Put one piece of the dough between sheets of plastic wrap or parchment (it's slightly sticky). Roll the dough into a rectangle about 15 inches (38 cm) long and 4 inches (10 cm) wide ●.

Spread one-third of the filling in a line about 1 inch (2.5 cm) wide down the rectangle of dough ●. Using the plastic wrap or parchment as an assist, lift each long side of the dough up and over the filling toward the center to form a tube 15 inches (38 cm) long ●. The dough should overlap a bit in the center to fully enclose the filling.

Flip the log so that it's seam side down on the parchment-lined sheet pan. Repeat the process with the remaining 2 portions of dough and remaining filling, spacing the logs evenly on the sheet pan. Brush the tops with the egg wash and sprinkle with the turbinado sugar ●.

Bake just until firm and barely darkening in color, about 15 minutes; the dough needs to be fully cooked but not browned or

crisp. Let the cookies cool on the sheet pan for about 5 minutes and then use a sharp knife to cut crosswise into 1½-inch-wide (4 cm) cookies (or whatever length you like) while still hot ●. Store the cookies in an airtight container at room temperature for up to 5 days.

Variation

Fresh Fig Newtons: Make the dough as directed above. For the filling, mix 3 cups fresh Black Mission figs (about 1 lb/450 g), halved, ¼ cup firmly packed (50 g) dark brown sugar, 2 teaspoons fresh lemon juice, and ¼ teaspoon kosher salt in a heavy-bottomed pot. Cook over medium-high heat until the sugar dissolves and the figs start to get juicy, smashing the figs up a bit with a wooden spoon. Reduce the heat to medium-low and cook until the figs have turned a deep shiny purple and the mixture is fairly thick, 15 to 20 minutes. Let cool completely.

Roll, fill, and bake as directed above.

Super Fudgy Chocolate Oat Layer Cake with Chocolate Oat Milk Frosting

Softened butter or baking
   spray, for the cake pans

1⅓ cups (280 g) granulated
   sugar

¾ cup (90 g) oat flour

¾ cup plus 2 tablespoons
   (105 g) whole wheat flour

½ cup (45 g) unsweetened
   cocoa powder

1¼ teaspoons baking powder

1¼ teaspoons baking soda

1 teaspoon kosher salt

¾ cup (180 ml) unsweetened
   oat milk

⅓ cup (80 ml) olive oil or
   vegetable oil

1 large egg, at room
   temperature

1½ teaspoons pure vanilla
   extract

⅓ cup (80 ml) boiling water

Chocolate Oat Milk Frosting
   (recipe follows)

The cake layers are very moist and will be quite fragile, especially if you accidentally underbake them. But the fudgy frosting is there to cover any mishaps, so if your layers rip, just piece them back together as you assemble the cake and know that they will taste perfect. If you make the cake ahead, you can keep it in the refrigerator, but be sure to give it at least 1 hour to come to room temperature before serving, or the texture will be too crumbly. The cake is gorgeous as is, but you can finish it with a sprinkle of toasted rolled oats. —**Makes one 9-inch (23 cm) two-layer cake**

Adjust an oven rack to the middle position. Heat the oven to 325°F (160°C). Grease the sides and bottoms of two 9-inch (23 cm) cake pans with butter or baking spray. Line the bottoms with rounds of parchment and grease the parchment.

Sift into a medium bowl the sugar, oat flour, whole wheat flour, cocoa powder, baking powder, baking soda, and salt and whisk to combine.

Whisk together the oat milk, oil, egg, and vanilla in a large bowl. Whisk the sugar-flour mixture into the wet mixture and stir or whisk vigorously for about 1 minute. Stir in the boiling water and mix until combined. The batter will be thinner than you might expect!

Divide the batter evenly between the prepared cake pans (it may seem like there's not quite enough batter, but it will rise, and the layers are meant to be thin). Bake until the cakes start to feel firm and just start to pull away from the sides of the pans, 25 to 30 minutes. (Note that the traditional "toothpick" test doesn't work well for this cake because it is so fudgy; the crumbs will always look wet on the toothpick.) Cool completely in the pans.

The cake layers will be fragile because they're so moist, so handle with care. Run a knife around the edge and flip a layer of cake out onto a serving dish. Remove and discard the parchment. Spread about one-third of the frosting over the layer, stopping about ¼ inch (6 mm) from the edge. Flip the other layer of cake onto the first layer. Remove and discard the parchment. Top the sides and top of the cake with the remaining frosting.

Store leftovers loosely wrapped in the refrigerator, but allow the cake to warm up at room temperature for at least 30 minutes before serving; the texture gets firm and crumbly when cold.

continues

Chocolate Oat Milk Frosting

If you're a milk chocolate fan, feel free to use milk instead of dark. And if you don't have oat milk, another nut milk, coconut milk, or dairy milk will work just fine.

Makes enough for one 9-inch (23 cm) two-layer cake

½ cup (120 ml) **unsweetened oat milk**

1½ cups (170 g) **good-quality semi- or bittersweet dark chocolate, finely chopped**

4 ounces (115 g) **unsalted butter, at room temperature**

1 cup (120 g) **powdered sugar, sifted**

½ cup (45 g) **unsweetened cocoa powder**

½ teaspoon **kosher salt**

Bring the oat milk to a simmer in a medium saucepan over medium heat. Remove the pan from the heat and add the chocolate. Let the mixture sit untouched for a few minutes so the chocolate can melt, then whisk until smooth. Cool to room temperature or just barely warm.

In a stand mixer fitted with the paddle, combine the butter, powdered sugar, cocoa powder, and salt and mix on low speed until it comes together like cookie dough, about 2 minutes. Add the chocolate mixture gradually in about four additions, mixing after each addition until smooth. This frosting stiffens up when it sits; if you won't use it within about 30 minutes, hold it in a warm place.

Quinoa

Quinoa

Chenopodium quinoa

▸ GLUTEN-FREE ◂

•▷ ***Why I love it:*** I'll admit it, I got a little sick of quinoa showing up in every magazine and blog post—the grain has one heck of a marketing campaign behind it—but this pseudo-grain earned the popularity contest win on its own merits.

•▷ ***What it tastes like:*** To put it simply, quinoa is delicious. It's crunchy when toasted, and has a unique springy, fluffy texture when cooked in liquid. It has a mild but slightly beany flavor that works well with so many other ingredients. And though quinoa comes in colors, they're very similar in flavor.

•▷ ***Common forms:*** White or tan is most common, but red, black, or a blend (tricolor) is easy to find.

•▷ ***How to prepare it:*** One reason quinoa was so quick to catch on is that it's so fast to cook. Unlike many other whole grains, it can be on the table in 15 minutes with no soaking required. I usually use the absorption method to cook quinoa, because the boil-like-pasta method can produce soggy quinoa.

•▷ ***How it's good for you:*** A lot of the credit for quinoa's popularity goes to its nutrients. A super-powered pseudo-grain, it provides complete protein, meaning it contains all the essential amino acids our bodies can't make on their own.

Details

→ 1 cup uncooked quinoa weighs 6½ ounces (185 g).

→ Use 1¾ parts liquid to 1 part quinoa as a rule of thumb for the absorption method.

→ Cook quinoa for 10 to 18 minutes.

→ 1 cup (185 g) uncooked quinoa yields 3 cups (515 g) cooked.

Quinoa and Watermelon Salad with Pistachios and Spicy Pickled Peppers

⅔ cup (120 g) uncooked quinoa

1¼ cups (300 ml) water

Kosher salt

2 cups (300 g) cubed ripe but firm watermelon, chilled

⅓ cup (75 g) cored, seeded, and sliced Quick-Pickled Chiles (page 277) or other pickled peppers, such as pepperoncini

¼ cup (40 g) finely chopped red onion

½ teaspoon dried oregano

Freshly ground black pepper

1 cup (30 g) lightly packed whole leaves and tender stems from a mix of fresh herbs (choose among basil, mint, parsley, cilantro, shiso)

1 lime

1 tablespoon pickling liquid from whatever chiles you're using

Extra-virgin olive oil

½ cup (60 g) roasted pistachios (salted or not), roughly chopped

This recipe is dead simple but so satisfying. The tender texture of quinoa plays nicely with watermelon's unique soft-but-crunchy consistency, and it soaks up all the tangy-sweet juices, making every bite flavor-packed. The watermelon tends to give off juice as it sits, however, so the dish is best right after you toss in the final ingredients. If you want to make this one ahead, keep the chunks of melon separate and toss everything together only at the last minute. The salad is also delicious with cantaloupe or another melon instead of watermelon. —Serves 4

Put the quinoa in a small saucepan with a lid, along with the water and ½ teaspoon salt. Bring to a boil, then quickly reduce the heat to a simmer. Cover and cook at a simmer until the quinoa is tender and the liquid has been absorbed, 15 to 18 minutes. If the quinoa is tender but there's liquid left, just drain it off; if the water has been absorbed but the quinoa isn't fully tender, add a few tablespoons more water and keep cooking until tender. Cool completely.

Put the watermelon, sliced chiles, onion, and oregano in a large bowl (it can be the serving bowl). Season generously with salt and pepper and toss gently.

Add the quinoa and fresh herbs. Finely grate the zest of the lime into the bowl, then squeeze the juice from one half onto the salad. Sprinkle on the pickling liquid and about 2 tablespoons olive oil and toss again. Taste and adjust with more salt, pepper, lime juice, pickle juice, or olive oil—you want the flavors to be very zingy.

Finish by tossing with the pistachios. Serve right away.

Roasted Carrot, Avocado, Pistachio, and Quinoa Salad

⅔ cup (120 g) uncooked quinoa

1¼ cups (300 ml) water

Kosher salt

8 ounces (225 g) carrots, cut into small chunks

Extra-virgin olive oil

¼ teaspoon dried chile flakes

½ medium red onion, cut into 4 wedges

Freshly ground black pepper

½ cup (60 g) pistachios, toasted and roughly chopped

1 cup lightly packed (30 g) fresh flat-leaf parsley leaves

About ⅓ cup (80 ml) Fresh Orange and Garlic Confit Vinaigrette (page 319), or freshly squeezed orange juice mixed with extra-virgin olive oil in a ratio of about 1:2

1 large or 2 smaller avocados

This salad is delicious just as it is, but you can make it a meal by adding grilled shrimp, chicken, or tofu. For a real upgrade, whisk a little lime juice (plus a bit of water and salt) into cashew butter until it's spreadable and use it to make a creamy base on your plate before piling on the salad. —Serves 2

Put the quinoa in a small saucepan with a lid, along with the water and ½ teaspoon salt. Bring to a boil, then quickly reduce the heat to a simmer. Cover and cook at a simmer until the quinoa is tender and the water has been absorbed, 15 to 18 minutes. If the quinoa is tender but there's liquid left, just drain it off; if the water has been absorbed but the quinoa isn't fully tender, add a few tablespoons more water and keep cooking until tender. Cool completely.

Heat the oven to 400°F (200°C).

Put the carrots in a bowl and toss with a nice glug of olive oil, the chile flakes, and 1 teaspoon salt. Spread onto a sheet pan.

Put the onion wedges in the same bowl. Drizzle on a bit of olive oil, season with ½ teaspoon salt and a few twists of black pepper, and toss gently to coat with oil but not break up the onion layers too much. Put the onion on another sheet pan or in a smaller baking dish.

Roast the carrots until tender and starting to brown around the edges, about 20 minutes. Roast the onion until it's also tender and starting to caramelize around the edges but not drying out, 15 to 25 minutes, depending on the size of your onion.

Put the roasted carrots and onion, quinoa, pistachios, and parsley in a bowl and toss gently. Drizzle on about half the vinaigrette and toss again.

Halve and pit the avocado(s) and, with a spoon, scoop out chunks of the flesh into the bowl. Toss again gently, trying not to smash up the avocado too much. Taste and season with more vinaigrette, chile flakes, salt, or black pepper.

Quinoa and Chicken Soup with French Lentils and Herbs

3 pounds (1.35 kg) bone-in, skin-on chicken parts, or a whole chicken, patted dry with paper towels

Extra-virgin olive oil

Kosher salt and freshly ground black pepper

1½ cups (240 g) finely diced carrots

1½ cups (225 g) finely diced celery

1½ cups (225 g) finely diced onion

6 garlic cloves, smashed and peeled

2 tablespoons roughly chopped fresh thyme

2 tablespoons roughly chopped fresh rosemary

1 tablespoon coriander seeds, toasted and finely ground

3 bay leaves

2 dried chiles, such as chiles de árbol

3 quarts (3 liters) chicken broth, homemade (page 311) or low-sodium store-bought, or water

¾ cup (135 g) dried French green lentils

¾ cup (135 g) uncooked quinoa

A couple of big handfuls of mixed fresh herbs and greens: choose from fresh parsley, cilantro, arugula, torn escarole, thinly sliced cabbage (optional)

Adding quinoa to soups (tricolor quinoa looks great here) pumps up the nutrition but keeps the soup's texture light. Making chicken soup always feels old school to me, like I'm someone's Jewish grandma, so I go all-in and render the chicken skin to make schmaltz, a wonderful fat for frying potatoes in later (see Note). —**Makes 3 quarts (3 L), serves 6 to 8**

Pull the skin off the chicken and set aside for making schmaltz (see Note). Or leave the skin on during cooking (for flavor) and pull it off and discard when you're picking off the chicken meat.

Heat a glug of olive oil in a large Dutch oven or heavy-bottomed soup pot over medium-high heat. Season the chicken lightly with salt and pepper, add to the pot, and brown nicely on all sides. Remove the chicken and set aside.

Add the carrots, celery, onion, garlic, thyme, rosemary, coriander, bay leaves, and chiles. Reduce the heat and cook until the vegetables are softer and lightly golden, about 10 minutes.

Return the chicken to the pot, add the chicken broth, and season with a big pinch of salt (unless your chicken broth is salty) and black pepper. Increase the heat and bring to a boil, then reduce the heat so the liquid simmers merrily but is not at a rolling boil (which would emulsify the fat from the chicken). Simmer, skimming off any foam from time to time,

until the chicken is cooked, 35 to 45 minutes. Remove the chicken and transfer to a tray. When it's cool enough to handle, pick off all the meat, pulling or cutting the larger parts (like the breasts, if using) into bite-size pieces.

Meanwhile, add the lentils to the simmering soup and cook for 10 minutes, then add the quinoa. Simmer until the lentils and quinoa are both cooked, another 15 minutes or so. Return the chicken to the pot to simmer for a few more minutes to heat the chicken through.

Taste the broth and adjust the salt and pepper to your taste. Discard the bay leaves. When it's time to serve the soup, toss in the herbs and greens, let them wilt, and then serve the soup in big bowls.

Note: To make schmaltz, simply put the uncooked chicken skin in a small pot over very low heat. Let it cook slowly until all the fat has rendered from the skin and you're left with golden fat and a few bits of crunchy skin. (These crunchy bits are called gribenes. They are a perfect snack for the cook.)

Crispy Quinoa Beet Cakes

1 large beet (about 6 oz/170 g), scrubbed

Kosher salt

⅔ cup (120 g) uncooked quinoa

1¼ cups (300 ml) water

2 cups (100 g) panko breadcrumbs (use whole wheat, if you like)

½ cup (75 g) finely chopped onion

¼ cup (40 g) roughly chopped drained capers

1 garlic clove, finely minced or grated on a rasp-style grater

1 teaspoon chopped fresh thyme

3 ounces (85 g) fresh goat cheese

3 large eggs, beaten

Extra-virgin olive oil

Freshly ground black pepper

These savory little patties can play a number of roles in your meal plan. A large size on a lovely brioche roll with some tender greens makes a fine sandwich, while "silver dollar"–size patties are perfect stuffed into a Whole Wheat Pita (page 245) as you would falafel, with some Turmeric Mayo (page 315) and Tzatziki (page 318). The quinoa adds substance to the grated beets, along with a nice portion of complete protein. —Makes 12 little patties

Put the beet in a small saucepan with about 1 inch (2.5 cm) water and a pinch of salt. Cover and simmer until the beet is completely tender when you poke it with a knife, 35 minutes to 1 hour, depending on whether your beet has a stubborn personality (check the water level during cooking and add more if needed). Cool until you can handle it, then slip off the skin and grate the beet on the large holes of a box grater.

Meanwhile, put the quinoa in a small saucepan with a lid, along with the water and ½ teaspoon salt. Bring to a boil, then quickly reduce the heat to a simmer. Cover and cook at a simmer until the quinoa is tender and the water is absorbed, 15 to 18 minutes. If the quinoa is tender but there's liquid left, just drain it off; if the water has been absorbed but the quinoa isn't fully tender, add a few tablespoons more water and keep cooking until tender. Cool completely.

Put the grated beet, cooked quinoa, panko, onion, capers, garlic, thyme, and 1 teaspoon salt in a large bowl. Toss to mingle the ingredients. Break up the goat cheese into bits, add them, and work them into the mixture.

When everything is nicely blended, add the eggs and toss once more to blend.

Let the mixture sit for about 15 minutes so the panko can fully hydrate. If it seems very wet and soggy, add a few more breadcrumbs, but the wetter the mixture is, the lighter and more tender the patties will be. Test for seasoning by frying a mini-patty in a little olive oil. Taste the patty, and if it's underseasoned, add pepper or more salt.

Shape the mixture into patties. These can be whatever size you like, just be sure they're all about the same size so that they cook evenly. Heat a healthy glug of olive oil in a large skillet over medium-high heat, carefully place as many patties as will fit without crowding, and cook until nicely browned and heated through, about 5 minutes per side. Serve hot or warm.

Leftover patties will keep in the fridge for up to 3 days; reheat them in a dry skillet for a few minutes. You can freeze the uncooked patties, individually wrapped well, for up to 2 months. Thaw in the fridge before cooking.

Crispy Quinoa "Tempura," Two Ways

**FOR FISH, SHRIMP,
AND OTHER SEAFOOD:**

1⅔ cups (200 g) whole wheat
flour

½ cup (90 g) uncooked red
quinoa

1 tablespoon baking powder

2 tablespoons cornstarch

½ teaspoon kosher salt

1 cup (240 ml) sparkling water

FOR VEGETABLES:

1⅔ cups (200 g) whole wheat
flour

⅔ cup (100 g) rice flour

½ cup (90 g) uncooked red
quinoa

2 tablespoons cornstarch

½ teaspoon kosher salt

1½ cups (360 ml) sparkling
water

Flaky salt, lemon wedges,
Turmeric Mayo (page 315),
and Tzatziki (page 318), for
serving

Here I give traditional batter even more crunch by adding uncooked quinoa, which pops during frying. I found that different ingredients ask for different batters: The one designed for fish has leavening, making it light and puffy, resulting in a fish-and-chips type of coating. The vegetable-specific batter is closer to a Japanese tempura batter, with rice flour along with whole wheat flour creating an exceptionally light crust.

I like to use sparkling water in both of these for extra lightness, but plain tap water will give you perfectly fine results. Make these batters right before you're ready to fry; they don't hold well. —**Makes enough to coat about 1 pound (450 g) of seafood or vegetables**

In a large bowl, whisk together the whole wheat flour (for the seafood version) or whole wheat and rice flour (for the vegetable version), quinoa, baking powder, cornstarch, and kosher salt to blend thoroughly.

Whisk in enough sparkling water to make a thin batter; you may not need the full amount of water, or you may need a few drops more. You want the consistency to be like thin pancake batter; you may need to fry a couple of tests to get it exactly right.

TO USE: Cut your ingredients into even pieces, so they will all cook at about the same rate. Cut dense vegetables thin, so they will cook fully before the batter burns. You may need to cook a few tests in order to get the optimal sizing and timing.

Line a plate or tray with a double layer of paper towels. Fill a medium or large saucepan or deep skillet with about 2 inches (5 cm) of vegetable oil and heat to 365°F (185°C).

Dip your ingredient in the batter and hold it over the bowl for a few seconds so the excess can drip off. Carefully lower into the hot oil and fry until the ingredient is fully cooked and the batter is crisp and deep golden brown; the timing will depend on the density of the ingredient. If the batter is browning deeply before the item is cooked, lower the oil temperature and try again.

Drain on paper towels, sprinkle with flaky salt, and serve right away, while crisp and hot, with lemon wedges and sauces on the side.

Snack Bars with Quinoa, Mango, Nuts, and Coconut

1 cup smallish torn pieces dried mango (about 3 oz/85 g)

½ cup (90 g) uncooked quinoa

½ cup (60 g) roughly chopped raw pistachios

½ cup (70 g) roughly chopped raw peanuts

¼ cup (35 g) raw sunflower seeds

¼ cup (20 g) unsweetened shredded coconut

Extra-virgin olive oil

Kosher salt

3 tablespoons brown rice syrup

COATING

¼ cup (20 g) lightly toasted unsweetened shredded coconut (optional)

I like to use red quinoa in these bars because the color adds eye appeal. If you can't find brown rice syrup, use another sweet syrup, such as honey, maple, or Lyle's Golden Syrup, a British favorite that's maybe not super "natural" but is super delicious.
—**Makes thirty-six 1 × 3-inch (2.5 × 7.5 cm) bars**

Put the mango pieces in a small bowl, sprinkle about 1 tablespoon hot water over them, and toss to coat. Let sit until the water has been absorbed and the mango is softer and more hydrated, adding a bit more hot water if you need to. The mango won't actually get soft, but it should be more pliable than its original state. Set aside.

Heat the oven to 350°F (175°C).

Dump the quinoa, pistachios, peanuts, sunflower seeds, and coconut into a bowl. Drizzle on a glug of olive oil, add ½ teaspoon salt, and toss until everything is well distributed and coated with oil.

Spread onto a sheet pan and bake—stirring from the outside to the inside occasionally—until the ingredients are slightly darkened and smelling nutty, 8 to 12 minutes. Take care not to overbake or the quinoa will be bitter. Remove the sheet pan from the oven and let the ingredients cool. If you're worried that they'll get a bit too toasted, transfer them ASAP from the sheet pan to a plate or tray so they don't keep cooking.

Reduce the oven temperature to 200°F (98°C). With a little olive oil, lightly grease a 9 × 13-inch (23 × 33 cm) baking dish.

Put the mango, brown rice syrup, and ¼ teaspoon salt in a food processor and blend until you have a chunky paste, scraping down the sides as needed. This could take a couple of minutes if your mango is tough. You could add another few sprinkles of water if need be, but don't let the mixture get soupy; it should be a thick, stiff paste.

Put the cooled quinoa mixture back into the bowl, add the mango paste, and knead it all together. It will be sticky, so you can dampen your hands lightly if you like. Once the bits are all nicely blended with the paste, transfer the mixture to the baking dish and press firmly to form an even, nicely compacted layer.

Bake to dry out the bar a bit, another 20 to 30 minutes.

Remove from the oven, let cool, and cut into 36 bars. If you like, spread the toasted coconut on a tray and press both sides of the bars into the coconut for a crunchy coating ●. Keep the bars in an airtight container or wrapped tightly in plastic for up to 1 week.

Eat whenever you want a snack, with no guilt whatsoever.

Quinoa-Coconut Power Cookies

½ cup (90 g) uncooked quinoa

1 large egg

1 cup (160 g) coconut butter

½ cup (120 ml) pure maple syrup or ½ cup (100 g) granulated sugar, or ¼ cup of each

½ teaspoon kosher salt

¼ teaspoon baking soda

1⅓ cups (175 g) peanuts, pecans, walnuts, or other favorite nut, lightly toasted and roughly chopped

1 cup (120 g) dried sour cherries, cranberries, strawberries, or other favorite dried fruit

Bring these on your next hike or camping trip, as they do an excellent job as breakfast on the trail, satisfying the munchies while providing some long-lasting nutrition.

Make sure you're buying coconut butter and not coconut oil or cocoa butter. Coconut butter is made from coconut flesh, not just the oil that's pressed out of the coconut. It's crazy delicious on its own, so if this is your first time using it, I suspect it won't be your last. Note that the texture of the cookie changes depending on the sweetener you use. All maple syrup makes a cakier cookie, while all sugar makes a crisper one. I often use half and half. —**Makes about 1 dozen cookies**

Heat the oven to 350°F (175°C).

Spread the quinoa on a sheet pan and bake until lightly golden and nutty smelling, about 10 minutes. (If you're using a darker-colored quinoa, you won't see much of a color change.) Remove from the oven but leave the oven on; let the quinoa cool.

Put the egg, coconut butter, maple syrup and/or sugar, salt, and baking soda in a food processor and pulse until well blended. Scrape the mixture into a bowl and fold in the nuts, dried fruit, and toasted quinoa.

Line the sheet pan with parchment or lightly grease with coconut butter. Using a ¼-cup (60 ml) ice cream scoop or measuring cup, scoop out just a bit less than ¼ cup (60 ml) dough and drop onto the lined sheet pan. Press down lightly to make a round "patty" about ½ inch (1.25 cm) thick. The cookies won't spread much.

Bake until the cookies just start to turn golden around the edges, 12 to 14 minutes. Let them cool for a few minutes on the pan before moving them to a rack—they are very fragile but will firm up as they cool. Store in an airtight container at room temperature for up to 1 week.

Rye

Rye

Secale cereale

▸ CONTAINS GLUTEN ◂

•▷ **Why I love it:** The flavor of rye transports me to another part of the world, probably due to my early tastes of Jewish rye breads from Eastern European traditions. Rye is also a scrappy grain, which I admire, growing well in wet and cold conditions that other grains can't handle, hence its popularity in Scandinavian, Russian, and other Northern European cuisines.

•▷ **What it tastes like:** Rye berries are chewy, nutty, and just slightly sour, so they are more powerfully flavored than, say, barley. Rye flour has a deep and assertive flavor.

•▷ **Common forms:** Whole rye berries and rye flour, which may be labeled light, medium, dark, or pumpernickel. Most dark ryes include all the bran and germ, making them whole grain, though some have part of the bran sifted out. For true whole-grain rye flour, choose pumpernickel. Light rye is closer to all-purpose wheat flour and medium is somewhere in the middle.

•▷ **How to prepare it:** As with many grains, you can enjoy rye as a whole berry or milled into flour and a few stops in between—rye flakes and rye grits, which I've actually never cooked with. Rye berries are quite hard, so give yourself plenty of cooking time; some people soak them first, but I usually skip that step and just simmer a bit longer. I like them in salads, in soups, and as a nutritious addition to meatballs and meat stuffings, such as Toasted Rye Cabbage Rolls (page 166). The flour is hearty, and while it does contain a type of gluten, it's a challenge to swap wheat flour one for one for rye flour in baking because you won't get the same crumb structure and loft as you do with a gluten-rich grain like wheat. Save the rye flour for denser baked goods or crackers (see Rye Caraway Crackers, page 169).

•▷ **How it's good for you:** Rye is exceptionally high in fiber, with the fiber not only in the bran but also the endosperm. This means rye has a low glycemic index, making it a good choice if you're watching your blood sugar. All that fiber also keeps you feeling full longer. Rye is a great source for magnesium, phosphorus, copper, selenium, and niacin (B3), and contains at least half of the recommended daily value of manganese, which helps metabolize protein and other macronutrients.

Details

→ 1 cup uncooked rye berries weighs 6 ounces (170 g).

→ Use 3½ parts liquid for 1 part rye berries as a rule of thumb for the absorption method, though I prefer the boil-like-pasta method because the berries can be quite hard and take a lot of time and liquid to soften.

→ Cook rye berries for 1 hour after an overnight soak, longer if unsoaked.

→ 1 cup (170 g) uncooked rye berries yields 2½ cups (385 g) cooked.

→ 1 cup rye flour weighs 4¼ ounces (120 g).

Grain Bowls for Every Season

A grain bowl brings together all the things we want in a healthy meal: satisfying substance from the grains, crunch from fresh vegetables, plus more textural delights from a range of accents and add-ins. Having cooked grains in the fridge or freezer means prep is a breeze. Aim for about half the dish to be grains and the other half to be those add-ins and accents. Season your grain bowl with intention—you want each bite to be lively—and serve at cool room temperature rather than straight from the refrigerator, as a little warmth will bring out the flavor of the grains.

How to assemble your grain bowl:

Refer to the foldout chart for ingredients by season.

1. In a small bowl, toss the **GRAIN** with the **HERBS**, **ACID**, **HEAT**, and **FAT**.

2. Season to taste with **SPICE**. Toss the ingredients together, if desired.

3. Spread some **CREAMINESS** on the base of your serving bowl.

4. Mound the seasoned grain mixture on top of the creamy element, arrange the **VEGETABLES/FRUIT** around the bowl, and top with the **CRUNCH** and **PROTEIN**.

Dress **GRAINS** well so they don't taste starchy.

Caramelize **VEGETABLES** for deeper flavor.

ACID from fresh citrus brightens winter grain bowls.

PROTEIN—animal or vegetable—adds substance to a grain bowl.

Leave tender **HERBS** whole for a pop of intensity.

Pictured here: Winter grain bowl (see chart)

Rye Berry and Roasted Cauliflower Salad with Walnuts and Dried Cranberries

1 cup (170 g) uncooked rye berries

1 quart (1 liter) water

Kosher salt

1½ to 2 pounds (675 to 900 g) cauliflower, cut or broken into florets (no bigger than about 1½ inches/3.75 cm)

Extra-virgin olive oil

⅛ teaspoon dried chile flakes

1 cup (120 g) roughly chopped lightly toasted walnuts

½ cup (60 g) dried cranberries, preferably unsweetened, soaked in warm water for 30 minutes or until softened, then drained

½ cup (15 g) lightly packed roughly chopped fresh flat-leaf parsley leaves and tender stems

10 to 12 pepperoncini or other pickled peppers, seeded and sliced

1 teaspoon fresh thyme leaves, roughly chopped

3 tablespoons red wine vinegar, or more to taste

1 tablespoon pepperoncini brine, or more to taste

Freshly ground black pepper

½ cup (115 g) plain whole-milk yogurt

I'm calling this a salad, but it's a main dish that you can serve any time of day, and it can come together in about 30 minutes, provided you've got some cooked rye berries in the fridge or freezer—always a good idea! (The salad also tastes great with spelt or farro.) You're likely to have most of the ingredients in the pantry already, so just pick up some cauliflower at the farmers' market or grocery store, and there's dinner. If you're going to cook the rye berries on the day you want to serve the salad, be sure to allow plenty of cooking time to get them plump and tender, as rye berries can be stubborn. —**Serves 4**

Put the rye berries into a medium saucepan with a lid. Add the water and 1 teaspoon salt. Bring to a boil, adjust the heat to a lively simmer, cover, and cook until the rye berries are fully tender and most of the grains have opened up, 60 to 75 minutes, checking occasionally to be sure the water hasn't cooked off. Drain thoroughly and cool. If you're cooking the rye berries ahead, keep them in the fridge, but take them out to warm up at least 30 minutes before serving.

Heat the oven to 375°F (190°C).

Put the cauliflower in a large bowl, add ¼ cup (60 ml) olive oil, ½ teaspoon salt, and the chile flakes and toss to coat all the florets. Spread them out on a sheet pan. Roast until tender and nicely browned around the edges, 20 to 30 minutes. Let cool slightly.

When ready to assemble the salad, put the rye berries in a large bowl. Add half the walnuts, all the cranberries, half the parsley, the sliced pepperoncini, thyme, vinegar, and pepperoncini brine, and toss to combine. Season generously with salt and pepper, taste, and adjust all the seasonings, adding more vinegar or brine if needed to make the flavor punchy. Add 3 tablespoons olive oil, toss, taste, and adjust the seasonings one more time.

In a small bowl, season the yogurt with salt and pepper to taste.

Spread the rye berry mixture in the bottom of a wide serving bowl or platter. Mound the cauliflower on top, drizzle everything generously with the seasoned yogurt, and finish with the remaining walnuts and parsley. Serve while the cauliflower is still warm, though the salad will also be good at room temperature.

Toasted Rye Cabbage Rolls

ROLLS

Extra-virgin olive oil

⅔ cup (115 g) uncooked rye berries

1 quart (1 liter) water

Kosher salt

2 tablespoons unsalted butter

2 cups (300 g) finely chopped onion

5 garlic cloves, finely chopped

1 tablespoon caraway seeds

1 tablespoon fennel seeds

1 teaspoon sweet or hot paprika

½ pound (225 g) ground beef, preferably grass-fed

½ pound (225 g) ground pork

1 cup (125 g) chopped drained sauerkraut

1 cup (50 g) panko breadcrumbs

¼ teaspoon dried chile flakes

Freshly ground black pepper

2 large eggs, beaten

SAUCE

One 28-ounce (794 g) can whole peeled tomatoes, undrained

1 cup (60 ml) extra-virgin olive oil

1 teaspoon kosher salt

FOR ASSEMBLY

1 small head savoy or green cabbage

2 tablespoons unsalted butter

A comfort food favorite, for sure, and while these meat-and-grain-filled rolls do take some time to prepare, the process is fun and you can do some of the steps ahead. I get satisfaction with every little bundle of savory goodness that I roll up. Typical cabbage roll recipes use white rice in the filling, but here I bring a lot more personality—and nutrition—with toasted rye berries and chopped sauerkraut. —**Serves 4 or 5**

MAKE THE ROLLS: Heat a glug of olive oil in a large skillet or Dutch oven over medium heat. Add the rye berries and cook until the rye is dark and smells toasty, about 5 minutes. Add the water and 1½ teaspoons salt and bring to a boil. Reduce the heat to a simmer and cook until the rye berries are very tender, 60 to 75 minutes. Drain thoroughly and cool completely. You can cook the rye berries up to 3 days ahead.

Meanwhile, heat the butter in a large skillet over medium heat. Add the onion and a pinch of salt. Cook until the onion is soft and translucent, stirring occasionally so it cooks evenly and doesn't brown. Add the garlic, caraway, fennel, and paprika and cook for another couple of minutes to soften the garlic. Cool completely.

Put the beef and pork in a large bowl and break up the meat into smaller pieces so it will be easier to incorporate the other ingredients. Add the cooled rye berries, cooled onion mixture, sauerkraut, panko, 1 tablespoon salt, the chile flakes, and many twists of black pepper. Work the ingredients together gently with clean hands until well blended. Pour on the eggs and, with your hands or a wooden spoon, incorporate them.

To check the seasoning, fry a small nugget of the filling and taste, adjusting with more salt, black pepper, or chile flakes as needed.

MAKE THE SAUCE: Put the tomatoes with their juices, olive oil, and salt in a blender and process until smooth. You can make the sauce up to 2 days ahead.

ASSEMBLE AND BAKE THE ROLLS: Bring a large pot of water to a boil. Cut the core from the cabbage and peel off any damaged outer leaves. Gently separate the cabbage leaves, taking care not to rip them, but if a few do rip, no worries. "Shave" off any thick ribs so that the leaves are close to a uniform thickness. You probably won't use any very tiny leaves, but you will use smallish ones, piecing two together.

continues

Blanch a few cabbage leaves at a time until just pliable, then drain on clean kitchen towels or paper towels.

Heat the oven to 400°F (200°C).

Lay out a large leaf or piece two smaller ones together. Put a generous ¼ cup (60 g) filling in the center, fold the bottom of the leaf up over the filling, fold the sides in, and roll to make a compact cylinder. You should be able to make 16 rolls, but depending on your cabbage and how much filling you use, you could make more or fewer. Aim for rolls of similar size, but don't stress if they aren't identical.

Lay the cabbage rolls seam side down in the bottom of a 9 × 13-inch (23 × 33 cm) baking dish, or the equivalent. Pour the sauce on top and dot the surface with the butter. Bake until the filling is thoroughly cooked and the sauce has thickened and the whole dish is browning and bubbling around the edges, about 45 minutes.

Let the cabbage rolls cool for about 10 minutes, then serve hot, with the cooking juices spooned over.

Rye Caraway Crackers

¾ cup (90 g) dark rye flour

2 teaspoons kosher salt

2 teaspoons ground caraway seed

½ teaspoon cracked black pepper

3 tablespoons extra-virgin olive oil

⅓ cup (80 ml) water

I love the husky flavor combination of rye flour and caraway in these crackers, with a little kick from the black pepper. The thinner you roll these, the crispier they will be, but even when they're not quite wafer-thin, they are delicious. The most important thing is to roll them evenly so they cook evenly.
—**Makes 2 dozen 2-inch (5 cm) square crackers**

Heat the oven to 350°F (175°C).

Whisk together the rye flour, salt, caraway, and black pepper in a bowl. Stir together the olive oil and water in a spouted measuring cup and pour into the dry ingredients. Stir to form a soft dough, adding a touch more flour if needed to make the dough workable.

Transfer to a lightly floured work surface and knead a couple of strokes to smooth out the dough. Divide into two pieces.

Roll each piece of dough as thin as you can make it, dusting with a bit more flour as needed to keep it from sticking. Cut into squares—or whatever shape you like—and transfer to a baking sheet.

Bake until the crackers look dry and are crisp and lightly browned around the edges, 18 to 20 minutes. You might want to bake off a few test crackers to determine the precise timing before you commit to the entire batch.

Cool on a rack, eat as many as you want, and store the rest in an airtight container at room temperature.

Chocolate Rye Brownies with Cashew Swirl

CASHEW SWIRL

6 tablespoons (85 ml) water

3 tablespoons sugar

½ cup (120 g) cashew butter

BROWNIE BATTER

6 tablespoons (85 g) unsalted
butter, cut into 6 pieces,
plus more for the baking
dish

3 cups (500 g) dark chocolate
chips (preferably 70%
cacao)

2¼ cups (450 g) sugar

4 large eggs, at room
temperature

1½ teaspoons pure vanilla
extract

⅓ cup (80 g) cashew butter

1 cup (120 g) dark, medium, or
light rye flour

¼ cup plus 2 tablespoons
(30 g) unsweetened cocoa
powder, sifted if lumpy

2 teaspoons kosher salt

¾ teaspoon (3 g) baking
powder

1 cup (120 g) roasted cashews

1 teaspoon flaky sea salt

These brownies are ooey-gooey and fudgy, but they have a
sophisticated complexity from the combination of rye flour
and dark chocolate. Let them cool completely before you cut
them . . . if you can wait that long. They are actually in their
prime the day after baking, when the texture has had a chance
to get nice and chewy. —**Makes twenty-four 2-inch (5 cm) squares**

Heat the oven to 350°F (175°C).

MAKE THE CASHEW SWIRL: Heat
the water and sugar in a small
saucepan and stir until the sugar
dissolves. Stir in the cashew
butter and whisk until smooth.
Set aside.

MAKE THE BROWNIE BATTER:
With a little butter, grease a
9 × 13-inch (23 × 33 cm) baking
dish and line with parchment,
leaving a few inches overhanging
on two sides (to make lifting out
the brownies easy). Melt the
chocolate and butter in a double
boiler and hold over low heat
to keep warm. (You can make
a double boiler by simmering
a couple of inches of water
in a saucepan and setting a
stainless-steel bowl over the pan;
be sure the water isn't actually
touching the bottom of the bowl.)

Meanwhile, in a stand mixer
fitted with the whisk, combine
the sugar, eggs, and vanilla
and whisk on medium speed
until very thick and pale, about
5 minutes. Add the cashew

butter and whisk to incorporate.
In a separate bowl, whisk
together the rye flour, cocoa
powder, kosher salt, and baking
powder.

Scrape the warm melted
chocolate-butter mixture
into the egg mixture and fold
gently to blend. Fold the dry
ingredients into the eggs and
chocolate and mix just to
combine. Pour the batter into
the prepared pan and spread
evenly ⬤. Dollop the cashew
swirl over the brownie batter ⚪
and use a knife or skewer to
make a swirl pattern ⬤. Top the
whole thing with the roasted
cashews and flaky salt.

Bake until the brownies just
begin to puff and crack around
the edges, about 25 minutes.
Let cool completely in the pan,
then lift out of the pan and cut
into squares. Store in an airtight
container at room temperature
for up to 4 days; the brownies
will get firmer and chewier as
time goes on, but they will still be
delicious.

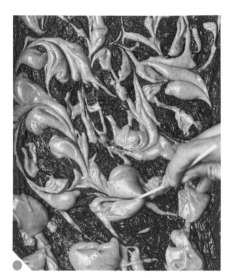

Rye and Cream Cheese Kringle

SPONGE

⅓ cup (80 ml) milk, at room temperature

¼ cup (60 ml) water, at room temperature

1 tablespoon granulated sugar

2¼ teaspoons (7 g) active dry yeast

⅓ cup (40 g) dark, medium, or light rye flour

1 large egg

FINAL DOUGH

2 teaspoons kosher salt

2 tablespoons granulated sugar

2 cups (240 g) white bread flour

½ cup (60 g) rye flour

4 tablespoons (60 g) unsalted butter, at room temperature

BUTTER BLOCK

6 ounces (180 g) unsalted butter, at room temperature

2 tablespoons white bread flour

CREAM CHEESE FILLING

8 ounces (225 g) cream cheese, at room temperature

2 large egg yolks

⅓ cup (65 g) granulated sugar

Finely grated zest of 1 lemon (optional)

1 teaspoon pure vanilla extract

¼ teaspoon kosher salt

FILLING AND BAKING

Egg wash: 1 large egg, beaten with a little splash of water

2 tablespoons turbinado sugar or granulated sugar

GLAZE

2 cups (240 g) powdered sugar, sifted

¼ cup (60 ml) heavy or whipping cream

Pinch of kosher salt

Warning: Making a kringle is "project baking" at its finest! The dough needs at least one overnight rest, and there is lamination involved, plus a filling, a glaze, and shaping into a ring or a half-moon. But the resulting tender, flaky, tasty pastry will likely be the best Danish you've ever had. Nothing about the technique is difficult, so even if you're a novice, go for it—just know that you need time and counter space. **—Serves 6 to 8**

MAKE THE SPONGE: Whisk together the milk, water, granulated sugar, and yeast. Whisk in the flour until smooth, then whisk in the egg. Cover and let sit in a warm place until bubbly and slightly risen; the sponge will have almost a Jell-O-like texture when you give the bowl a shake, about 1½ hours.

MAKE THE FINAL DOUGH: In a stand mixer fitted with the dough hook, combine the risen sponge, salt, granulated sugar, bread flour, rye flour, and butter. Knead on medium speed just until the dough is evenly mixed and the butter is incorporated, about 4 minutes.

Transfer the dough to an oiled bowl, cover, and let rise in a warm place until almost doubled in volume, about 1 hour. Punch down the dough by gently pressing on the dough to deflate it, wrap, and refrigerate overnight.

WHILE THE DOUGH IS RISING, MAKE THE BUTTER BLOCK: In a stand mixer fitted with the paddle, mix the butter and flour. With a spatula, scrape out the butter mixture onto a piece of parchment and shape into a rough 6-inch (15 cm) square.

Wrap and chill overnight with the dough.

The next day, take the butter block out of the fridge and let it soften slightly. The dough and the butter should be about the same texture. Pat and roll the dough into a 9-inch (23 cm) square. Put the butter block on top of the square so that it fits diagonally (like a square within a diamond) ●. Pull the sides of the dough up and over to enclose the butter ●.

On a lightly floured surface, roll the dough out into a rectangle about 8 × 18 inches (20 × 46 cm) ●. Fold the dough in thirds (like a business letter), rotate 90 degrees, and repeat the rolling and folding three more times ●. If the dough feels like it's getting too elastic and is pulling back, give it a 20-minute rest. On a cool day, you can leave the dough on the counter to rest. If it's warm, put it in the fridge. After the last fold, wrap the dough and chill for at least 3 hours or up to 3 days; the flavor improves with time.

At last, you can now make the kringle!

continues

MAKE THE CREAM CHEESE FILLING: In a bowl with an electric mixer or a wooden spoon, beat the cream cheese, egg yolks, granulated sugar, lemon zest (if using), vanilla, and salt until smooth. Set aside at room temperature.

FILL THE KRINGLE: Roll the dough out on a lightly floured surface until it measures about 8 × 30 inches (20 × 76 cm). Give the dough a rest if it feels too tight to roll. If desired, lay a sheet of parchment on the work surface and slide the dough onto it (the dough will be bigger than the parchment for now, but that will be easier than transferring it later).

Spread the cream cheese filling over the dough, leaving a couple of inches of border around all of the sides ●. Brush the edges with some of the egg wash ● and fold the dough over lengthwise to make one long rectangle measuring about 4 × 30 inches (10 × 76 cm) ●.

Using a fork dipped in flour, press along all of the edges to seal the pastry ●. Curve the dough around to form a ring or a half-moon. Slide the parchment onto a baking sheet, cover loosely with plastic, and let rise in a warm place until puffy, 1½ to 2 hours.

About 20 minutes before the kringle has finished rising, heat the oven to 400°F (200°C).

Brush the kringle with more egg wash and sprinkle with the turbinado sugar. Make diagonal slits along the pastry to let steam escape. Bake for 10 minutes, then reduce the oven temperature to 350°F (175°C) and bake until the kringle is deep brown, about 25 more minutes. Don't worry if some of the filling seeps out, it's part of the charm!

MEANWHILE, MAKE THE GLAZE: In a stand mixer fitter with the paddle, beat the powdered sugar, cream, and salt together until smooth.

Let the kringle cool and spread with the glaze. This is best served within a few hours of baking, but it will recrisp well in a 350°F (175°C) oven.

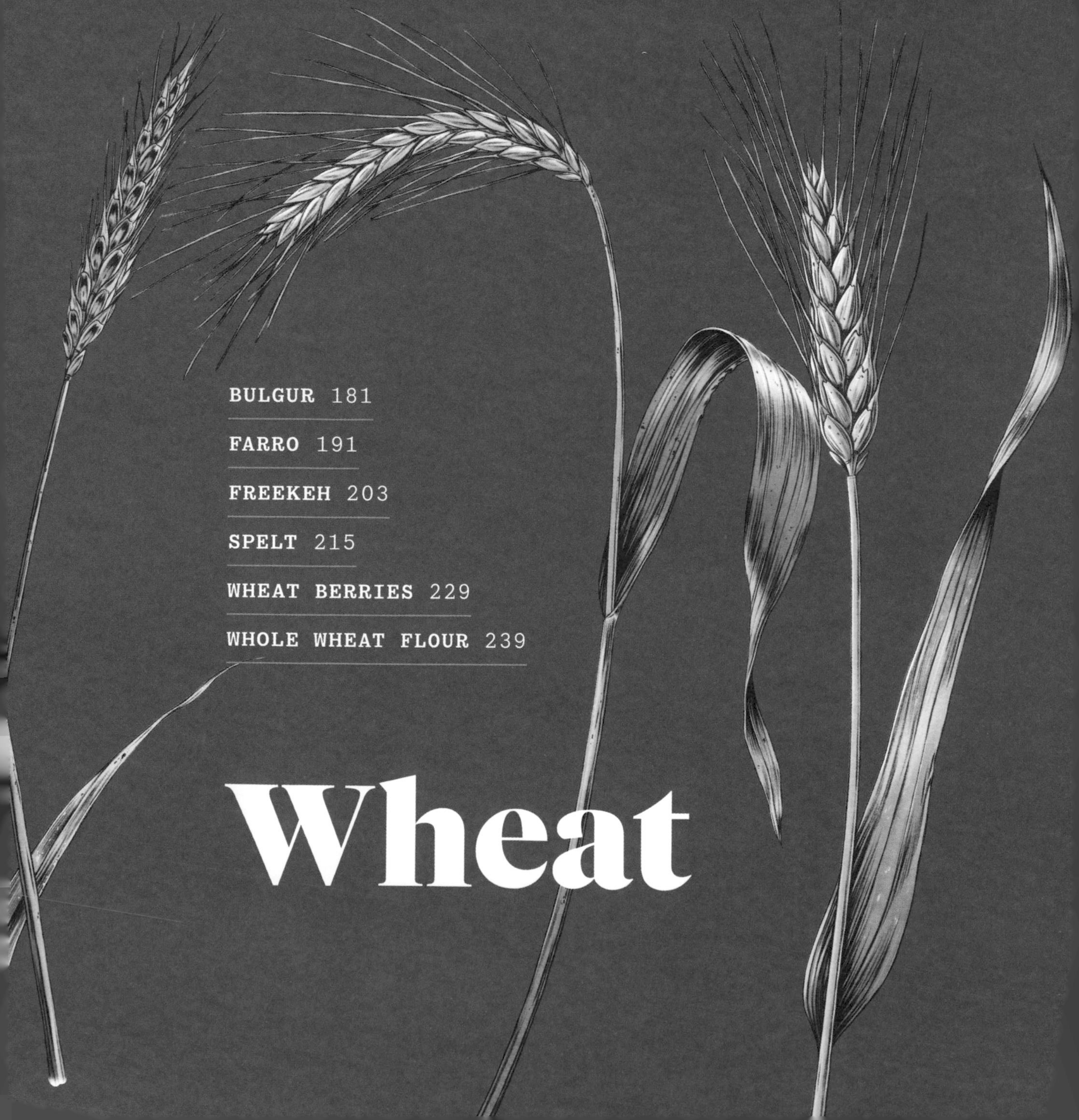

Wheat

Wheat

Triticum aestivum

▶ CONTAINS GLUTEN ◀

•▷ **Why I love it:** For centuries, wheat has been integral to many cooking traditions around the world, especially in Eurocentric cuisines, which is my background. And no wonder—wheat is delicious and immensely versatile. The wheat family is vast, though most of the wheat produced around the world is either "common wheat" (*Triticum aestivum*) or (a much smaller proportion) durum wheat (*Triticum durum*), which is generally higher protein and used for commercial pastas. But in recent years, as cooks have grown passionate about ancient grains, more wheat relatives have made the scene, such as farro (also known as emmer), spelt, einkorn, and Kamut (a wheat variety with a brand name!). I cook with a lot of farro and spelt, both in whole kernel and milled flour forms, as well as bulgur and wheat berries. And course flour from "common" wheat is always in my pantry and is the basis of my pastas, pizzas, and other breads.

•▷ **What it tastes like:** Wheat is generally sweet and mild, which makes it so versatile. Some whole wheat flours have a slightly bitter flavor, which I like; it's more assertive in flavor than refined white flour, which is all but tasteless, if you ask me.

•▷ **Favorite ways to prepare it:** All the various forms of the wheat family contain a type of gluten that is well suited for breads, pastries, and pasta. Those gluten proteins (mostly glutenin and gliadin) produce a structure for leavened or layered baked goods that we love, and a springy chewiness that makes pasta the sensuous food that it is.

Baking or making pasta with 100 percent whole-grain wheat flours and getting an excellent result takes some experimentation. Swapping cup-for-cup whole wheat flour for white all-purpose flour (or cake flour!) may yield some disappointment in terms of texture and rise, but plenty of super-talented bakers and chefs have worked out formulas and methods using high-quality flours that produce delectable breads, pastries, and pastas. (See Sources, page 332, for some favorites.)

I take a hybrid approach, because I'm more of a cook than a baker, and my interest is in creating good food that's better for you than food with no whole grains. I'll use all whole-grain flour where I can, but most of the time I hedge my bets by blending whole-grain flour with unbleached white all-purpose. Just because it's white flour doesn't mean it can't be high quality. I try to use freshly milled flour from wheat that's locally grown using good growing practices.

But there's good eating to be had from wheat beyond the dishes we make with wheat flours. The whole kernels of wheat and its cousins provide a delicious base for salads, give substance to soups and stews, and make nutritious yet indulgent-seeming side dishes, such as Farrotto (page 194). In these whole-grain forms, the gluten content is relevant only to those trying to avoid it; the cooking and eating properties come from the actual type of wheat and how it's processed.

•▷ **How it's good for you:** Each wheat variety contains a different combo of nutrients, but all these whole grains are nutritional powerhouses, providing good sources of protein, minerals, and vitamins, including iron, magnesium, phosphorus, zinc, and the B vitamins thiamin (B1) and niacin (B3). Whole wheat, like all whole grains, contains tons of good fiber and at least half of the recommended daily value of manganese, which helps metabolize protein and other macronutrients.

Bulgur

Triticum durum

▶ CONTAINS GLUTEN ◀

Bulgur comes from wheat kernels that have been precooked and then broken into pieces, which is why it cooks so fast. In fact, the most typical way to "cook" bulgur is to steep it: Simply add boiling liquid, cover the bowl, and let the bulgur absorb the liquid and become soft. I will sometimes dry-toast the bulgur before steeping to deepen the flavor. Bulgur comes in various levels of coarseness, though you may only find the full range at a Middle Eastern store. The coarser it is, the longer the cooking/steeping time required.

Details

→ 1 cup uncooked bulgur weighs 6 ounces (170 g).

→ For fine and medium bulgur, use 1¾ parts liquid to 1 part bulgur; for coarse bulgur, use 2 parts liquid to 1 part bulgur.

→ Steep for 10 to 20 minutes.

→ 1 cup (170 g) uncooked bulgur yields 3 cups (485 g) cooked.

RECIPES

Tabbouleh for Every Season 183

Spiced Beef and Bulgur Hand Pies 184

Lamb and Bulgur Meatballs in Lemony Yogurt Sauce 187

Tabbouleh for Every Season

2 cups (340 g) uncooked fine
  bulgur (see Note)

3 cups (720 ml) boiling water

2 cups (60 g) roughly chopped
  fresh flat-leaf parsley leaves

1 tablespoon finely grated
  orange zest

Juice of ¼ small orange

Splash of red wine vinegar

Kosher salt and freshly
  ground black pepper

Dried chile flakes

2 cups (300 g) diced roasted
  winter squash

½ cup (85 g) diced celery

½ cup (30 g) lightly packed
  tender celery leaves

3 tablespoons lightly packed
  1-inch (2.5 cm) chive pieces

½ cup (70 g) Toasted Pumpkin
  Seeds (page 306; optional)

Extra-virgin olive oil

Note: You can use any coarseness
level of bulgur, but medium
and coarse will require longer
soaking.

Think of the traditional Middle Eastern dish, which uses
bulgur, as a jumping-off point for a whole range of fresh,
wholesome grain salads that you'll customize depending on
what's in your pantry and what's fresh at the market. This is my
favorite combination for cooler fall and winter days. I'll often
use freekeh, farro, wheat berries, or quinoa instead of bulgur,
keeping in mind the most essential aspect of this dish, which is
the ratio of grain to parsley. I like equal amounts, which means
a lot of parsley—so much healthy chlorophyll (the green stuff)!
—Serves 4

Put the bulgur in a large
heatproof bowl and cover with
the boiling water. Soak for
about 15 minutes, then drain
well, pressing on the bulgur to
squeeze out as much water as
possible.

Put the drained bulgur and
parsley in a large serving bowl
and season lightly with the
orange zest, orange juice,
vinegar, ½ teaspoon salt, several
twists of black pepper, and
a pinch of chile flakes. Toss,
taste, and adjust the seasoning,
knowing you'll season a bit
more after you add the other
ingredients.

Add the roasted squash, celery,
celery leaves, chives, and
toasted pumpkin seeds, if using.
Toss again and dial in the final
flavoring with more orange
juice, vinegar, salt, black pepper,
or chile flakes. Finish with a
generous drizzle of olive oil and a
final toss. Serve within an hour.

Variations

Summer Tabbouleh: Instead of
winter squash and celery, use diced
tomatoes, cucumbers, and bell
peppers. Instead of parsley and
chives, use a mix of some or all of
these: basil, mint, hyssop, cilantro,
dill, or shiso. A sliced habanero
would add wonderful tropical
flavor and plenty of heat. A bonus
ingredient could be diced grilled
and cooled onion or even grilled
eggplant.

Spring Tabbouleh: Instead of
winter squash and celery, use
thinly sliced scallions, raw English
peas, and sliced sugar snap peas.
Instead of celery leaves, use fresh
mint leaves. Instead of orange juice,
vinegar, and orange zest, season
with lemon juice and zest.

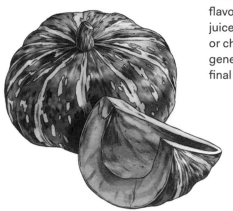

Spiced Beef and Bulgur Hand Pies

Extra-virgin olive oil

1 cup (150 g) finely chopped onion

1 cup (120 g) chopped scallions, white and most of the green parts

2 teaspoons kosher salt

3 or 4 garlic cloves, chopped

2 teaspoons chopped fresh thyme

1 small hot fresh chile, such as habanero, deribbed, seeded, and finely chopped

8 ounces (225 g) ground beef chuck

1 teaspoon ground allspice

1 teaspoon smoked paprika, hot or mild

1 teaspoon curry powder, hot or mild

1 teaspoon sugar

½ teaspoon freshly ground black pepper

½ cup (80 g) bulgur, any grind

1¾ cups (420 ml) beef broth or chicken broth, homemade or low-sodium store-bought, or water

Whole Wheat Flaky Pastry Dough with Turmeric (page 313)

1 egg, beaten

Inspired by a Jamaican street food snack called beef patties, which I ate a lot of when I lived in Brooklyn, these savory hand pies—flaky turmeric-scented pastry wrapped around a spiced beef and bulgur filling (the bulgur's not traditional)—make a fine lunch or dinner.

I like using ground chuck in the filling because that cut of beef has such great beefy flavor, but what's most important is to use good meat—humanely raised and preferably local.

Making and shaping these hand pies does take a bit of time, but they freeze so nicely that I suggest making a batch and freezing some before cooking, so that you have near-instant joy at hand. To cook frozen hand pies, don't thaw, just reduce the oven temperature to 350°F (175°C) and cook about 10 minutes longer. Test by poking one with the tip of a knife to be sure the filling is fully heated through. —**Makes sixteen 5-inch (13 cm) hand pies**

Heat a generous glug of olive oil in a large skillet over medium-high heat. Add the onion, scallions, and salt and cook, stirring frequently, until the onion starts getting juicy and fragrant, about 2 minutes. Add the garlic, thyme, and chile and keep cooking until all the aromatics are quite soft and translucent, another couple of minutes.

Add the beef to the pan, breaking it up into smaller bits with a spatula or wooden spoon, and cook until no longer pink, but don't let it get brown and crusty. Add the allspice, smoked paprika, curry powder, sugar, and black pepper and cook for another minute.

Stir in the bulgur and broth. Reduce the heat to a gentle simmer, cover, and cook, stirring occasionally, until the bulgur has softened and swelled up and all the liquid has been absorbed, about 30 minutes. Taste and adjust the seasoning with more salt or any of the spices—you want the filling to be zesty.

Let the filling cool completely, first on the counter and then in the fridge.

To assemble the hand pies, divide the dough into 16 pieces. Gently shape each piece into a round and flatten the round by pressing with your fingertips until you have a disk that's about 3 inches (7.5 cm) across. If the dough is sticking as you're working, dust it lightly with more flour.

Lightly flour the work surface and roll one disk of dough into a round about 7 inches (18 cm) across; it's okay if it's not perfectly round or the dough is ripping a bit; you can just press it back together.

Scoop out a couple of generous tablespoons of cooled filling (one-sixteenth of the filling, to be precise) and pile it onto the

lower half of the dough, leaving a border all around.

Brush the border lightly with water using a pastry brush or your finger. Fold over the top half of the dough round, pressing it gently around the filling, and then press gently to seal the two layers of dough. Again, if the dough rips a bit, don't stress, just pinch or press to repair. These are rustic!

Repeat with the rest of the dough and filling; if your kitchen is warm, pop the assembled pies in the fridge as you work. Chill for at least 30 minutes before baking. If you want to freeze some, do it now: Arrange them on a tray and put into the freezer. Freeze until they are firm, then put them into zip-top freezer bags. (If you don't think you'll be consuming these in a month or so, wrap each hand pie individually in plastic wrap before putting them into the zip-top bag.) Press out all the air and freeze, and take out only the number you need at one time.

When ready to cook the pies, heat the oven to 375°F (190°C).

Brush the tops of the pies with the beaten egg, cut three little slits in the top to release steam during cooking, and arrange on a baking sheet (you can line it with parchment, but you won't need to). Bake until the pastry is a rich deep golden, the underside is lightly brown, and the filling is heated through and bubbling a bit at the seams, 18 to 25 minutes. Let the hand pies cool for a few minutes, then enjoy, plain or with a hot sauce.

Lamb and Bulgur Meatballs in Lemony Yogurt Sauce

1 cup (170 g) uncooked bulgur, preferably fine

1 pound (450 g) ground lamb

1½ cups (335 g) plain whole-milk Greek yogurt or labneh

½ cup (15 g) lightly packed chopped fresh flat-leaf parsley

¼ cup (7 g) lightly packed chopped fresh mint

¼ cup (35 g) finely chopped toasted hazelnuts

¼ cup (30 g) chopped scallions, white and light-green parts only

2 tablespoons Spice Mix (recipe follows)

1½ teaspoons kosher salt

1 large egg, beaten

Extra-virgin olive oil

3 medium garlic cloves, smashed and peeled

¼ teaspoon dried chile flakes, or 2 whole small dried chiles, such as chiles de árbol

1¾ cups (420 ml) chicken broth or vegetable broth, homemade or low-sodium store-bought

1 teaspoon finely grated lemon zest

1 tablespoon fresh lemon juice, or more to taste

One of the many splendors of meatballs is that they freeze beautifully, giving you a complex dinner in minutes. I shape my meatballs, arrange them on a parchment-lined sheet pan, and then freeze the raw meatballs "naked" until quite firm. At that point, I pile them into a good freezer container or bag. The individual freezing method means I can pull out the number I want at any time, leaving the rest for the next meatball meal. The bulgur keeps the texture light and tender, and it of course adds more nutritional value. Serve the meatballs and sauce with some plain cooked grains or whole wheat couscous.

This recipe makes more seasoning than you'll need for the meatballs, but if you're going through the process, you might as well make enough for your next meatball batch . . . because you *will* want to make these again! You can use the spice mix for a quick tagine, rice pilaf, or kebab, but to save time, use a ready-made North African or Middle Eastern blend such as ras el hanout or baharat. —**Makes 24 meatballs**

Put the bulgur in a small bowl and cover generously with cool water. Soak until the bulgur has softened, though it should still have some toothiness to it, about 30 minutes. Drain in a fine-mesh sieve and shake and tap the sieve until you've got all the excess water out.

Break up the lamb with your fingers and toss into a large bowl. Add the drained bulgur, ½ cup (115 g) of the yogurt, half the parsley, the mint, hazelnuts, scallions, spice mix, and salt, distributing them well as you add them so it's easier to blend everything together.

With clean hands, work the ingredients together to blend the seasonings; work gently so you keep the texture light. Add the beaten egg and work the mixture a bit more until the egg is incorporated.

Fry a test portion (about 2 tablespoons) in a nonstick skillet until the mixture is fully cooked and then taste for seasoning, adding more of anything to your liking.

Shape the mixture into 1½-ounce (42 g) meatballs (just a hint smaller than a golf ball) and arrange on a tray. If you want to freeze the meatballs to eat later, see the instructions in the headnote.

Heat a generous glug of olive oil in a large heavy-bottomed skillet over medium heat. Add the garlic and cook slowly to toast it so it's very soft, fragrant, and nicely golden brown—but not burnt—about 5 minutes. Add the chile flakes, increase the heat to medium-high, and add enough meatballs to form a single layer with plenty of room for your

Lamb and Bulgur Meatballs
in Lemony Yogurt Sauce,
continued

spatula so you can roll and flip the meatballs.

Brown the meatballs all over, shaking and flipping so they are evenly colored and more or less keep their shape; this will take about 10 minutes per batch. Transfer to a plate or tray, wipe out any burnt pan juices, add a touch more olive oil if things look dry (or, if there's a lot of grease, pour it off), and fry another batch. Repeat until you've browned all the meatballs.

Return all the meatballs to the pan, add the broth, and adjust the heat to a nice simmer. Simmer the meatballs, rolling them around a bit, until they are fully cooked, about 15 minutes, depending on how long you browned them. The broth should reduce during this process. If the meatballs are totally cooked but you still have a lot of liquid (like more than ½ cup/120 ml) in the pan, scoop out the meatballs, continue to reduce the broth, then put the meatballs back in.

Remove the skillet from the heat and add the remaining 1 cup (225 g) yogurt, shaking the pan to blend the yogurt with the pan juices and coat the meatballs. The meatballs are fragile, so be gentle with them. Toss in the remaining parsley, the lemon zest, and the lemon juice. Serve hot.

Spice Mix

I love the complex perfume that long peppers (also called *pipli*) bring to this mix, so if you can find them, please use them. Otherwise any black peppercorn will work; Tellicherry is a good choice.

Makes about 5 tablespoons

2 teaspoons cumin seeds

1½ teaspoons coriander seeds

1½ teaspoons long pepper (pipli) or black peppercorns

1½ teaspoons allspice berries

1 teaspoon cardamom seeds (out of the pods)

1 whole star anise

2 teaspoons Aleppo pepper

2 teaspoons ground cinnamon

1½ teaspoons ground turmeric

1 teaspoon ground sumac

1 teaspoon freshly grated nutmeg

Toast the cumin seeds, coriander seeds, long pepper, allspice berries, and cardamom in a small dry skillet over medium-high heat, shaking the pan frequently to avoid burning, until the spices are very fragrant; some will darken slightly but not all, so go by smell rather than color. Immediately dump them onto a plate or tray to stop the cooking and let cool.

When they're cool, grind them, along with the star anise, in a spice grinder. Transfer the ground spices to a bowl and add the Aleppo pepper, cinnamon, turmeric, sumac, and nutmeg. Store in an airtight jar.

Farro

Triticum turgidum ssp. *dicoccum*

▶ CONTAINS GLUTEN ◀

Among all the whole-grain kernels, farro is the one that I cook with the most. The Italians love farro, and hence I do, too. It's nutty and earthy and retains a lovely chewy texture without being slightly, er, slick like barley is (don't get me wrong, I love barley, too). Farro flour is also delicious and easy to bake with.

You see farro in hulled (meaning it includes all the bran), semipearled, or pearled forms. Much farro is imported from Italy and not all the packaging is labeled clearly, so you may have to use trial and error to determine cooking times.

Details

→ 1 cup uncooked farro weighs 7 ounces (200 g).

→ Use 1¾ parts liquid to 1 part farro as a rule of thumb for the absorption method; the boil-like-pasta method also works well with farro.

→ Cook farro for 20 to 50 minutes, depending on whether the grains are pearled or not; hulled farro can take a long time to cook and benefits from an overnight soak before cooking.

→ 1 cup (200 g) uncooked farro yields 2½ cups (390 g) cooked.

→ 1 cup farro flour weighs 4¼ ounces (120 g).

RECIPES

Farro Salad with Pepperoncini, Sun-Dried Tomatoes, Salami, and Almonds 192

Farrotto, in the Style of Cacio e Pepe 194

Spring Peas and Calamari Stew with Toasted Farro 197

Farro con Pollo 198

Farro, Brown Butter, and Honey Cake 201

Farro Salad with Pepperoncini, Sun-Dried Tomatoes, Salami, and Almonds

⅔ cup (130 g) uncooked farro

1¼ cups (300 ml) water

Kosher salt

2 cups (80 g) Torn Croutons (page 306)

¼ small red onion, thinly sliced, soaked in ice water for 20 minutes, and drained thoroughly

¼ cup (40 g) roughly chopped sun-dried tomatoes in oil (or dry-packed ones plumped in warm water for 20 minutes and drained)

5 or 6 medium pepperoncini, deribbed, seeded, and sliced

1 tablespoon pickling liquid from pepperoncini

About ½ cup (120 ml) Italian Salad Dressing (page 318) or basic vinaigrette of your choice

2 ounces (60 g) sliced salami (about 8 slices), cut into strips

Freshly ground black pepper

2 cups lightly packed (60 g) fresh flat-leaf parsley leaves and tender stems

½ cup (70 g) Brined and Roasted Almonds (page 307), roughly chopped

Turmeric Mayo (page 315), for serving (optional)

I like this salad because you can make it any time of year, no fresh stuff required beyond parsley. But you can add more freshness and crunch with a handful of crisp lettuce, such as sliced romaine or iceberg, and the addition of grilled onions, scallions, or red bell pepper would be terrific. —Serves 4

Put the farro in a small saucepan with a lid, along with the water and ½ teaspoon salt. Bring to a boil, then quickly reduce the heat to a simmer. Cover and cook at a simmer until the farro is tender and the water has been absorbed, 30 to 40 minutes for pearled, 50 to 60 for hulled. If the farro is tender but there's liquid left, just drain it off; if the water has been absorbed but the farro isn't fully tender, add a few tablespoons more water and keep cooking until tender. Cool completely.

Put the croutons in a large bowl (this can be the serving bowl). Add the red onion, sun-dried tomatoes, and pepperoncini. Sprinkle on the pickling liquid and about ¼ cup (60 ml) of the salad dressing and toss to distribute. Let sit for 15 minutes so the croutons start soaking up some of the liquid.

Add the farro, salami, and another couple tablespoons of dressing. Toss again, taste, and season with salt and pepper as needed (the dressing is well seasoned).

Just before serving, add the parsley and almonds, toss, and adjust the consistency with a bit more dressing if needed.

Serve right away, as is or with a drizzle of turmeric mayo on top, if you wish.

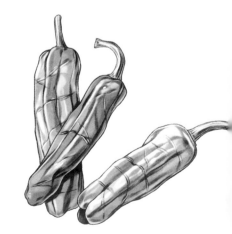

Farrotto, in the Style of Cacio e Pepe

1 cup (200 g) uncooked pearled farro

7 cups (1.7 liters) chicken broth or vegetable broth, homemade or low-sodium store-bought

Extra-virgin olive oil

2 medium shallots, minced

2 or 3 garlic cloves, chopped

3 tablespoons unsalted butter

½ cup (60 g) finely grated Parmigiano-Reggiano cheese

¼ cup (30 g) finely grated pecorino cheese

Kosher salt and freshly ground black pepper

¼ cup (7 g) chopped or torn fresh herbs, such as parsley, basil, tarragon, or a combination (optional)

Despite my devotion to Italian cooking, I do not like risotto. But I love making this farro dish that uses the same technique: Toast the grain and some aromatics in oil and then cook the grain by gradually adding broth until the texture is tender and creamy.

I first encountered this method in a recipe by food writer and whole-grain champion Martha Rose Shulman, and over the years have adapted it to my own tastes. This basic cheese-and-black-pepper version is a good foundational recipe from which you can go crazy with variations.

Farro is a lot denser than the polished white Arborio rice typically used in risotto, so you need to take measures to allow the kernels to become tender and encourage the creamy starch to develop. I usually use pearled farro, which has had the tough hull removed, and I break up the kernels by spinning it in a food processor for a few pulses. You want the grains broken up into irregular bits, but you don't want them too fine. Hulled farro (which still has the bran coating the kernels) will work fine, especially after a trip through the food processor, but will take longer to cook and may not give you as creamy a result. —**Serves 4**

Put the farro in a food processor and pulse a few times until the grains are broken up, but don't turn it into a fine meal. (Depending on your processor blade, your farro may not actually look super chopped up, but it will at least be "scored," which will allow it to absorb liquid more easily.)

Put the broth in a saucepan and bring to a very low simmer.

Pour a generous glug of olive oil into a heavy-bottomed saucepan or deep sauté pan and heat over medium-high heat. Add the shallots, garlic, and cracked farro. Cook, stirring constantly so nothing actually browns, until the farro is lightly toasted and the shallots and garlic are soft and fragrant, about 4 minutes.

Add a ladleful of the warm broth, adjust the heat so everything simmers merrily, and cook, stirring every few moments, until the farro has absorbed all the liquid. Add another ladleful of broth and repeat. Continue until the farro is plump and the mixture is starting to get creamy, about 40 minutes. Start tasting after a few ladlefuls so you can gauge the doneness of the farro. You may not use all the broth, or you may need to use it all then add more; you can use water if you don't have any more broth.

When the farro is a nice tender-but-chewy texture, stir in a final bit of liquid so the mixture is a little looser than your final desired texture, because when you add the cheese, the farrotto will become thicker and tighter.

Add the butter, Parmigiano, pecorino, and a few big twists of black pepper and stir for a few

seconds until well incorporated and creamy. Taste and adjust the flavor and consistency with salt, more pepper, or more liquid.

Fold in the herbs, if using, and serve right away.

Mushroom Farrotto: Sauté 1 pound (450 g) sliced mushrooms (wild varieties, if you have them, but creminis or white button mushrooms will be fine) in about 1½ tablespoons butter, seasoning them lightly with salt and black pepper. When they are browned, transfer to a bowl and set aside while you proceed with the main recipe. Fold the sautéed mushrooms into the farrotto when you add the cheese.

Seasonal Vegetable Farrotto: Create your own combo with the vegetable mix of your choice. Cook them separately (roasted or charred under the broiler), or simmer the vegetables in the chicken broth and add to the farrotto toward the end of cooking.

Kale Farrotto: Fold about 1 cup (240 ml) Updated Kale Sauce (page 319) into the farrotto when you think you're about midway through cooking. You will probably need to add less chicken broth, because the kale sauce counts as added liquid.

Seafood Farrotto: Fold some cooked crab, shrimp, lobster, or scallops into the farrotto when you add the cheese. And don't worry about the "Italians don't eat cheese with seafood" rule, because seafood and cheese is delicious.

Pork Farrotto: Some diced prosciutto, cooked pancetta or bacon, or ham is delicious in farrotto, especially with the mushroom version. Fold it in toward the end of cooking.

Spring Peas and Calamari Stew with Toasted Farro

Extra-virgin olive oil

5 garlic cloves, smashed and peeled

Dried chile flakes

1 cup (200 g) uncooked farro

1 quart (1 liter) water

1 bay leaf

Kosher salt

3 or 4 scallions, trimmed (including ½ inch/1.5 cm off the green tops) and thinly sliced

¼ cup (60 g) tomato paste

1 pound (450 g) cleaned squid, tentacles left whole or halved if large, bodies sliced across into ¼-inch-thick (6 mm) rings

1 cup (240 ml) dry white wine

1 cup (145 g) English peas (fresh or frozen)

1 cup (145 g) diced sugar snap peas

Freshly ground black pepper

Small handful fresh mint leaves, torn

Small handful fresh flat-leaf parsley, roughly chopped

Lemon wedges, for squeezing

When spring finally arrives, I roll out every form of pea and eat as many as I can. Here I'm using English peas and sugar snaps, but you could use just one of them. If you find pea tendrils, add them along with the peas. No need to chop (unless they seem very tough); I like a big tangle of tendrils!

I toast up my farro nice and dark to deepen its flavor and contrast with all those bright green vegetables. —Serves 3 or 4

Pour a small glug of olive oil into a heavy-bottomed saucepan with a lid and heat over medium heat. Add 2 cloves of the garlic and a pinch of dried chile flakes. Cook slowly until the garlic is getting soft, fragrant, and nicely golden brown, about 3 minutes. Add the farro and cook, stirring constantly so the grains toast evenly, until slightly darkened and fragrant.

Add the water, bay leaf, and 2 teaspoons salt. Bring to a boil, then reduce to a simmer. Cover and cook until the farro is tender and all the water has been absorbed, 15 to 30 minutes, depending on the farro. Drain off any remaining liquid, taste, and adjust with more salt if needed. Set aside and keep warm.

Put a generous glug of olive oil, another small pinch of chile flakes, and the remaining 3 cloves garlic in a large skillet. Cook slowly over medium heat until the garlic is getting soft, fragrant, and nicely golden brown, about 3 minutes. Add the scallions and cook until they start to soften, another 2 minutes.

Add the tomato paste and stir it into the scallions and garlic. Cook, stirring and scraping the pan constantly, until it has concentrated and darkened slightly, about 3 minutes.

Add the squid rings and tentacles and toss to get all the squid coated with tomato. Increase the heat to high, add the wine, and stir and scrape until the tomato paste is dissolved in the wine.

Add the English peas, sugar snaps, and a few twists of black pepper and cook for another minute or two, shaking the pan and moving your ingredients around. You want the squid to be just cooked, the peas crisp-tender, and the liquid reduced; the dish should still be quite "saucy."

Remove from the heat, taste, and adjust with more chile flakes, salt, or black pepper. Add the mint and parsley and toss again.

Pile the warm farro in a serving bowl and top with the squid and pea stew. Drizzle the dish with a little more olive oil, and serve right away, with lemon wedges.

Farro con Pollo

1 tablespoon ground coriander

1 tablespoon ground cumin

1 tablespoon ground turmeric

½ teaspoon Aleppo pepper or dried chile flakes

2½ pounds (1.125 kg) bone-in, skin-on chicken parts (6 big chicken thighs work nicely)

Kosher salt and freshly ground black pepper

Extra-virgin olive oil

1 medium onion, finely chopped

4 garlic cloves, chopped

1 cup (200 g) uncooked farro

½ cup (120 ml) dry white wine or dry hard cider

1 dried red chile, such as chile de árbol

1 bay leaf

One 3-inch (7.5 cm) sprig rosemary

One 14.5-ounce (410 g) can whole peeled tomatoes, drained and roughly chopped (save the juice for another use; it freezes well)

1½ cups (360 ml) chicken broth, homemade (page 311) or low-sodium store-bought, or water

Small handful fresh flat-leaf parsley and mint, torn or roughly chopped

Lemon wedges, for serving

Chicken and whole grains make a superb team because chicken's mild flavor doesn't overpower the flavor of the grain, and the ever-thirsty grains drink up all those good chicken juices and fats. My starting point for this dish is the traditional arroz con pollo, of which many Latin cuisines have versions. I'm using farro, but barley would work well. In either case, pearled grains will cook faster than hulled.

You may need to finesse the timing a bit, orchestrating the cooking so that all the liquid is absorbed, the grains are fully tender, and the chicken is properly cooked at the same time. Fortunately, chicken thighs are difficult to overcook, so you've got some wiggle room (but don't undercook them!). For chicken breast fans, use breasts on the bone, which will protect against overcooking, always a challenge with breast meat.
—Serves 4 to 6

Mix the coriander, cumin, turmeric, and Aleppo pepper together in a small bowl. Trim off any big pockets of chicken fat (and save to use for cooking something delicious). In a large bowl, toss the chicken with half the spice mix, and season with salt and black pepper.

Heat a medium glug of olive oil in a large deep broilerproof skillet or wide Dutch oven over medium-high heat. Lay the chicken pieces in the pan, skin side down, with a comfortable amount of room between them; do this in batches if your pan isn't large enough. Cook until both sides of the chicken are nicely browned, about 5 minutes per side. Transfer the chicken to a plate or tray and set aside.

If there's less than about 2 tablespoons of fat left in the pan, add a touch more olive oil. Reduce the heat to medium, add the onion, and stir and scrape to dissolve any nice browned bits left from cooking the chicken.

Season lightly with salt and stir in the remaining spice mix. Cook until the onion is soft and fragrant but not browned, about 4 minutes. Add the garlic and cook another minute.

Add the farro and cook, stirring, until lightly toasted, about 3 minutes.

Increase the heat to medium-high, pour in the wine, and add the dried chile, bay leaf, and rosemary. Simmer for a minute or two to let the wine reduce by about half. Add the tomatoes and chicken broth.

Nestle the chicken into the pan, skin side up; adjust the heat to a strong simmer and cover the pan (use foil if your pan doesn't have a lid). Cook until the chicken is fully cooked (the tip of a paring knife will go through easily and the temperature will register at least 170°F/77°C on an instant-read thermometer) and the farro is tender, about 45 minutes.

If the farro is tender but too soupy, turn up the heat and boil, uncovered, for a few minutes to cook off excess liquid. If the farro isn't quite tender but the pan looks dry, add water or broth, cover, and cook until tender.

When the chicken and farro are done to your liking, heat the broiler and adjust a rack so the chicken will be 4 inches below the heating element. Slide the pan under the broiler and broil, turning the pan as needed, until the chicken skin looks nicely bronzed.

Shower the chicken and farro with the herbs and serve with lemon wedges for each diner.

Farro, Brown Butter, and Honey Cake

6 ounces (170 g) unsalted
butter

Butter and flour, for the pan

½ cup (60 g) unbleached all-
purpose flour

1 cup (120 g) farro flour

1 teaspoon baking powder

1 teaspoon kosher salt

½ teaspoon ground cinnamon

1 cup plus 2 tablespoons (225 g)
sugar

¼ cup (80 g) honey

3 large eggs

½ cup (120 ml) whole milk, at
room temperature

Simple and elegant, this cake is just waiting for some Malted Whipped Cream (page 308) and gently stewed dates, figs, or other fruit compote as a garnish. You can make this honey cake with another flour in place of the farro—spelt is excellent, as is regular whole wheat—but I like the nutty flavor of farro flour.
—**Makes one 9-inch (23 cm) cake**

Melt the butter in a small saucepan over medium heat and then continue to cook, swirling the pan occasionally until the butterfat turns amber, the milk solids at the bottom of the pan are golden, and the butter smells deliciously nutty. This should take 2 to 4 minutes, but take your time so you don't burn anything.

Remove from the heat and pour the butter and any browned bits into the bowl of a stand mixer. Set aside and let cool until the butter has solidified but is still soft. To speed this up, put the bowl in the fridge or over a bowl of ice water.

Heat the oven to 350°F (175°F).

Butter a 9-inch (23 cm) cake pan, line the bottom with a round of parchment, and butter the parchment. If you don't have parchment, make sure the butter layer is generous and even and dust the interior of the pan with all-purpose flour, tapping out the excess.

Whisk together the all-purpose flour, farro flour, baking powder, salt, and cinnamon in a small bowl and set aside.

Add 1 cup (200 g) of the sugar to the mixer bowl with the soft but solidified brown butter. Mix with the paddle on medium-high speed until pale and fluffy, about 3 minutes.

With the mixer running, drizzle in the honey and mix for another 30 seconds. Add the eggs to the mixer one at a time, mixing just until incorporated. Add the dry ingredients and the milk in this order: one-third of the dry ingredients, half of the milk, one-third of the dry ingredients, the remaining milk, and finally the remaining dry ingredients. Mix after each addition just until blended.

Scrape the batter into the prepared pan and sprinkle with the remaining 2 tablespoons sugar. Bake until the cake pulls away from the sides of the pan and a toothpick inserted into the center comes out clean, 25 to 35 minutes, rotating the pan front to back halfway through baking. Let the cake cool in the pan for about 15 minutes, then run a knife between the cake and the edge of the pan and slide onto a serving plate; you want the sugared side up.

This cake is best eaten while still warm but will keep for a day or two wrapped in plastic at room temperature.

Freekeh

Triticum turgidum var. durum

▸ CONTAINS GLUTEN ◂

Freekeh is a form of wheat that I can't get enough of, partly because two of my favorite farmers—Anthony and Carol Boutard of Ayers Creek Farm in Gaston, Oregon—produce freekeh locally. Freekeh traditionally starts with durum wheat, the hard (high-protein) variety that's used for the best pastas. The magic happens when the wheat is harvested while still "green," rather than letting the kernels come to full maturity and dry on the stalk.

The green wheat is harvested and then the hulls are removed by burning them off. Then it gets threshed, and the resulting grain is at once slightly vegetal and smoky in flavor, with a tender chew. You'll usually find freekeh in cracked form, which makes cooking quicker, but whole-kernel freekeh exists.

Details

→ 1 cup uncooked freekeh weighs 6 ounces (170 g).

→ Use 1 part freekeh to 2 parts liquid as a rule of thumb for the absorption method.

→ Cook freekeh for 15 to 20 minutes.

→ 1 cup (170 g) uncooked freekeh yields 2½ cups (370 g) cooked.

RECIPES

Freekeh, Shredded Collards, and Your Favorite Fruit

Extra-virgin olive oil

1 cup (170 g) uncooked freekeh

2 cups (480 ml) water

Kosher salt

1 bunch (about 10 oz/280 g) collard greens

½ bunch scallions, trimmed (including ½ inch/1.5 cm off the green tops), sliced on a sharp angle, soaked in ice water for 20 minutes, and drained well

2 to 3 tablespoons red wine vinegar

Freshly ground black pepper

Dried chile flakes (or fresh chiles when in season)

3 cups (510 g) chunks or slices ripe fresh fruit

½ cup (70 g) roughly chopped lightly toasted nuts

I love the way the gentle smokiness of the freekeh plays with tangy, succulent fresh fruit in this salad. Here I'm using apples, with pecans as the nutty accent, but other combinations are an option, too: plums and walnuts, strawberries and peanuts, peaches and almonds. —**Serves 4 to 6**

Heat a glug of olive oil in a large skillet over medium-high heat, add the freekeh, and toast, stirring frequently, until it smells toasted and smoky, a good 5 minutes. Add the water and 1 teaspoon salt, bring to a boil, reduce to a simmer, cover, and simmer until the freekeh is tender and the liquid has been absorbed. If the freekeh is tender but there's liquid left, just drain it off; if the water has been absorbed but the freekeh isn't fully tender, add a few tablespoons more water and keep cooking until tender. Cool completely.

Cut out the thick midrib from each collard leaf and compost or discard it. Stack a few leaves on top of one another and roll them into a tight cylinder. With a sharp knife, slice across the roll to cut the collards into very thin strips (this is called a chiffonade).

Put the collards in a large bowl along with the freekeh and scallions and toss to mix. Pour on the vinegar and ¼ cup (60 ml) olive oil, toss again, and season with about ½ teaspoon salt, a few twists of black pepper, and a big pinch of chile flakes. Toss.

Add the fruit and toss again gently. Taste and adjust the seasoning with more salt, pepper, chile flakes, or vinegar. Top with the nuts and serve right away.

Seafood Chowder with Freekeh, Potatoes, and Corn

Extra-virgin olive oil

1 leek, trimmed, halved lengthwise, cleaned well, and cut crosswise into half-moons ¼ inch (6 mm) thick

2 to 3 largeish inner celery stalks, preferably with some leaves attached, thinly sliced, leaves roughly chopped

2 garlic cloves, smashed and peeled

Kosher salt

2 tablespoons unsalted butter

1 pound (450 g) new potatoes, peeled only if the skins are thick, halved or quartered if large

1 habanero chile, halved

1 bay leaf

2 large ears sweet corn, kernels sliced off, cobs cut in half and reserved

2 quarts (2 liters) water

½ cup (85 g) uncooked freekeh

4 ounces (115 g) hot-smoked salmon or trout, skin and bones removed, broken into large flakes

Freshly ground black pepper

Hot sauce

1 lemon, half for juice, half for wedges

8 ounces (225 g) dry-packed scallops, halved or quartered if large

8 ounces (225 g) mild white-fleshed fish such as cod, halibut, or rock fish, cut into 1-inch (2.5 cm) chunks

1 cup (240 g) heavy cream or crème fraîche

Yes, a classic corn chowder is an unusual place to find freekeh, but I wanted to bring some attitude to what's often a too-bland soup, all sweet vegetables and creamy broth.

Here I use potatoes as per the traditional soup, which I let fall apart a bit so they thicken the broth, and I use the corn in three ways: the cobs will flavor the base broth, half the kernels will get cooked a long time to add body and sweetness, and a final handful of kernels will go in just at the end, so they retain their juicy freshness and add some contrast.

The freekeh contributes a smoky meatiness that I love, especially when echoed by the hot-smoked salmon. I think the salmon, scallops, and chunks of white fish make a great combination, but you can use whatever seafood you have on hand. When shopping for the scallops, try to buy "dry-packed"; if not labeled as such, ask the fishmonger. —**Serves 6**

Pour a glug of olive oil into a large soup pot and heat over medium-high heat. Add the leek, celery stalks, garlic, and 1 teaspoon salt and cook, stirring, for a couple of minutes. Add the butter and cook, stirring, until the vegetables become slightly golden, another 3 or 4 minutes.

Add the potatoes, habanero, bay leaf, 1 teaspoon salt, the corn cobs, and the water. Bring back to a boil, reduce to a simmer, and cook, uncovered, for 10 minutes. Add the freekeh and half the corn kernels and simmer until the freekeh and potatoes are both tender, another 15 to 20 minutes. Don't worry if the potatoes are done before the freekeh; you want them to fall apart a bit and thicken the chowder.

Add the smoked salmon, several generous twists of black pepper, a few shakes of hot sauce, and a big squeeze of the lemon half. Taste and adjust the seasoning. Remove and discard the corncobs, scraping them to remove any soup and to squeeze out the tender pulp clinging to the cobs. Set the soup aside.

Heat a large skillet over medium-high heat. Add a small glug of olive oil, the scallops, and the white fish and season lightly with salt and black pepper. Once added, don't move them for at least 1 minute; this will help them get a browned exterior and prevent them from sticking to the pan. Flip the seafood and add some soup broth to the pan to deglaze. Add the cream and bring to a simmer, then add all of this back to the soup pot.

Gently reheat the soup if needed, then add the celery leaves (if using) and the remaining raw corn. Taste and adjust the seasoning. Serve with the lemon wedges and more hot sauce.

Freekeh Falafel

⅓ cup (55 g) uncooked freekeh

⅔ cup (160 ml) water

Kosher salt

One 15-ounce (420 g) can chickpeas, rinsed, drained well, and roughly chopped

1 cup (30 g) roughly chopped fresh flat-leaf parsley leaves

1 cup (30 g) roughly chopped fresh cilantro leaves and tender stems

1 cup (150 g) finely chopped onion

4 garlic cloves, roughly chopped

1 small fresh hot chile, such as serrano or jalapeño, deribbed and finely chopped

½ cup (60 g) whole wheat flour or chickpea flour

2 teaspoons ground cumin

1½ teaspoons baking powder

1 teaspoon ground cardamom

Freshly ground black pepper

Finely grated zest and juice of 1 lemon

Vegetable or olive oil, for deep-frying

FOR SERVING

Whole Wheat Pitas (page 245)

Chopped cucumber

Chopped tomato

Spicy Creamy Green Sauce (page 314)

Note: You'll be chopping the ingredients in a food processor, but in order to control the texture—you don't want things to get too mushy—you need to roughly chop the chickpeas, herbs, and vegetables first, so that you're not forced to overprocess the whole shebang in order to get just one ingredient, such as your onion, small enough.

Freekeh originated in the Middle East, as did falafel, so I thought why not marry the two for a falafel with some added texture and slightly smoky flavor? I like to serve these stuffed in a pita as a sandwich, but also on top of a big salad full of chopped cucumbers, tomato, celery, and crisp lettuce, or maybe in a grain bowl, dressed with some Spicy Creamy Green Sauce. —**Makes about 2 dozen 2-inch (5 cm) falafels, serves 4 to 6**

Put the freekeh in a small saucepan with the water and a pinch of salt. Bring to a boil, reduce to a simmer, cover, and simmer until the freekeh is tender and the liquid has been absorbed, 15 to 20 minutes. If the freekeh is tender but there's liquid left, drain it off; if the water has been absorbed but the freekeh isn't tender, add a bit more water and keep cooking until tender. Cool completely.

Put the chickpeas in a food processor and pulse a few times to roughly chop. Put the freekeh, parsley, cilantro, onion, garlic, chile, whole wheat flour, 1 tablespoon salt, the cumin, baking powder, cardamom, and ¼ teaspoon black pepper into the processor and pulse, scraping down the sides until you get a nice uniform consistency that is about the texture of chopped nuts. *Do not go all the way to a puree.*

Transfer the mixture to a bowl, stir in the lemon zest and juice, taste, and add more salt, black pepper, cumin, or cardamom if you like. Chill for at least 30 minutes and up to overnight.

Pour 3 inches (7.5 cm) of oil into a large, deep, heavy-bottomed pot; make sure the pot is tall enough that there's room for the falafels and for oil to bubble up without spilling over. Heat over medium-high heat to 330°F (165°C) on a deep-frying thermometer.

While the oil is heating, shape the falafels using a small ice-cream scoop or two tablespoons. Aim for round, but with a few rough edges, to get nice and crispy. Line a tray with paper towels.

Working in batches, carefully slide a few falafels into the oil. Don't overload the pot or the oil temperature will cool too much and the falafels will end up being greasy. Cook until they are richly browned and crisp, flipping them over from time to time, about 5 minutes. Lift them out of the oil with a spider or slotted spoon and drain on the paper towels. Repeat with the rest of the mixture.

Serve the falafels in pitas with cucumbers, tomatoes, and green sauce.

Stir-Fries for Every Season

A stir-fry is the epitome of a quick meal, especially when you start with already-cooked and cooled grains. Leftovers are perfect. When stir-frying, use high heat (but make sure nothing burns), move your ingredients actively around the pan, and stop when the vegetables are just tender—some crunch is good. Cutting your vegetables fairly small will make them cook quickly and will help all your elements integrate well. This is a game of timing, so make sure you have all your ingredients ready to go when you start cooking.

How to assemble your grain stir-fry:

Refer to the foldout chart for ingredients by season.
Use a very large, heavy wok or skillet, and don't overcrowd the pan.

1. Add a glug of extra-virgin olive oil to the pan and heat over high heat. Add the **PROTEIN** and sauté quickly to brown the exterior. Remove and set aside.

2. Add more oil if needed, then add the **AROMATICS** and cook for a few seconds until fragrant. This is important to build flavor.

3. Add the **VEGETABLES** one type at a time, starting with the most densely textured. Sauté quickly until crisp-tender (unless otherwise noted).

4. Add the **GRAIN** and toss to heat. Return the protein to the pan; season with salt, pepper, and dried chile flakes; and toss until fully cooked.

5. Add the **CRUNCH** and **SEASONING**; taste, and adjust the seasoning.

6. Top with the **FINISHING** and serve while nice and hot.

Fold a scrambled egg into your stir-fries at the last minute for more **PROTEIN** and tender texture.

Cut skinny ingredients like **AROMATICS** and **VEGETABLES** at a sharp angle to give you more surface area.

To cook **VEGETABLES** more quickly, add a splash of water, cover the pan, and steam until tender.

Pictured here: Midsummer stir-fry (see chart)

Spelt

Triticum aestivum ssp. spelta

▶ CONTAINS GLUTEN ◀

Whole spelt kernels are delicious and versatile, behaving like farro—tasty, chewy, mild-flavored—in soups, stews, and side dishes. But I think spelt shines brightest as a flour. The flavor is rich and nutty and the baking qualities make it a good substitute in any recipe calling for whole wheat flour.

Details

→ 1 cup uncooked spelt weighs 6½ ounces (180 g).

→ Use 2 parts liquid to 1 part uncooked spelt as a rule of thumb for the absorption method.

→ Cook spelt between 40 and 90 minutes.

→ 1 cup (180 g) uncooked spelt yields 2 cups (370 g) cooked.

→ 1 cup spelt flour weighs 4¼ ounces (120 g).

RECIPES

Beef and Swiss Chard Soup with Spelt

2 pounds (900 g) boneless beef chuck roast, cut into two or three pieces

Kosher salt and freshly ground black pepper

Extra-virgin olive oil

1 large (12 oz/350 g) onion, sliced as thin as possible

4 large garlic cloves, smashed and peeled

1 cup (240 ml) dry white wine

2 quarts (2 liters) chicken, beef, or vegetable broth, homemade or low-sodium store-bought, or water

2 bay leaves

A few small sprigs thyme

1 bunch Swiss chard, ends trimmed, stems cut out from the leaves and thinly sliced, leaves cut into 1-inch (2.5 cm) ribbons

2 large carrots, cut into ¼-inch (6 mm) dice (1 generous cup/180 g)

1 cup (180 g) uncooked spelt

One 14.5-ounce (410 g) can whole peeled tomatoes, drained and roughly chopped

Horseradish cream (optional): ½ cup (120 g) crème fraîche or sour cream mixed with 2 tablespoons prepared horseradish

Note: Grains are thirsty, so keep an eye on liquid levels. If the spelt has drunk up a lot of broth, just add a bit more broth or water, simmer to incorporate, and you'll be fine.

Most beef soup recipes ask the cook to cut the beef into bite-size pieces before cooking, but I find that you can end up with dry bits of beef, with all the flavor cooked out of them. Instead, I simmer big ol' chunks of chuck roast slowly until fully tender and then pull them into smaller shreds and pieces. This keeps the beef more succulent, and it's frankly easier! You can also use the shredding step as a time to locate and discard any big pieces of fat, silver skin, or gristle. —**Makes 3 quarts (3 liters), serves 6 to 8**

Season the beef generously all over with salt and pepper. Pour a glug of olive oil into a large, heavy-bottomed soup pot or Dutch oven and heat over medium-high heat. Add the beef and cook until nicely browned on all sides, about 15 minutes for the whole process. Cook the beef in batches if necessary to avoid crowding the pan, which will inhibit browning (properly browned beef will add a ton of flavor to the soup).

Remove the beef and set it aside. Add the onion and garlic to the pot, reduce the heat to medium, and cook, stirring frequently and making sure you dissolve the meat juices with the moisture from the onion so it doesn't burn, until the onion is soft and fragrant, about 8 minutes.

Add the wine, increase the heat to high, and simmer rapidly until the wine has reduced to under ½ cup (120 ml). Add the broth, bay leaves, and thyme. Return the beef chunks to the pot, immediately reduce the heat to a gentle simmer, cover, and simmer until the beef is very tender, anywhere from 1 to 3 hours, depending on your cut of beef. Remove the beef, let it cool, and pull it apart into generous bite-size chunks, discarding any big pockets of fat or gristle.

While the beef cools, add the chard stems, carrots, and spelt to the broth and simmer for 15 minutes. Add the chard leaves and tomatoes and simmer until all the vegetables are tender and the spelt is fully cooked and tender, another 10 to 15 minutes.

Return the beef to the pot, taste, and adjust the seasoning and the amount of liquid; you may need to add up to a pint or more.

Serve simply or with a spoonful of horseradish cream drizzled over the soup. Store in the refrigerator for up to 3 days or freeze for up to 3 months.

Tender Spelt Buttermilk Biscuits

2 cups (240 g) spelt flour

1 tablespoon baking powder

1 teaspoon baking soda

2 teaspoons kosher salt

4 ounces (115 g) unsalted butter, very cold

1 cup (240 ml) buttermilk, plus more for brushing

I used to make these biscuits using all white flour, but once I was introduced to spelt flour, I made the switch. Because spelt is a type of wheat, it's fairly easy to swap in for white flour, and the flavor of spelt is addictive—nutty, mellow, with the finished biscuit just begging to be topped with some butter and honey, Honey Butter with Bee Pollen (page 307), or Maple Butter (page 307). —**Makes eight 3-inch (7.5 cm) biscuits**

Heat the oven to 425°F (220°C).

Whisk together the spelt flour, baking powder, baking soda, and salt in a large bowl. On the large holes of a box grater, grate the cold butter into the dry ingredients. With your hands, toss the dry ingredients and butter together so the butter is fully distributed.

Pour in the buttermilk, stirring gently to moisten the flour. Turn the dough onto a lightly floured work surface. Press lightly to flatten the dough slightly, then fold it over on itself a couple of times; this will complete the mixing and help create some flaky layers.

Press the dough out until it's about 1 inch (2.5 cm) thick. Cut out rounds with a 2½-inch (6.5 cm) cutter, then gently pat the scraps together and cut a final biscuit. (Or press the dough into a rectangle and cut square biscuits with a large knife.)

Arrange the biscuits on a sheet pan and chill for 15 minutes.

Brush the tops lightly with more buttermilk and bake until they are a rich brown, puffed, and no longer doughy in the center (you may need to break one open to verify), 12 to 15 minutes. Cool on a rack until you're tired of waiting, then split and spread with something buttery.

Handy Spelt-Flour Pancake Mix

DRY PANCAKE MIX

3⅓ cups (400 g) unbleached all-purpose flour

2½ cups (300 g) spelt flour or other whole-grain flour

1½ cups (225 g) buttermilk powder

⅓ cup (65 g) sugar

1 tablespoon plus 2 teaspoons baking powder

1½ teaspoons baking soda

1 tablespoon kosher salt

TO MAKE PANCAKES

1 cup (240 ml) water or milk

3 tablespoons vegetable oil or melted unsalted butter, plus more for cooking pancakes

1 large egg

Warm maple syrup and good salted butter, or jam or Honey Butter with Bee Pollen (page 307) or Maple Butter (page 307), for serving

This mix uses buttermilk powder, for both tenderness and a little extra flavor, which allows you to use plain water in the final mix for extra convenience, though milk adds richness and flavor. Keep the mix in an airtight container in your pantry and it'll be ready to go, quick enough even for school-day breakfasts. The mix should also go with you on every camping trip. —**Makes 6 batches, about 10 pancakes per batch**

MAKE THE DRY PANCAKE MIX: Whisk together all of the ingredients in a large bowl. Store in an airtight container for up to 3 months.

TO MAKE THE PANCAKES: Whisk the milk, oil, and egg in a medium bowl. Add 1¼ cups (150 g) of the dry pancake mix and stir just to combine . . . leave those lumps!

Heat a heavy-bottomed pan or griddle (cast iron works great) over medium-high heat and add a thin film of oil or butter.

Scoop or pour about ¼ cup (60 ml) of batter per pancake into the pan, adding as many as will comfortably fit. Cook until the pancakes are bubbling on top and golden brown when you peek under them with a spatula, about 2 minutes. Flip and cook until cooked through, another minute or so.

Serve right away with maple syrup and butter, jam, or honey butter or maple butter.

Cast-Iron Skillet Spelt Cinnamon Rolls

DOUGH

½ cup (120 ml) whole milk

1 cup (120 g) spelt flour

¼ cup (60 ml) barely warm water

1½ teaspoons (5 g) active dry yeast

1 cup (120 g) unbleached all-purpose flour

4 tablespoons (60 g) unsalted butter, cut into 4 pieces, at room temperature

1 large egg, at room temperature

1 tablespoon granulated sugar

2 teaspoons kosher salt

FILLING

½ cup firmly packed (105 g) light or dark brown sugar

2 teaspoons ground cinnamon

¼ teaspoon kosher salt

3 tablespoons unsalted butter, very soft

FOR BAKING

1 tablespoon unsalted butter, very soft, for the pan

¼ cup (60 ml) heavy or whipping cream

FROSTING

½ cup (60 g) powdered sugar

3 ounces (85 g) cream cheese, at room temperature

¼ cup (60 ml) heavy or whipping cream

Fresh-from-the-oven cinnamon rolls, their tops spread with creamy frosting just starting to melt and get gooey, are undisputed breakfast favorites. They do, however, take some planning, as the dough needs an overnight rise. This dough gets its supremely tender crumb from a *tangzhong*, an awesome technique in which you cook flour and milk into a paste that's then added to the main dough. Tangzhong is originally Chinese, but many people know it from Japanese Hokkaido milk bread. Here it gives a classic American cinnamon roll a real textural advantage. If you don't have a cast-iron skillet, you can use any 9- or 10-inch (23 or 25 cm) round baking dish or heavy ovenproof skillet. The cast iron just looks so good! —**Makes 9 cinnamon rolls**

MAKE THE DOUGH: Whisk together the milk and 2½ tablespoons of the spelt flour in a small saucepan. Cook the mixture over medium heat, whisking occasionally, until it boils. Whisking constantly, boil the flour paste until it's thick and starts to pull away from the bottom of the pan, about 30 seconds ●. Transfer the paste to a bowl, cover the surface directly with plastic wrap so a skin doesn't form, and let cool to room temperature.

When the flour paste is cool, put the warm water and yeast in a small bowl and let sit for about 5 minutes to hydrate the yeast ●. In a stand mixer fitted with the dough hook, combine the flour paste, the yeast mixture, remaining spelt flour, all-purpose flour, butter, egg, granulated sugar, and salt.

Knead on low speed for a few minutes until all of the ingredients are combined, scraping down the sides of the bowl as needed. Switch to medium speed and continue

kneading until the dough is smooth and springy, about 8 minutes, again scraping the bowl and the hook as needed ●. Scrape out the dough from the mixer and shape into a ball with your hands. Place the dough in an oiled bowl and cover with plastic or a damp towel. Let rise at room temperature until doubled, about 1½ hours, and then pop into the refrigerator for an overnight rest ●.

A couple of hours before you want to serve the cinnamon rolls, take the dough from the refrigerator.

MAKE THE FILLING: Mix together the brown sugar, cinnamon, and salt in a small bowl.

Lightly flour your work surface, transfer the dough to the work surface, and roll into an 18 × 12-inch (46 × 30 cm) rectangle ●.

Spread the softened butter evenly over the dough, taking care not to tear the dough; dot the butter rather than spread it. Sprinkle the brown sugar mixture

evenly over the surface, all the way to all the edges ●.

FOR BAKING: Beginning on a long side, roll the dough into a cylinder 18 inches (46 cm) long (it will be soft; just work gently and do your best) ● and cut crosswise into 9 even pieces ●. (Tip: Cut the dough cleanly with unflavored dental floss. Slide floss under the dough, bring both ends up, crisscross them, then pull taut.) Coat a 9- or 10-inch (23 or 25 cm) cast-iron skillet or cake pan with the 1 tablespoon soft butter and arrange the rolls cut side up in the pan ●. Cover loosely with a cloth and let rise in a warm place until the rolls are puffy and touching one another, 1½ to 2 hours.

About 20 minutes before the rolls are fully risen (just guesstimate!), heat the oven to 375°F (190°C).

Once the rolls have risen, brush the surface generously with the cream (it will pool in the cracks, which is fine). Bake until medium brown and dry-looking on the top, with no "raw dough" look in the folds, 20 to 25 minutes.

WHILE THE ROLLS ARE BAKING, MAKE THE FROSTING: In a stand mixer fitted with the paddle, combine the powdered sugar and cream cheese and beat on low speed until smooth. Gradually add the cream and mix until smooth.

Frost the cinnamon rolls while they're still in the pan, warm but not piping hot (which would melt the frosting too much). Eat as many as your heart desires.

Savory Morning Bun with Sausage, Fontina, and Broccoli Rabe

DOUGH

½ cup (120 ml) whole milk

1 cup (120 g) spelt flour

1½ teaspoons (5 g) active dry yeast

¼ cup (60 ml) barely warm water

1 cup (120 g) unbleached all-purpose flour

2 teaspoons kosher salt

1 large egg

4 tablespoons (60 g) unsalted butter, cut into pieces, at room temperature

FILLING

Kosher salt

8 ounces (225 g) broccoli rabe, tough ends trimmed off

Extra-virgin olive oil

3 garlic cloves, smashed and peeled

8 ounces (225 g) breakfast sausage, bulk or casings removed, shaped into 3 or 4 patties

1 tablespoon pure maple syrup

2 cups (240 g) grated Fontina cheese

½ teaspoon dried chile flakes

Freshly ground black pepper

FOR BAKING

1 tablespoon unsalted butter, at room temperature

1 large egg, beaten

¼ cup (40 g) sesame seeds

Call your friends now and invite them over for next Sunday morning, because you've just met the perfect brunch dish. The coiled presentation looks lovely on a spread, and the hearty filling means this plays the role of both main dish and pastry. The dough (essentially the same as for the Cast-Iron Skillet Spelt Cinnamon Rolls on page 221) requires advance planning—an overnight rest and a couple of hours of rising before baking—so be sure to read through everything to plan accordingly. While it's dreamy fresh from the oven, you can bake the morning bun a day ahead, refrigerate it, and then reheat in a 375°F (190°C) oven for 15 to 30 minutes, covered in foil at first, then uncovered to crisp up the edges. —Serves 6 to 8

MAKE THE DOUGH: Whisk together the milk and 2 tablespoons of the spelt flour in a small saucepan. Cook the mixture over medium heat, whisking occasionally, until it boils. Whisking constantly, boil the flour paste until it's thick and starts to pull away from the bottom of the pan, about 30 seconds. Transfer the paste to a bowl, cover directly with plastic wrap, and let cool to room temperature.

When the flour paste has cooled, put the yeast and water in a small bowl and let sit for about 5 minutes to rehydrate the yeast. In a stand mixer fitted with the dough hook, combine the paste, yeast mixture, remaining spelt flour, the all-purpose flour, salt, egg, and butter.

Knead on low speed for a few minutes until all of the ingredients are combined (you

may need to scrape down the bowl once or twice). Switch to medium speed and continue kneading until the dough is smooth and springy, about 8 minutes. Remove the dough from the mixer and shape into a ball. Place the dough in an oiled bowl and cover with plastic or a damp towel. Let rise at room temperature until doubled in volume, about 1½ hours, and then pop into the refrigerator for an overnight rest.

A couple of hours before you want to serve the morning rolls, take the dough from the refrigerator and make the filling.

MAKE THE FILLING: Bring a large pot of water to a boil and add enough salt that it tastes like the ocean. Add the broccoli rabe and boil until the stems are quite tender when you cut (or bite) them, 8 to 10 minutes. Drain well, let cool, then chop roughly,

Pictured on pages 226–27

making sure there are no long pieces of stem, which can be fibrous even when fully cooked. Set aside.

Heat a nice glug of olive oil in a large skillet over medium heat. Add the smashed garlic and cook slowly over medium heat until the garlic is very soft, fragrant, and nicely golden brown—but not burnt—about 5 minutes.

Add the sausage patties and cook, flipping occasionally, until browned on the surface and just cooked on the inside. Break into bite-size chunks with a spoon and cook until no longer pink. (You can leave the garlic in the pan as you cook the sausage, if it's not getting too dark. If it is, scoop it out and add back when you add the broccoli rabe. In either case, smash it further into small bits.)

Pour off any excess grease from the skillet and add the chopped broccoli rabe. Cook, stirring, for a minute to integrate the broccoli rabe and flavor it with the sausage grease. Stir in the maple syrup.

Transfer the mixture to a bowl, let cool completely, then add the Fontina and chile flakes and season with lots of black pepper. Taste and adjust the seasoning. Refrigerate while you roll out the dough.

BAKE THE ROLL: Coat a 9-inch (23 cm) cast-iron skillet or cake pan with 1 tablespoon butter.

Lightly flour your work surface and roll the dough into an 18 × 12-inch (46 × 30 cm) rectangle. Distribute the filling in an even layer over the whole surface of the dough.

Beginning with a long side, roll the dough into a tight cylinder (it will be soft, just work gently and do your best) and coil the cylinder into a loose spiral. Gently lift the spiral and place into the buttered pan; you may need to pat things back into place, but that's fine. Cover loosely with a cloth and let rise in a warm place until the dough is puffy and the coil is swollen, 1½ to 2 hours.

About 20 minutes before the dough is fully risen (just guesstimate!), heat the oven to 375°F (190°C).

Brush the morning roll with the beaten egg and sprinkle with the sesame seeds. Bake until medium brown and dry-looking on the top, with no "raw dough" look in the folds, 20 to 25 minutes.

Let cool for a few minutes so the filling can set, then cut into slices and serve.

Wheat Berries

Triticum aestivum/Triticum turgidum

▶ CONTAINS GLUTEN ◀

We mostly encounter "regular" wheat as a flour of some kind, but the whole kernels, or berries, of hard red spring or winter wheat are delicious eaten as a whole grain. They're nutty little nuggets that do require a long time to cook, up to 1 hour, but because they are so firm, they hold up beautifully in salads and soups.

Details

→ 1 cup uncooked wheat berries weighs 7 ounces (200 g).

→ Use 2½ parts liquid to 1 part wheat berries as a rule of thumb for the absorption method, though I prefer the boil-like-pasta method because the berries can be quite hard and take a lot of time and liquid to soften.

→ Cook wheat berries for 40 to 50 minutes, sometimes a bit longer.

→ 1 cup (200 g) uncooked wheat berries yields 2½ cups (450 g) cooked.

RECIPES

Grated Carrot Salad with Peanuts, Raisins, and Wheat Berries

1 cup (200 g) uncooked wheat berries

1 quart (1 liter) water

Kosher salt

4 cups (450 g) grated or shredded carrots

1 cup (150 g) golden raisins, plumped in warm water with a squeeze of lemon juice for 20 minutes, then drained

½ cup (60 g) scallions, trimmed (including ½ inch/1.5 cm off the green tops), sliced on a sharp angle, soaked in ice water for 20 minutes, and drained well

1 cup (30 g) lightly packed roughly chopped fresh flat-leaf parsley

2 tablespoons fresh lemon juice

2 tablespoons sherry vinegar or red wine vinegar

Freshly ground black pepper

¼ cup (60 ml) extra-virgin olive oil

1 cup (140 g) chopped toasted peanuts or other nuts

Serve this salad the next time you have friends over for some summer grilling. It's fresh, colorful, and best when made about an hour ahead of serving, which allows time for the carrots to soften just a touch and become more "slaw-like." Add the nuts at the last minute, however, to keep their crunch. —**Serves 6 to 8**

Put the wheat berries in a medium saucepan with the water and 1 teaspoon salt. Bring to a boil, reduce the heat to a lively simmer, cover, and cook until the wheat berries are fully tender and most of the grains have opened up, about 45 minutes. All the water won't be absorbed, so drain thoroughly. Cool completely.

Put the wheat berries in a medium serving bowl and add the carrots, drained raisins, scallions, and parsley. Toss to mix, then add the lemon juice and vinegar, season generously with salt and pepper, and toss again.

Let the salad rest for about 15 minutes, taste, and adjust the seasoning with more lemon, vinegar, salt, or pepper. Add the olive oil, toss again, then finish by adding the nuts and giving it all one final toss. Serve right away.

Freshest Chicken Salad with Chile Peppers and Wheat Berries

1 cup (200 g) uncooked wheat berries

1 quart (1 liter) water

Kosher salt

2 limes (maybe 3, if they're not very juicy)

2 tablespoons rice vinegar or white wine vinegar

A few fresh hot chiles, such as jalapeños (or Anaheims if you want milder), deribbed, seeded, and thinly sliced

½ cup (15 g) torn or roughly chopped fresh cilantro leaves and tender stems, plus a handful of 4-inch (10 cm) stems (8 to 10) for poaching the chicken

6 black peppercorns

1 bay leaf

About 1½ pounds (675 g) chicken pieces: 4 bone-in, skin-on chicken thighs or 2 bone-in, skin-on chicken breasts

½ cup (75 g) chopped red onion

1 teaspoon sugar

1 pint (360 g) cherry tomatoes, halved or quartered if large

1 red, orange, or yellow bell pepper, cut into small dice or strips

Freshly ground black pepper

Extra-virgin olive oil

2 cups lightly packed (200 g) shredded crisp lettuce, such as romaine or iceberg

This dish is perfect for summer entertaining, because you can cook the chicken and wheat berries in the cool of the morning or the night before, and everything else in the dish is raw. A dollop of Spicy Creamy Green Sauce (page 314) on this salad would be delish. —Serves 4 to 6

Put the wheat berries in a medium saucepan with the water and 1 teaspoon salt. Bring to a boil, reduce the heat to a lively simmer, cover, and cook until the wheat berries are fully tender and most of the grains have opened up, about 45 minutes. All the water won't be absorbed, so drain thoroughly. Cool completely.

Cut 2 or 3 thin slices off one of the limes and place in a medium pot (reserve the other half of the lime for later). Add 3 cups (720 ml) water, the vinegar, 3 or 4 slices of one of the hot chiles, the cilantro stems, peppercorns, bay leaf, and 2 teaspoons salt. Bring to a boil, then reduce the heat to a simmer and simmer for about 10 minutes so the flavors develop.

Slide the chicken into the simmering liquid and adjust the heat to a gentle simmer. If the chicken is not covered by the liquid, add some hot water. Poach until just cooked—no longer pink in the center but not cooked much past that; the internal temperature should be 170°F (77°C) for thighs or 160°F (71°C) for breasts; the temperature will rise several degrees after cooking. Do NOT let the liquid actually boil, which can dry out the chicken. The actual time needed will vary according to your chicken's thickness, but count on 12 to 30 minutes.

When the chicken is cooked, take it from the liquid and set aside to cool, then shred, discarding any skin or bones (or pop them back into the poaching liquid, simmer another 45 minutes or so, and use it as a tasty broth). Chill the meat, covered, in the fridge.

Meanwhile, grate the zest from a whole lime into a small bowl. Add the onion, then squeeze the juice from one lime over the onion. Add the sugar and a big pinch of salt. Toss and leave to "pickle" while you make the rest of the dish.

Put the chicken in a big serving bowl, add the wheat berries, tomatoes, bell pepper, hot chiles, onion–lime juice mixture, and cilantro and toss. Season with salt and pepper, squeeze on the juice from the reserved lime half, and drizzle with about ¼ cup (60 ml) olive oil. Toss again, taste, and adjust with more salt, pepper, lime juice, and olive oil until really zingy. Fold in the shredded lettuce and serve right away.

Roasted Delicata Squash with Wheat Berries and Romesco Sauce

1 cup (200 g) uncooked wheat berries

1 quart (1 liter) water

Kosher salt

1 large or 2 small delicata squash (about 1½ lb/675 g total)

Extra-virgin olive oil

Freshly ground black pepper

½ teaspoon dried chile flakes

1 lemon, halved

½ cup (70 g) Toasted Pumpkin Seeds (page 306)

½ cup lightly packed (15 g) fresh cilantro leaves

¼ cup lightly packed (7 g) fresh mint leaves

½ cup (120 ml) Romesco Sauce (page 315)

I'd like to thank whoever developed the delicata squash, because its small size makes it easy to handle and the skin is so tender you don't need to peel it . . . a perfectly behaved winter squash! This dish is hearty enough to be a vegetarian main dish, and would look inviting to any diner on the Thanksgiving table. —Serves 4

Put the wheat berries in a medium saucepan with the water and 1 teaspoon kosher salt. Bring to a boil, reduce to a lively simmer, cover, and cook until the wheat berries are fully tender and most of the grains have opened up, about 45 minutes. All the water won't be absorbed, so drain thoroughly.

While the wheat berries are cooking, heat the oven to 400°F (205°C).

Scrub the squash (you're going to leave the edible skin on) and halve lengthwise (if the squash is long, cut it in half crosswise first, for easier handling). Scoop and scrape out the seeds and then cut crosswise into half-moons ½ inch (1.25 cm) thick.

Pile into a bowl, add 2 tablespoons olive oil, ½ teaspoon salt, several twists of black pepper, and the chile flakes and toss to coat. Spread onto a baking sheet (use two sheets if one seems crowded—you don't want the squash slices to overlap at all) and roast until golden brown and tender, 25 to 30 minutes. You can flip halfway through cooking, if you like, but the squash will also be nice if it's browned on one side only.

To assemble the dish, toss the cooked wheat berries with the juice of half the lemon, a nice glug of olive oil, some salt, and a few twists of black pepper. Add the toasted pumpkin seeds, cilantro, and mint and toss again. Taste and add more lemon, olive oil, salt, or pepper; you want the grains to be totally tasty before you add the squash. Spread the wheat berry mixture onto a platter or shallow serving bowl and arrange the squash slices on top. Top the whole dish with dollops of the romesco sauce and serve.

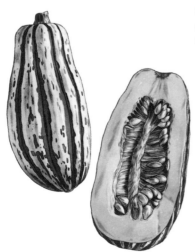

Broccoli, Tuna, and Wheat Berry Gratin

1 cup (200 g) uncooked wheat berries

1 quart (1 liter) water

Kosher salt

1 bunch broccoli, stems trimmed and peeled, cut into long florets

4 tablespoons (60 g) unsalted butter

¼ cup (30 g) all-purpose flour

3 garlic cloves, finely chopped

2 cups (480 ml) whole milk

Freshly ground black pepper

Hot sauce

1½ cups (225 g) grated cheese, such as Comté, Gruyère, Emmenthal, Swiss, or extra-sharp cheddar

Two 6-ounce (170 g) cans tuna, drained

1 cup (120 g) finely grated Parmigiano-Reggiano cheese

Garlic-Chile Crunch (page 306; optional)

Here's your new tuna casserole (because everyone needs a tuna casserole in their weeknight repertoire, correct?), made ultranutritious by the addition of broccoli and nutty wheat berries. I prefer light (not white) tuna in olive oil. If you want to splurge a bit, try an imported tuna, such as one from the Spanish producer Ortiz. —Serves 4 to 6

Put the wheat berries in a medium saucepan with the water and 1 teaspoon salt. Bring to a boil, reduce to a lively simmer, cover, and cook until the wheat berries are fully tender and most of the grains have opened up, about 45 minutes. All the water won't be absorbed, so drain thoroughly. Cool.

Meanwhile, boil or steam the broccoli until just tender, about 8 minutes. Drain and cool.

Heat the oven to 400°F (200°C).

Melt the butter in a large saucepan (or deep ovenproof skillet, in which you can bake the final casserole) over medium heat and add the flour. Stir to make a smooth paste, then add the garlic and cook for about 2 minutes to cook off the raw floury taste and soften the garlic.

Whisk in the milk to make a smooth sauce. If you get some lumps, don't worry, just whisk a bit more; any remaining lumps will even out during cooking. Season to taste with salt, black pepper, and a few dashes of hot sauce. Fold in 1 cup (120 g) of the cheese. Stir over low heat until the cheese is melted. Taste again and adjust the seasoning.

Fold the steamed broccoli, tuna, and wheat berries into the sauce. Pile into a 9 × 13-inch (23 × 33 cm) baking dish, top with the remaining cheese, including the Parmigiano, and bake until heated through, golden brown on top, and bubbling around the edges, 30 to 40 minutes. Let the casserole cool for about 10 minutes before you serve it. For extra excitement, top with a spoonful or two of garlic-chile crunch.

Whole Wheat Flour

Triticum aestivum/Triticum turgidum

▸ CONTAINS GLUTEN ◂

Whole wheat flour is obviously not a grain but rather a milled form of wheat. Yet whole wheat flour is such a big player in my kitchen that I wanted to highlight my favorite recipes using this versatile ingredient.

As I've explained elsewhere, I'm not a purist when it comes to whole-grain baking. Using 100 percent whole wheat or other whole-grain flour can be tricky, especially if you're not an experienced baker, and it doesn't always result in the flavor or texture that I want, so I'm totally fine with using some good ol' white all-purpose flour in my baked goods and pastas when I feel it will make the dough easier to work with and give me better results. I do make sure my all-purpose flour is unbleached (which preserves more nutrients than bleached flour) and I use all-purpose from local mills, though there are plenty of respectable brands in grocery stores, including King Arthur and Bob's Red Mill.

I encourage you to play around with the proportions of whole wheat to white, and see how far you can nudge the recipes toward more whole-grain, less refined flour, for increased nutritional value and, as always, for flavor's sake.

RECIPES

Tender, Flaky Whole Wheat Flour Tortillas

2 cups (240 g) whole wheat flour

½ cup (60 g) all-purpose flour

1½ teaspoons baking powder

1½ teaspoons kosher salt

5½ tablespoons (70 g) lard, chilled and cut into small pieces

Scant ¾ cup (180 ml) barely warm water

Homemade flour tortillas are a huge upgrade from the kind you buy in the store, which are usually uninspiring at best, not much more than neutral delivery vehicles for whatever you're wrapping them around. These homemade ones, in contrast, are tender and flaky, with all the right puffed and browned bits and the nutty taste of whole wheat flour.

The most amazing thing is that they are super simple to make. You do need lard, however, which is traditional in most Mexican flour-tortilla-making. Once you get past the name, you'll realize that lard is just another all-natural animal fat, like butter or schmaltz; lard actually contains less saturated and more monounsaturated fat than butter. The best lard for baking is leaf lard, a very delicate white fat from a certain part of the pig. It can be hard to find other than online (though you can make your own), but mass-market brands such as Armour are widely available. Just be sure you buy it from the refrigerated section and that it contains only pork fat. The shelf-stable brands often contain hydrogenated vegetable shortening. Or play with another type of fat. Some superstar Mexican chefs are making tortillas using avocado oil or duck fat. Yum.

I like to make a batch of tortilla dough, portion it, cook up a few tortillas, then keep a couple of dough balls in the fridge for the next day and the rest in the freezer. Let the frozen dough thaw on the counter for a couple of hours, and you have fresh warm tortillas whenever you want. —**Makes ten 9-inch (23 cm) tortillas**

Stir together the whole wheat flour, all-purpose flour, baking powder, and salt in a large bowl. Toss the lard pieces in the flour to coat them and then work the lard into the flour as you would for a pie crust, pinching the flour and lard between thumb and fingers to break it into smaller bits and sort of smear the lard into the flour ⬤. Do this until the mixture looks like very coarse cornmeal; it's okay if a few larger bits remain.

Pour in about half of the water, stirring gently to moisten all the flour. Add more until all the dry powdery bits have been incorporated and you have a dough that holds together easily when you squeeze it; it should feel like soft Play-Doh. Depending on your flours, you may need to add a few more teaspoons of water.

Knead gently for one or two more strokes ⬤, then wrap the dough in plastic and refrigerate for at least 20 minutes or up to overnight.

Divide the dough into 10 pieces and roll each into a ball. Work with 1 portion at a time and

Pictured on pages 242–43

keep the rest covered loosely with plastic wrap. You'll need to use a bit of flour to keep it from sticking, but the dough should be fairly easy to work with, so don't overflour.

Flatten the dough ball with your fingers and press it out to a disk that's 4 or 5 inches (10 or 13 cm) across, then switch to a rolling pin and roll until very thin and about 9 inches (23 cm) in diameter. Roll between sheets of parchment to manage stickiness ●.

Heat a heavy skillet—a cast-iron pan is ideal—over medium-high heat until the pan is quite hot. Flop the tortilla into the pan; if you get a few pleats, try to straighten them out quickly, but don't stress if your first few aren't perfect.

Cook the tortilla until you see bubbles forming and the underside looks dry and has plenty of brown spots, then flip and cook the second side. Total cooking time will only be 1½ to 2 minutes. You can flip a few times if needed to get the tortilla cooked evenly. You want it fully cooked, but cooking it too long will make it brittle and harder to roll. Tuck into a clean cloth napkin to keep warm and continue shaping and cooking the remaining tortillas.

If you don't want to serve all 10 tortillas now, only cook what you want and wrap the other dough balls individually in plastic and refrigerate for up to 1 day, or wrap and freeze for up to 2 months. Thaw at room temperature for a few hours, then cook per the instructions.

Whole Wheat Pitas

1 cup (120 g) unbleached all-purpose flour

3 cups (360 g) whole wheat flour, spelt flour, or a combination

2¼ teaspoons (7 g) active dry yeast

1 tablespoon kosher salt

2 teaspoons sugar

1½ cups (360 ml) water

½ cup (115 g) plain whole-milk yogurt

2 tablespoons extra-virgin olive oil

Pitas are such fun breads to make because they don't require long fermentation or tricky shaping. With a quick mix and a couple hours of rising, you have freshly baked bread to eat with something like Beef and Swiss Chard Soup with Spelt (page 217), Lamb and Bulgur Meatballs in Lemony Yogurt Sauce (page 187), and of course Freekeh Falafel (page 211). Or simply dip them in good olive oil and enjoy on their own.
—**Makes ten 6-inch (15 cm) pitas**

Whisk together the all-purpose flour, whole wheat flour, yeast, salt, and sugar in a large bowl. Whisk together the water, yogurt, and olive oil in another bowl.

Add the liquid mixture to the dry ingredients and stir with a wooden spoon or silicone spatula until you have a cohesive dough; it will be quite wet and sticky at this point.

Cover the bowl and refrigerate the dough for about 1 hour. Remove from the fridge and let rise at room temperature until close to doubled in volume, another hour or so, depending on the temperatures of your fridge and your room.

Generously dust your work surface and a sheet pan with either of the flours. Transfer the dough to the work surface and dust the dough with more flour. With a bench scraper or large chef's knife, cut the dough into 10 even pieces. Working with one piece at a time and keeping the rest covered loosely with a clean towel or plastic, shape into balls and arrange on the flour-dusted sheet pan. Let the balls rest until slightly puffy and risen, about 30 minutes.

Heat the oven as hot as you can get it—550°F (290°C) is ideal. Put your heaviest baking sheet on the bottom rack to heat. You can also use a large cast-iron skillet or a pizza stone.

Press the dough into 6-inch (15 cm) rounds (no need to actually roll them out, these are thick pitas). Carefully take out your heated pan and flop one or two pitas onto it. Return immediately to the oven and bake until the pitas are puffed and lightly browned, about 5 minutes. You can bake all on one side, or turn the pitas after a few minutes for more evening browning, but you risk losing oven temperature by opening the oven door a lot, so I usually just bake them on one side.

Continue with the rest of the dough. Serve as soon as you can. To save for more than one day, wrap well and freeze. You can also freeze the raw dough balls, thaw overnight in the fridge, and bake whenever you want fresh pita.

Whole Wheat English Muffins

1½ cups plus 2 tablespoons (200 g) whole wheat flour

1½ cups plus 2 tablespoons (200 g) unbleached all-purpose flour

1½ tablespoons kosher salt

1¾ cups (420 ml) buttermilk (see Note), at room temperature

2¼ teaspoons (7 g) active dry yeast

2 tablespoons pure maple syrup, honey, or molasses

1 tablespoon extra-virgin olive oil

1 large egg white, at room temperature

Optional add-ins (see below)

About ¼ cup (45 g) semolina flour or fine cornmeal, for dusting

Note: If you have dry buttermilk powder left over from making the Handy Spelt-Flour Pancake Mix (page 220), use it here as a substitute for buttermilk: Stir ¼ cup (30 g) of the dry buttermilk into 1¾ cups (420 ml) water.

+ ADD-INS:

Add either of these to your dough, as described in the recipe:

½ cup (75 g) raisins

½ cup (60 g) very roughly chopped pitted Kalamata or other brined olives

This dough is sticky and may take some practice to work with, but the reward is light, crispy muffins with all of the requisite nooks and crannies. If a dozen seems too many to eat in the next two days, split the extra baked muffins and freeze them; thaw by wrapping in foil and heating in a 350°F (175°C) oven.

For a fabulous brunch, go crazy with an array of these spreads: Honey Butter with Bee Pollen (page 307); Maple Butter (page 307); Bacon, Scallion, and Black Pepper Cream Cheese (page 308); Dill, Cucumber, and Celery Cream Cheese (page 308); Beet, Smoked Salmon, and Caper Cream Cheese (page 311), and Pickled Pepper Cream Cheese (page 311). —**Makes 12 muffins**

Whisk together the whole wheat flour, all-purpose flour, and salt in a large bowl.

Pour the buttermilk into the bowl of a stand mixer, but don't connect it to the mixer yet. Sprinkle on the yeast and let sit for about 5 minutes to rehydrate. Add the maple syrup, olive oil, and egg white and whisk to combine.

Add the flour mixture to the mixer bowl with the wet ingredients, then attach the bowl to the mixer and snap on the dough hook. Knead just until the dough comes together. Cover the bowl loosely and let the dough rest for 10 minutes. Continue kneading on medium speed until the dough is smooth and pulls away from the sides of the bowl, 8 to 10 minutes. (You can knead this dough by hand, but it's very wet and sticky.) If using either of the optional add-ins, add now and knead just until the additions are incorporated. They may not be perfectly distributed; that's okay.

Coat the inside of a bowl with olive oil, transfer the dough to it, cover, and let rise for about 4 hours at room temperature, until it's more than doubled in size. Cover and refrigerate overnight or for up to 2 days. This dough is sticky and will be easier to handle after a rest in the fridge, and the slow cold rise develops more flavor in the dough.

Lightly flour a work surface and scrape the dough onto it. Divide into 12 pieces (helpful, though perhaps obvious, tip: First cut the dough in half, then cut each half into two, and finally cut each of those quarters into 3 pieces). Shape each piece into a ball, adding as little flour as possible ●.

Line two sheet pans with parchment and dust generously with the semolina flour. Place the dough balls onto the sheet pans, keeping them at least 1 inch (2.5 cm) apart; they will spread a bit. Cover the dough balls loosely with plastic wrap and let rise in a warm place for about 1 hour ●. They should be very puffy and *almost* to the point of collapsing.

After the dough has been rising for about 30 minutes, heat the oven to 350°F (175°C).

When the dough balls are done rising, heat a large ungreased cast-iron skillet, griddle, or other flat, heavy pan over medium-high heat. Very gently transfer the muffins to the pan a few at a time, depending on how much space you have. Keep the remaining dough balls covered.

Cook until nicely browned on one side, about 2 minutes ●. Gently flip the muffins and cook for another minute or two on the other side. (If the semolina starts to burn in the pan, wipe it out with a paper towel.) Return the muffins from the skillet to the sheet pan (or use a new one). Once all the muffins have been browned, transfer the sheet pans

to the oven and bake until cooked through and slightly puffier, 8 to 10 minutes.

Let the muffins cool completely, preferably on a rack ●, and then split them open with a fork for maximum nooks and crannies. These will keep well wrapped at room temperature for 2 days or for a few months in the freezer.

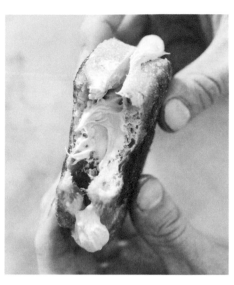

Super-Crisp Flatbread
That Tastes Like Cheez-Its

1 cup (120 g) unbleached all-purpose flour

1 cup (120 g) whole wheat flour

1 scant cup (110 g) finely grated Parmigiano-Reggiano cheese

1 scant cup (110 g) finely grated pecorino cheese

1 tablespoon kosher salt

1 tablespoon ground turmeric

1 tablespoon garlic powder

1 teaspoon dried chile flakes or other dried hot chile, such as Aleppo pepper

About ½ cup (120 ml) cool water

Flaky salt

The dough for these crackers is very stiff and dry; you may think you've done something wrong at first, but just press on, it'll all be fine. And to roll this stiff dough to the thinness that you need, you really should have a pasta roller. You can use the hand-crank kind, or if you're lucky enough to have a pasta attachment for your stand mixer (or your neighbor does), use that, which will leave both hands free to feed the dough strips in and out.

You should bake off a few smaller test crackers in order to get the timing right, because so much depends on your oven and your baking sheet. You want the crackers just browned on the edges, ombréing their way into a golden center. If the crackers are underbaked—too golden—they won't be crisp, but if they are too browned, they will be extremely bitter—from the turmeric, among other things. Just try a few and then you'll get the precise timing for your equipment. —**Makes about 16 large freeform crackers**

In a stand mixer fitted with the paddle or in a bowl using a wooden spoon, mix the all-purpose flour, whole wheat flour, Parmigiano, pecorino, salt, turmeric, garlic powder, and chile flakes.

Slowly stream in ½ cup (120 ml) cool water ●. Mix a few times and then drizzle in up to another 3 to 4 tablespoons water, just until the dough holds together. It will still look shaggy, but it shouldn't be powdery ●.

Dump the dough onto a work surface and knead it by pushing away with the heel of your hand and then turning and folding. Continue to knead until the dough is smoother, though it will still be very stiff and not super smooth ●. Wrap tightly in plastic and refrigerate for at least 2 hours and up to overnight. This

lets the flours fully absorb the liquid and develop a smoother consistency.

Take the dough from the fridge about 30 minutes before you plan to roll and bake it.

Fit a stand mixer with the pasta rolling attachment (see Note) set to the widest setting. Cut a small chunk of dough and pass it through the rollers. (Once you see how long a sheet that size chunk produces, you can cut the remaining dough into the size that is easiest to handle.) Fold that sheet crosswise in thirds and roll again. Adjust the pasta roller to a tighter setting after each couple of passes, as you would when making pasta, stopping after you use setting number 4, or whatever setting gives you a very thin, translucent sheet. The actual thickness isn't critical, though the thinner the dough, the crispier the cracker. It's important that each sheet be a consistent thickness, however, so that it bakes evenly.

Heat the oven to 350°F (175°C).

Arrange the dough sheets in a single layer on parchment-lined baking sheets. Brush or spritz each sheet with a tiny amount of water and sprinkle with flaky salt.

Bake for about 8 minutes. Switch the pans from the top rack to the bottom and at the same time rotate the pans front to back; these gyrations are to promote even baking. The crackers are done when they are gently browned along the edges and smell good ●. Take care not to overbake, which can make the crackers bitter.

Let the crackers cool on a rack (they won't get fully crisp until cool) and then break them into groovy shapes. You can store the crackers in an airtight container at room temperature for up to 2 weeks.

Note: If you don't have a pasta roller, you can roll the dough using a rolling pin, but it will require some muscle and you likely won't get it paper thin. But your crackers will still be delicious!

Chanterelles and Wilted Kale Quiche in Whole Wheat Flaky Pastry Dough

½ recipe Whole Wheat Flaky Pastry Dough (page 313)

Extra-virgin olive oil

1 pound chanterelles or other wild mushrooms, wiped clean and chopped or torn into large pieces

Kosher salt and freshly ground black pepper

½ medium onion, thinly sliced

2 cups lightly packed (140 g) finely sliced kale (I like to use lacinato kale, aka Tuscan kale)

3 large eggs

2 large yolks

1 cup (240 ml) milk

1 cup (240 ml) heavy or whipping cream

Pinch of freshly grated nutmeg

1 cup (120 g) grated Fontina cheese

¼ cup (30 g) finely grated Parmigiano-Reggiano cheese

I always have a batch of ultraversatile whole wheat pastry dough in the freezer (divided in two), so that I can whip up a quiche, pie, galette, or other dish that wants buttery, flaky pastry. The crust gives a comforting embrace to whatever you put in the filling. I love this hearty combination of autumn ingredients, but you can make the quiche with whatever vegetable combination you have on hand; you'll need about 2 cups (about 500 ml) total, once they're cooked. —Makes one 10-inch (25 cm) quiche (not deep-dish)

Heat the oven to 325°F (160°C).

On a lightly floured surface, roll out the pie dough into a round about 14 inches (36 cm) across. Transfer the dough to a 10-inch (25 cm) tart pan with a removable bottom by folding the dough in half and then laying it over the pan and opening it up. Gently press the dough into the corners and up the sides of the pan. Trim any excess dough so that you're left with about ½ inch (1.25 cm) of overhang all around. Fold the dough overhang so the tart shell walls are a double thickness (I like to fold outward, away from the center of the quiche) and tuck and pinch so that the top rim of the tart shell is about ¼ inch (6 mm) taller than the edge of the pan—this is insurance in case your crust shrinks a little. Refrigerate the tart shell for at least 30 minutes to chill.

Line the tart shell with parchment and fill with pie weights or dried beans, making sure that the beans reach into the corners of the shell. Put the tart shell on a baking sheet and bake until the edges are golden and the bottom is starting to set, about 30 minutes. Remove the parchment and weights and continue baking until the crust is dark golden all around, another 10 to 20 minutes. Remove from the oven but leave the oven on. Let the tart shell cool on a rack. (If you pour the filling into a hot crust, the crust will get soggy and you'll lose the crisp, flaky texture.)

While the crust is cooling, prepare the filling. Pour a generous glug of olive oil into a large skillet or Dutch oven and heat over medium-high heat. Add the chanterelles in an even layer and season with a nice sprinkling of salt and pepper. (Cook the mushrooms in batches if your pan can't accommodate them all in one layer.) Don't disturb the mushrooms until they're nicely browned on one side, then flip them over and cook until all are browned and slightly crisp at the edges. Depending on the mushrooms, they may give off a lot of liquid; if so, just keep cooking until it has evaporated and the mushrooms will brown. Scrape the mushrooms out of the pan into a bowl and set aside.

Return the pan to the heat, reduce the heat to medium, and add a hint more oil and the onion. Cook over medium heat until soft and fragrant but not actually browned, about 4 minutes. Add the kale and about 2 tablespoons water, cover the pan, and cook, stirring occasionally, until the kale is tender and the onion is very soft and jammy. Season to taste with a bit more salt and pepper and let cool.

Whisk together the eggs, egg yolks, milk, cream, salt, and nutmeg in a medium bowl.

When the crust has cooled, put it back on the baking sheet (it's easier to handle this way), distribute the chanterelles, onion-kale mixture, Fontina, and Parmigiano in the crust, and pour on the egg mixture.

Return the pan to the oven and bake until just set and maybe barely puffing, about 35 minutes. Cool to warm room temperature, cut, and serve.

Whole Wheat Dough for Tagliatelle and Other Long Pastas

2 large eggs, at room
  temperature

1 tablespoon extra-virgin
  olive oil

1 cup (120 g) tipo "00" flour

1 cup (120 g) whole wheat flour

3 large egg yolks, at room
  temperature

Semolina, for dusting

Making pasta from scratch is a bit of a project, so plan your time accordingly. Fortunately, the tagliatelle freezes nicely, so make more than you'll need for one meal to maximize your efficiency. You can make these long noodles totally by hand, but you'll get the best results if you have a pasta machine. The hand-crank kind is fine, but once you've tried the pasta attachment that works with a stand mixer, you'll never go back. Not only does the motor do all the hard work, but not needing to turn the crank gives you both hands to guide the dough strips through the rollers.

In this pasta, by using two flours, we get depth of flavor and more nutrients from the whole-grain flour and a chewy, silky, springy texture from the white tipo "00" flour, an extra-fine flour you can find in many well-stocked grocery stores or online. If you can't find it, an all-purpose white will work just fine.

This dough will work for other noodle widths, though I wouldn't go narrower than about ⅛ inch (3 mm) or you risk the noodles breaking. The wider the noodle, the thinner the sheet of pasta should be.

Of course fresh pasta is sublime with just butter and a shower of grated Parmigiano-Reggiano, but I also love these tagliatelle with the Beef and Pork Ragù (page 320) or even the Perfect Simple Tomato Sauce (page 275) that I use for my pizzas. —**Makes just less than 1 pound (455 g)**

Whisk the eggs and olive oil in a small bowl to blend.

In a stand mixer fitted with the dough hook, mix both flours for a few seconds on low to blend. Pour in the egg–olive oil mixture and mix on low until the ingredients look like coarse sand.

Add the egg yolks, one at a time, mixing for a few seconds after each addition. The dough will become "chunkier" and then start sticking together as a mass.

Knead on low until the dough seems very dense and springy, about 5 minutes. Wrap the dough in plastic and let it rest for at least 20 minutes and up to 24 hours (put it in the refrigerator if you'll rest it for more than 1 hour). The rest helps the flour absorb the liquid in the eggs and fully hydrate.

To roll out the dough, attach the pasta roller to the stand mixer. Start with a golf-ball-size chunk of dough. You'll see how long a strip this produces and whether you can comfortably handle it. Make the next chunk bigger or smaller; it doesn't really matter how long your noodles are, but it does matter that you can manipulate the dough easily as you roll.

Flatten the dough chunk slightly with the heel of your hand. Insert the dough into your pasta roller set on the widest setting. For these instructions, we'll say 1 is the widest and 7 is the narrowest.

Run the chunk through on setting 1, then again on setting 2, and finally on setting 3. Don't worry if the dough doesn't look perfect; it might be streaky or a bit ripped, but the texture will improve with subsequent rolling.

Fold the pasta sheet in thirds crosswise. On the end that looks straightest, fold the corners over a tiny bit so the edge is now slightly angled. This will help you insert the dough strip into the rollers.

Repeat rolling through settings 1 through 3 ●. As you roll, try to keep the tension even between the portion of the dough sheet entering the rollers and the portion exiting the rollers. This will help create a sheet that is of even width, the full width of the rollers. While an even width isn't critical for long noodles like tagliatelle, it will make your noodles more uniform, and it's a good practice to develop.

Fold the pasta into thirds again, fold the corners of the leading

edge, and repeat for a third cycle. By now, the texture of the dough should be evening out; it should look smooth and uniform in color.

You can stop now or run the sheet through setting 4 and maybe 5, depending on how thick you like your noodles.

Generously dust a sheet pan with semolina and lay out your pasta sheet, folding it so it fits on the sheet pan and dusting with more semolina between the folds ●. Cover loosely with a dry towel or plastic.

Repeat with the remaining dough.

You can now run the pasta sheets through the cutting blade of your pasta maker, or cut noodles by hand: Stack a few sheets together

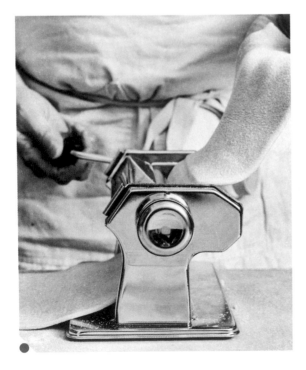
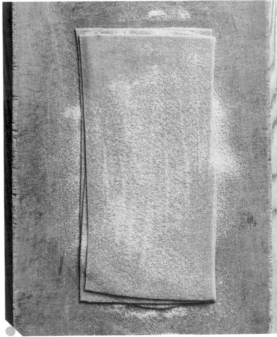

and roll into a loose cylinder, leaving about 1 inch (2.5 cm) unrolled, sticking out like a tab.

With a very sharp knife, cut across the cylinder into strips of your desired width. I think ⅜ inch (1 cm) is a good width for tagliatelle (but there's probably an Italian law that specifies the width to the precise millimeter).

Pick up the strips a few at a time by grabbing the unrolled tab

and letting the noodles dangle. Shake off the excess semolina. Shape the noodles into a loose "nest" and arrange back on the semolina-dusted sheet pan.

Let the tagliatelle rest on the counter loosely covered until you're ready to cook it, up to 4 hours. You can also freeze the pasta: Slide the sheet pan into the freezer until the pasta is solid, then transfer the nests into a freezer container. They will be

best protected if you put them into an airtight box, but a zip-top freezer bag will work also. Just take care that they don't get crushed by a bag of frozen peas in the freezer.

To cook, follow the instructions on page 262. When the tagliatelle is freshly made, the cooking time should be 4 minutes, so start checking at 3 minutes.

Whole Wheat and Ricotta Cavatelli

1½ cups plus 2 tablespoons (200 g) tipo "00" flour

1½ cups plus 2 tablespoons (200 g) whole wheat flour

1 large egg, whisked

1¼ cups (280 g) whole-milk ricotta (I like Calabria)

Semolina or cornmeal, for dusting

As in the dough for tagliatelle (page 257), we're pairing whole wheat flour with white tipo "00," an Italian finely milled flour with a moderate-to-high protein content, usually between 11 percent and 12 percent; you can find it in many well-stocked grocery stores or online. If you can't find it, an all-purpose white flour will work just fine, though you'll probably need to add the full amount of ricotta, and possibly a touch more.

Shaping the cavatelli can be done by hand, but there's also a dedicated hand-cranked machine for it. My model is Cousin Elisa's Cavatelli Maker from Fante's, and it's worth seeking it out just for the box, which sports vintage photos of the Fante family, including a 1960s passport photo of a very dapper-looking dude.

Cavatelli are excellent with any type of pesto, and in that fresh-and-green mode, the Updated Kale Sauce (page 319) would be mighty tasty. The cream sauce in Whole Wheat Pasta with Crab, Cream, Olives, and Habanero (page 265) is of course fantastic. —**Makes 1½ pounds (680 g)**

In a stand mixer fitted with the paddle, blend together the tipo "00" flour and the whole wheat flour at low speed. With the mixer running on low, add the egg. Then add 1 cup (225 g) of the ricotta and let the mixer run for a minute.

Test the consistency by taking a big pinch—does it stick together nicely or does it crumble? If crumbly, add up to ¼ cup (55 g) more ricotta 1 tablespoon at a time, testing after you incorporate each tablespoon.

The final texture should feel like Play-Doh—moist but not sticky, still slightly crumbly but not at all powdery.

Dump the pasta dough onto a clean counter and knead with the heel of your hand until it starts to get smooth and elastic, about 3 minutes. When you poke it with your finger, the dent

should spring back; if not, keep kneading a bit more.

Wrap the dough in plastic wrap and let rest for at least 20 minutes and up to a few hours (in the refrigerator if resting more than 1 hour). During this rest, the flours will absorb even more of the moisture from the egg and cheese and become fully hydrated.

After its rest, cut the dough in half. Flatten each half into a disk that's about 1 inch (2.5 cm) thick. Slice one disk into strips ¾ inch (2 cm) wide to yield 1 × ¾-inch (2.5 × 2 cm) pieces. Now roll each piece into a rope about ½ inch (1.25 cm) in diameter ●. Flatten the rope slightly by pressing with your fingers. If the pasta isn't getting good traction on the board when you roll it, spritz it with a tiny bit of water; that will help it grab better.

continues

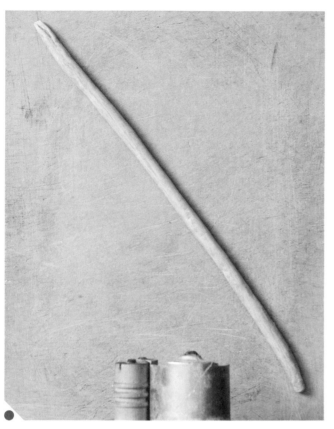

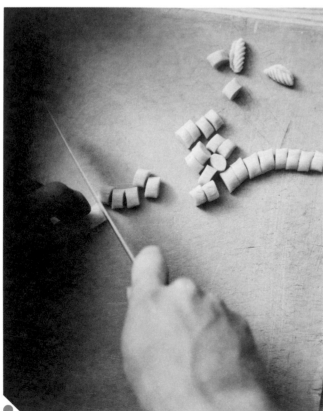

Repeat with the other disk of dough, keeping all your strips and ropes lightly covered to prevent them from drying out too much.

Dust a couple of baking sheets generously with semolina or cornmeal. Working with one rope at a time, shape the dough into cavatelli (by hand or machine; see below) and arrange them on the dusted baking sheets as you make them. With either of the following shaping methods, you're likely to need a few practice tries, but don't worry about the misshapen efforts—they will taste delicious.

TO SHAPE USING A HAND-CRANKED MACHINE: Follow the instructions on the box, which consist of simply feeding the dough rope into the machine and turning the crank, which cuts each cavatelli ●.

TO SHAPE BY HAND (WITH A GNOCCHI BOARD): Cut the ropes into ¾-inch (2 cm) lengths ●. Place a piece of dough on a gnocchi or cavatelli board (a finely ridged wooden paddle or board), press into it lightly with your thumb, and roll it away from you ●. Hopefully, this will create a curved piece of pasta with ridges on the outside and a little pocket on the inside . . . all in service of catching sauces.

TO SHAPE BY HAND (WITHOUT A BOARD): Cut the ropes into ¾-inch (2 cm) lengths. Put a piece of dough on the work surface in front of you, press your forefinger and middle finger into the center of the piece, and draw it toward you, again trying to make a concave curved shape with a little dimpled interior pocket.

When you've shaped all the dough, put the sheets of cavatelli in the freezer, unwrapped, and freeze until firm, about 1 hour. At that point, you can cook the cavatelli right away, or transfer them to a freezer bag, squeezing out as much air as possible, and freeze for up to 1 month.

To cook, bring a big pot of water to a boil and add enough salt that the water tastes very salty, like ocean water. Test a few cavatelli for cooking time; it should be about 6 minutes. Drop in the cavatelli, stirring a few times so they don't stick together. After you've added the last one, boil for exactly 6 minutes (or whatever you determined the best cooking time to be), but start tasting at about 5 minutes. You want the pasta to be thoroughly cooked so there's no white bit in the center, but of course you don't want it to get mushy. Drain, reserving about a cup (240 ml) of the pasta water to use to dial in the consistency of whatever sauce you're using.

Whole Wheat Pasta with Crab, Cream, Olives, and Habanero

Kosher salt

Extra-virgin olive oil

3 or 4 garlic cloves, smashed and peeled

1 tablespoon unsalted butter

¾ cup (180 ml) heavy or whipping cream or crème fraîche

1 habanero chile, seeded and cut into rings

8 ounces (225 g) whole wheat tagliatelle (page 257) or Whole Wheat and Ricotta Cavatelli (page 260) or store-bought fresh pasta, or 4 ounces (115 g) dried pasta

4 ounces (115 g) cooked crabmeat, picked through to remove any bits of shell

2 tablespoons finely grated Parmigiano-Reggiano cheese

1 teaspoon finely grated lemon zest

Freshly ground black pepper

½ lemon

Small handful arugula (optional)

Several fresh mint leaves, torn (optional)

¼ cup (15 g) toasted breadcrumbs (optional)

These days, we don't often give ourselves permission to indulge in a straight-up cream sauce, but every so often we should—it's good for the soul. And when it's time to indulge, may I recommend this dish? It's crazy simple to make, with over-the-top flavor from the habanero chile—bright, fruity, tropical, and yes, hot! But I leave the habanero in rings, which are easy to fish out if you want to avoid full-on fire. Use either the whole wheat tagliatelle (page 257) or the Whole Wheat and Ricotta Cavatelli (page 260), or even your favorite store-bought fresh pasta shape. —Serves 2

Bring a large pot of water to a boil for the pasta; add a big handful of salt so that the water tastes as salty as the ocean.

While the water is coming to a boil, heat a small glug of olive oil in a heavy-bottomed skillet over medium heat, add the garlic, and cook until the garlic is very soft, fragrant, and nicely golden brown—but not burnt—about 5 minutes. Scoop out the garlic so it doesn't burn; you can add it back along with the cream or simply discard it.

Add the butter and cook gently until it starts to turn light brown and smells very nutty—you're making browned butter. Go slow so it doesn't burn. Pour in the cream and adjust the heat to a very gentle simmer. Add the habanero and cook to reduce the cream slightly and infuse the chile flavor into it. Set aside off the heat while you cook the pasta.

Add the pasta to the boiling water and cook until almost al dente. When the pasta is about 30 seconds from being fully cooked, scoop out a mugful of cooking water, then drain the pasta well. Dump the pasta into the pan of cream sauce, along with the crab. Toss for a minute or so, to let the pasta absorb some sauce and finish cooking, adding a few splashes of the pasta water to keep the consistency from getting too gloppy. Add the Parmigiano, lemon zest, several twists of black pepper, and a nice squeeze of lemon juice.

Taste and adjust with more salt, black pepper, or lemon juice; note that the heat from the chile rings will continue to increase a bit as the dish sits.

Divide between two pasta bowls. If desired, top with the arugula, mint, and/or breadcrumbs. Serve immediately.

Variation

Chicken and Artichoke Pasta: This is an easy one to whip up because you can use rotisserie or other leftover chicken and canned artichoke hearts or bottoms. Omit the crab. Omit the habanero for a more mellow dish, or keep it if you like spicy. Add 1 cup (140 g) shredded or chopped cooked chicken and 3 to 5 rinsed and dried artichoke hearts or bottoms (the number depends on how big they are, as sizes vary from can to can), cut into smaller chunks. Add the chicken and artichokes when you add the cream to the browned butter, so the ingredients have time to get warm. Season with extra pepper.

Whole Wheat Focaccia

STARTER

¾ cup plus 1 tablespoon (200 ml) room-temperature water

½ teaspoon (2 g) active dry yeast

¾ cup plus 1 tablespoon (100 g) white bread flour

¾ cup plus 1 tablespoon (100 g) whole wheat flour

DOUGH

5½ cups (660 g) white bread flour

2½ cups (300 g) whole wheat flour

¼ cup plus 2 tablespoons (50 g) rye flour or other whole-grain flour (or use more whole wheat, but a different grain will add complexity)

3½ cups (840 ml) water

3 tablespoons kosher salt

Extra-virgin olive oil

Get ready to do some pro-level baking. The method in this recipe is almost exactly the way we make focaccia at the restaurant—no shortcuts—but the timing and stretching techniques are what make this an absolutely delicious bread, one that lets the whole wheat goodness really shine through. We use part white flour in order to get the consistency that we want, though you should feel free to change the ratio of whole-grain to white once you get used to the recipe.

The recipe makes a big slab, a half-sheet-pan size (13 × 18 inches/33 × 46 cm), so you can bake it, then cut into quarters and freeze what you don't eat in the next couple of days.

Serve the focaccia warm from the oven with a dipping bowl of good olive oil. Sliced and broiled or grilled, it makes excellent crostini. Or split a square of it in the middle, pile it with sliced meats, cheese, and vegetables (or skip the meat, or the cheese, for that matter), moisten with a dash of olive oil and vinegar, and wrap tightly with plastic wrap. Refrigerate for a few hours or overnight and you've got yourself a righteous sandwich, perfect for a picnic basket or camp cooler. And focaccia croutons are a treat (see Torn Croutons, page 306). —**Makes one 13 × 18-inch (33 × 46 cm) focaccia**

MAKE THE STARTER: Stir the water and yeast together in a small bowl. Whisk together the bread flour and whole wheat flour in a larger bowl. Stir the yeast mixture into the flours using a wooden spoon or spatula, then thoroughly mix it with your hands.

Cover the starter with a cloth or store in a lidded container and leave on the counter until doubled in size, at least 8 hours and up to overnight. If the starter has doubled but you're not ready to go to the next step, refrigerate the starter, covered with plastic, for up to 12 hours ●.

MAKE THE DOUGH: Whisk together the bread flour, whole wheat flour, and rye flour in a large bowl.

In a stand mixer fitted with the dough hook, combine the starter and water ●. Add the flours and mix on low speed for 2 minutes. It may take a few moments for the flour to get wet enough so the mixture looks like a dough, especially if your mixer bowl is small. Stop the mixer and scrape down the sides of the bowl thoroughly, making sure to scrape along the bottom, underneath the dough, where pockets of dry flour often form. Mix again for 30 seconds and then let rest, draped with a kitchen towel, for 30 minutes.

Turn the mixer to low speed and sprinkle in the salt, trying to distribute it evenly throughout the dough ●. Mix for 8 minutes.

Generously oil another large bowl and scrape the dough into it, rolling the dough around a bit to get it all coated in oil ●. Cover the bowl. Let the dough rest on the counter for 30 minutes.

DO A "STRETCH AND FOLD" ON ALL FOUR SIDES: Either with the dough still in the bowl or on the counter, slide your fingers or a flexible dough scraper under one side of the dough and gently pull it outward and over the top of the dough ball ●. Do the same on the other three sides, like you're trying to wrap up the dough in itself ●. The idea is to gently stretch all parts of the dough.

Return the dough to the bowl, if you removed it. Cover and let rest for another 30 minutes, then repeat at 30-minute intervals for a total of six "stretch and folds."

After the sixth time, let the dough rest for another 30 minutes at room temperature and then cover and refrigerate for at least overnight and up to 48 hours. Remove the dough from the fridge about 2 hours before you want to bake the focaccia.

Brush a half-sheet pan (13 × 18 inches/33 × 46 cm) with 3 tablespoons olive oil and transfer the dough to the pan.

continues

Brush more oil over the top of the dough so it's entirely coated . Leave at warm room temperature for 1 hour.

Press the dough gently with your fingertips to spread it out into the pan; it probably won't reach the corners yet because it springs back too much ⬤, which is fine. Don't force it; you want it to relax into the full dimension of the pan. Let rest for another hour; after 30 minutes, put your oven rack in the middle position and heat the oven to 450°F (230°C). You want to be sure it is fully heated, so give it a bit more preheating time than you might normally.

Now the dough should start looking a bit puffy and be easier to stretch. Press it all the way into all corners of the pan, in as even a layer as possible ⬤.

Dimple the dough by pressing your fingers deeply into it in an even pattern. Top with any seasonings (see Variations) and bake for 20 minutes. Rotate the pan front to back and bake until the focaccia is deep brown, including on the bottom; lift up a corner to check.

Transfer the baked focaccia from the pan to a rack and let cool at least most of the way. Serve while slightly warm or at room temperature. Wrap any leftovers tightly in plastic wrap, keep at room temperature for up to 2 days, and reheat in a 375°F (190°C) oven for a few minutes before serving. You can also freeze some of the focaccia as soon as it's fully cool. Be sure it's well wrapped in freezer wrap or zip-top bags. To serve from a frozen state, let thaw at room temperature for 1 hour, then continue thawing and crisping up in a 375°F (190°C) oven.

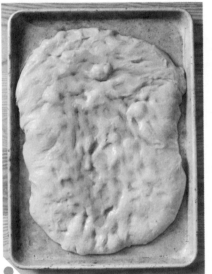

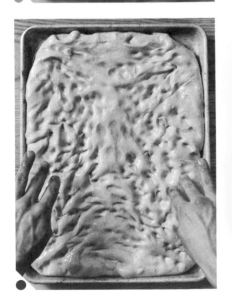

Variations

Classic Focaccia: Dimple the dough, drizzle with more extra-virgin olive oil, and scatter a good amount of roughly chopped fresh rosemary over the top. Finish with some flaky salt, such as Maldon.

Cherry Tomato and Garlic Focaccia: Dimple the dough, tuck halved or quartered garlic cloves into the dimples, then pop in some cherry tomatoes (you don't need a tomato for every dimple!). Drizzle with more extra-virgin olive oil, and finish with some flaky salt, such as Maldon. After the focaccia is finished baking, scatter torn basil leaves over the surface.

Pictured on page 270

Spring Onion and Olive Focaccia: Thinly slice about 6 ounces (180 g) tender spring onions, or other juicy sweet onion, such as Walla Walla or Vidalia, and toss with a glug of extra-virgin olive oil and 2 tablespoons roughly chopped fresh thyme. Sprinkle flaky salt on the dough, layer with the onions, and scatter 1 cup (120 g) good-quality pitted olives all over.

Plum, Honey, and Black Pepper Focaccia: Cut about 8 ounces (225 g) ripe but not mushy plums in half (or quarters, if large) and remove the pits. (Italian prune plums work nicely.) Push the plums into the dough, drizzle with 3 tablespoons honey, and crack tons of black pepper on top. Finish with a little sprinkle of flaky salt. This is so good served with dollops of fresh goat or sheep's cheese or ricotta; cool the bread so the cheese doesn't melt.

Pictured on page 271

Rhubarb Focaccia: This may be my favorite focaccia version, as I am devoted to rhubarb. Cut a few stalks of rhubarb into bits the size of grapes, sprinkle with sugar, and let sit for about 1 hour to macerate and soften. Discard that juice . . . or make some killer lemonade with it. Then follow the same method as the plum, honey, and black pepper focaccia above.

Caramelized Onion and Cheese Focaccia: This is my go-to in the winter; sometimes I'll just have a slice of this moist, oniony focaccia with a fried egg on top and call it dinner. Thinly slice a couple of yellow onions and pile them into a Dutch oven or large skillet with a big glug of extra-virgin olive oil and a pinch of kosher salt. Cook slowly, stirring frequently, until the onions are very soft and fragrant, about 15 minutes. Turn up the heat just a notch and cook until the onions turn deep golden brown and are sweet and slightly sticky-jammy. You should stir and scrape the bottom of the pan frequently as you approach this stage, so no onion juices burn. Let the onions cool completely, then top the focaccia with the onions and about 1 cup (120 g) finely grated Parmigiano-Reggiano or pecorino cheese or a blend.

Apple Butter Focaccia: In the depths of winter, give your focaccia a sweet fruity note even if there's no fresh fruit around, using apple butter. To do this, bake the focaccia half to three-quarters of the way, then take it from the oven, brush it all over generously with apple butter, sprinkle it with some herbs such as thyme or rosemary, and pop it back in the oven.

Serious Sheet Pan Pizza, Many Ways

I take pizza very seriously, as it is one of humankind's greatest inventions. I've been working on making the perfect pizza for years, and something I've learned along the way is that making pizza at home is often disappointing. With a normal home oven, people just can't achieve a crust like the crust at a good pizzeria—chewy-crisp with the right amount of char on the edges—and they end up with pizzas that are cardboard-y. That's because it's just not possible to get the high heat and thermal capacity of a wood-burning masonry oven by using a home oven.

So I say forget about Neapolitan-style pizza, leave that to the pizzerias, and make a sheet pan pizza. You can use the same types of toppings you'd use on any good pizza, and the crust is equally delicious, just different—slightly thick, meaning you get a lot of delicious whole-grain flavor. Sometimes I give it some extra crunch with a layer of grated cheese on the bottom.

The recipe for this dough is not a quickie one, but it's not hard to make; it just requires some time and advance planning.

The recipe makes two half-sheet-pan pizzas (13 × 18 inches/33 × 46 cm), so you can make two for a party or make one with half the dough (or even a smaller version) keeping the rest in the fridge for up to about 5 days, pulling out a portion whenever you want to cook up a 'za during the week.

Topping possibilities for pizza are endless, but I'm sharing a few of my favorites.

HERE ARE MY FOUR RULES OF PIZZA MAKING (SEE FACING PAGE, CLOCKWISE FROM TOP LEFT):

1 Do not oversauce your pizza. Pizza is about the dough; the sauce should just be an accent. No soggy pizzas, please. Exception to the rule: Pomodoro Pizza (page 275).

2 Do not use more than three main ingredients for your toppings (other than extra-virgin olive oil and some grated Parmigiano). The concept will just be muddled.

3 Bake your pizza hotter and longer than you think you should. You want your toppings to get good and browned for the most flavor and the bottom crust must be cooked and crisp.

4 Once the pizza is out of the oven, finish with a drizzle of olive oil and a big pinch of flaky salt as the final flourish.

continues

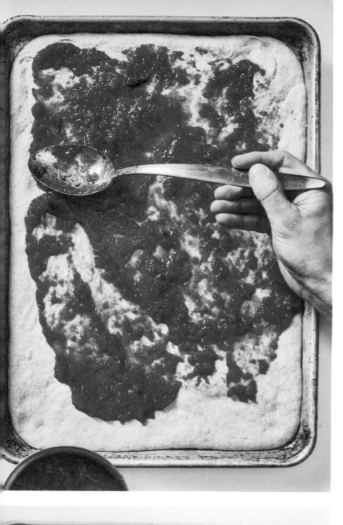

Sheet Pan Pizza Dough

**Makes enough for two
13 × 18-inch (33 × 46 cm) pizzas**

STARTER

7 tablespoons (100 ml) warm water
  (about 85°F/29°C)
⅛ teaspoon (0.4 g) active dry yeast
¼ cup plus 3 tablespoons (50 g)
  white bread flour
¼ cup plus 3 tablespoons (50 g)
  whole wheat flour

DOUGH

3 cups (720 ml) warm water (about
  85°F/29°C)
½ cup (120 ml) extra-virgin olive
  oil, plus more for the bowl
½ teaspoon (1.5 g) active dry yeast
5 cups (600 g) white bread flour
3 cups (360 g) whole wheat flour
¼ cup plus 3 tablespoons (50 g)
  durum flour, or ¼ cup (45 g)
  semolina flour
3 tablespoons kosher salt

FOR THE PAN

Olive oil
⅔ cup (80 g) finely grated
  Parmigiano-Reggiano cheese

MAKE THE STARTER: Whisk the water and yeast together in a medium bowl. Whisk the flours together in a separate bowl, dump into the water, and stir until mostly smooth; the starter will look lumpy.

Keep in a warm place until doubled in volume and looking very bubbly, at least 4 hours.

MAKE THE DOUGH: In a stand mixer fitted with the dough hook, combine the water, 200 g of the starter, the olive oil, and the yeast. Whisk together the bread flour, whole wheat flour, and durum flour in another bowl. Tip the flours into the water mixture and mix on the lowest speed for 2 minutes, stopping to scrape down the bowl to make sure all the flour is getting moistened and incorporated; be sure to scrape along the bottom.

Stop the mixer and let the dough rest for 30 minutes. Add the salt and mix on the lowest speed for 8 minutes.

Rub a film of olive oil on the inside of a bowl or other large container. Transfer the dough to the bowl and oil the top of the dough. Cover loosely with a lid or kitchen towel and let rest at room temperature until doubled in size, about 4 hours.

If you're making the dough ahead of time, transfer the dough to the fridge. The dough will be delicious for up to 5 days. Or if you're only going to use half the dough to make one pizza, divide the dough in half and return the other half of the dough to the bowl or put it in a large zip-top bag, oil it lightly, cover it well (if using a bowl), and return it to the fridge. When ready to make pizza, remove the dough from the refrigerator and let it rest, lightly covered, at room temperature for 30 minutes before proceeding.

To make the pizza, lightly flour your work surface and dump out the dough. Divide it in half. Each half will make one 13 × 18-inch (33 × 46 cm) pizza, but bake only one pizza at a time.

Adjust an oven rack to a lower position; if you have a large pizza stone or steel, arrange it on the rack. Heat the oven to 500°F (260°C). If your oven isn't clean, you might want to turn on the exhaust fan.

PREP THE PANS: Brush a half-sheet pan, or other 13 × 18-inch (33 × 46 cm) rimmed baking sheet, with enough olive oil to cover the bottom and sides generously. If you are baking two pizzas, oil a second sheet.

Distribute the grated cheese evenly over the bottom of the pan (⅓ cup/40 g per pizza). Plop the dough onto the sheet pan and press it out with your fingertips so it fills the whole pan ●. If the dough doesn't want to stretch easily and springs back, let it rest another few minutes. Be aware of the cheese layer; you don't want to disturb it too much. If not a couple of pieces will be cheesier than others!

Add your sauce and choice of toppings and bake until the bottom is nicely browned (lift up a corner for a peek), the edges are puffed and browned, and your toppings are bubbling a bit, 20 to 30 minutes.

Transfer the pizza to a rack as soon as possible, so the bottom crust stays crisp. Cut into squares and serve hot.

Pomodoro Pizza

This is truly one of my favorite pizzas and the only time you use more sauce than you should. You'll need to plan ahead a bit in order to marinate the garlic in oil.

Makes one 13 × 18-inch (33 × 46 cm) pizza

5 garlic cloves, sliced super thin, using a mandoline if you have one
Extra-virgin olive oil
½ recipe Sheet Pan Pizza Dough (page 274)
1¼ cups (300 ml) Perfect Simple Tomato Sauce (recipe follows)
2 tablespoons dried oregano
Flaky salt

Put the garlic in a small bowl or jar and cover with olive oil. Refrigerate for at least 24 hours and up to 1 week.

Make the pizza dough as directed. While the dough is having its 30-minute rest, brush a 13 × 18-inch (33 × 46 cm) sheet pan with some of the oil from the garlic. Do not dust the sheet pan with grated cheese; I don't use any cheese for this pizza.

Heat the oven as directed.

Just before the pizza is ready to go into the oven, spread the tomato sauce over the dough and distribute the sliced garlic evenly over the surface (save the garlicky oil for another use). Sprinkle with the oregano.

Bake until the bottom is nicely browned and the edges are puffed and browned and the sauce is bubbling a bit, about

20 minutes. Dress the hot pizza with a generous drizzle of olive oil and a sprinkle of flaky salt.

Transfer the pizza to a rack as soon as possible, so the bottom crust stays crisp. Cut into squares and serve hot.

Perfect Simple Tomato Sauce

This recipe is obviously all about the canned tomato, so use a good brand. I love Stanislaw, but it's not available in normal retail outlets, as they sell directly to food service; however, you might find it online. Another good choice is Muir Glen, and you can of course go crazy with imported Italian brands. This recipe makes enough sauce for more than three pizzas, but it freezes perfectly, so make the full batch (or double it), freeze what you don't use, and you're all set for your next pizza.

Makes 2⅔ cups (640 ml)

One 28-ounce (785 g) can whole peeled tomatoes, drained
2 tablespoons extra-virgin olive oil
1 teaspoon kosher salt

Put the tomatoes, olive oil, and salt in a blender and process until smooth. Use immediately, store in the refrigerator for up to 4 days, or freeze for up to 3 months.

Four-Cheese Pizza

I use two types of mozzarella here in order to get some complex texture happening. The low-moisture is the most important, however, as it will melt well and not give off liquid during cooking. While fresh mozzarella is delicious, it will get rubbery as it cooks, so I always drain it first and then combine it with the crappier stuff.

Makes one 13 × 18-inch (33 × 46 cm) pizza

½ recipe Sheet Pan Pizza Dough (page 274)
¾ cup (180 ml) Perfect Simple Tomato Sauce (above)
½ cup (60 g) low-moisture shredded mozzarella cheese
2 ounces (60 g) fresh mozzarella cheese, torn into chunks and drained on paper towels for about 1 hour
½ cup (60 g) freshly grated Parmigiano-Reggiano cheese
½ cup (60 g) freshly grated pecorino cheese
Extra-virgin olive oil
Flaky salt

Prepare the dough, heat the oven, and spread the dough in the sheet pan as directed.

Spread the tomato sauce over the dough and distribute both of the mozzarellas, half the Parmigiano, and half the pecorino evenly over the surface.

Bake until the bottom is nicely browned, the edges are puffed and browned, and your toppings are bubbling a bit,

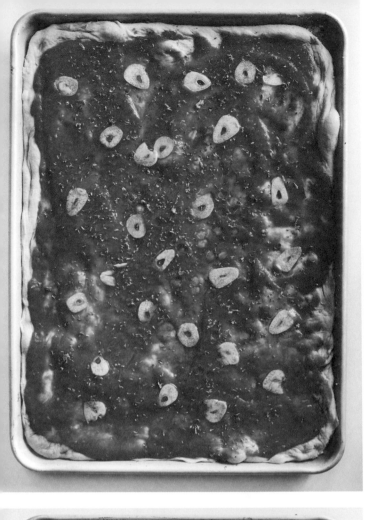

about 20 minutes. Dress the hot pizza with the rest of the Parmigiano and pecorino, a generous drizzle of olive oil, and a sprinkle of flaky salt.

Transfer the pizza to a cooling rack as soon as possible, so the bottom crust stays crisp. Cut into squares and serve hot.

Variation

Add sliced pepperoni before baking.

Crispy Kale and Pickled Chile Pizza

This is a cheese pie at heart, just with less cheese. Try to almost completely burn the kale to make it nice and crispy.

Makes one 13 × 18-inch (33 × 46 cm) pizza

Pictured on page 273

5 garlic cloves, sliced super thin, using a mandoline if you have one
Extra-virgin olive oil
½ recipe Sheet Pan Pizza Dough (page 274)
¾ cup (180 ml) Perfect Simple Tomato Sauce (page 275)
½ cup (110 g) chopped Quick-Pickled Chiles (recipe follows)
¼ cup (60 ml) juice from the pickled chiles

½ cup (60 g) freshly grated Parmigiano-Reggiano cheese
½ cup (60 g) freshly grated pecorino cheese
1 bunch Tuscan kale (about 8 oz/ 225 g), thick midribs torn or cut out, leaves torn into large pieces, left whole if small (they should look dramatic on the finished pizza)
Flaky salt

Put the garlic in a small bowl or jar and cover with olive oil. Refrigerate for at least 24 hours and up to 1 week.

Make the pizza dough as directed. Brush a 13 × 18-inch (33 × 46 cm) sheet pan with some of the oil from the garlic. Do not dust the sheet pan with grated cheese; I don't use any cheese for this pizza.

Spread the tomato sauce over the dough and distribute the drained sliced garlic evenly over the surface. Distribute the chiles and the pickling liquid over the pizza, sprinkle with the Parmigiano and pecorino, and arrange the kale leaves in a single layer over everything.

Bake until the bottom is nicely browned, the edges are puffed and browned, and the kale is getting crisp, about 20 minutes. Dress the hot pizza with a generous drizzle of olive oil and sprinkle with flaky salt.

Transfer the pizza to a rack as soon as possible, so the bottom crust stays crisp. Cut into squares and serve hot.

Quick-Pickled Chiles

Makes about 12 ounces (360 g) chiles, plus brine

1 pound (450 g) mixed fresh chiles (play with colors and heat levels)
5 garlic cloves, smashed and peeled
3 or 4 sprigs thyme
1½ cups (360 ml) water
½ cup (120 ml) rice vinegar
1 tablespoon white wine vinegar
5 tablespoons (65 g) sugar
1 tablespoon plus 1 teaspoon kosher salt

Find a jar (with a lid) that's large enough to hold all the chiles plus 2 cups (480 ml) liquid. Wash the jar and lid in hot soapy water and rinse well. Core, seed, and slice or chop the chiles and put them in the jar, along with the garlic and thyme sprigs. Pack down lightly.

Bring the water, rice vinegar, white wine vinegar, sugar, and salt to a boil in a small saucepan, stirring to dissolve the sugar and salt. Pour the liquid over the chiles to cover. Screw on the lid and let cool at room temperature, then refrigerate for at least 2 days before using. The chiles (in the pickling liquid) will keep in the fridge for up to a couple of months.

continues

Pizza for Every Season

We should all eat pizza year-round, so here are a few ideas to get you creating pizza through the seasons. These ingredient combinations are some of my favorites, but feel free to improvise according to what your garden or farmers' market tells you.

SPRING
Spring Onion and Pepperoncini Pizza

Assemble a Pomodoro Pizza (page 274) and before baking, top with a large amount (more than you think—they'll melt into the pie) of thinly sliced early-season onions (both white and green parts) and a generous scattering of thinly sliced cored and seeded pepperoncini. Sprinkle generously with a 50/50 mix of grated Parmigiano-Reggiano and Pecorino Romano, a pinch of dried chile flakes, and a pinch of fresh thyme leaves. Drizzle with some pepperoncini brine. Bake as usual, though these toppings are moist and will create quite a bit of steam, so you may need to cook the pizza a little longer than the recipe says.

EARLY SUMMER
Salad Pizza

Bake a Pomodoro Pizza (page 274). While it's baking, prep a salad of mixed greens and herbs (I love using Little Gem lettuce) and a creamy dressing, such as Yogo Ranch (page 313), with maybe some Garlic-Chile Crunch (page 306) stirred in. Let the pizza cool slightly so it's not crazy hot before putting the greens on top. Toss the greens with more dressing than you would otherwise and scatter it over the pizza. For a bonus, top with crunchy breadcrumbs and some anchovies.

MIDSUMMER
Summer Squash Pizza

Make ½ recipe Sheet Pan Pizza Dough (page 274) and press into the sheet pan (but don't add any tomato sauce). Scatter some shredded mozzarella, dollops of ricotta, and a generous sprinkling of 50/50 Parmigiano-Reggiano and Pecorino Romano over the dough. Lay super-thin ribbons of firm zucchini or other summer squash onto the pizza, twisting them into sinewy layers. (You'll need a mandoline to slice the squash thin enough to form tender ribbons.) Add some shredded squash blossoms, if you have them, along with some basil leaves, thinly sliced garlic, dried chile flakes, and a nice drizzle of extra-virgin olive oil. Bake as usual.

CAST-IRON PIZZA

A big cast-iron skillet is an ingenious way to deliver pizza goodness with an extra-crispy bottom crust. You'll need 12 ounces (360 g) dough—or a little less than one-quarter of the dough recipe on page 274. Heat the oven to 425°F (220°C). Press the dough into a rough round on the counter. Heat a cast-iron skillet on the stovetop over high heat. Add a very big glug of extra-virgin olive oil and when the oil is hot, carefully lay the pizza dough into the pan. Quickly spread on some tomato sauce (if using), top with cheese and other toppings. Here I'm using mozzarella, Parmigiano-Reggiano, pepperoni, crumbled sausage, and black olive. Quickly transfer the skillet to the oven and bake until the crust is puffed around the edges and the toppings are bubbling, 12 to 15 minutes.

LATE SUMMER

Fresh Tomato Pizza

Bake a Pomodoro Pizza (page 275). While it's baking, slice a variety of tomatoes (aim for lots of colors and shapes), season lightly with salt and pepper, and leave on a rack or in a colander to drain for 20 minutes. Tear a ball or two of burrata into pieces and let that drain as well. Let the finished pizza cool slightly, then layer the tomatoes all over and season with more salt and some dried chile flakes. Top with the burrata chunks, basil and/or mint leaves, and a generous drizzle of extra-virgin olive oil.

FALL

Mushrooms, More Mushrooms, and Sausage Pizza

This is a classic tavern-style pizza combo back in Wisconsin, where I grew up. Assemble a Four-Cheese Pizza (page 275) and, before baking, pile a lot of very thinly sliced cultivated white or cremini mushrooms on top in an even layer (use 20 to 35 percent more mushrooms than you think; they shrink). Scatter some crumbled uncooked sausage over the pizza, sprinkle heavily with 50/50 Parmigiano-Reggiano and Pecorino Romano, and bake as usual.

WINTER

Onion and Pancetta Pizza

Thinly slice 2 or 3 large onions and slowly cook in olive oil, stirring and scraping as they get darker, until deeply caramelized; this could take up to 1 hour. Let cool. Make ½ recipe Sheet Pan Pizza Dough (page 274) and press into the sheet pan (but don't add any tomato sauce). Scatter some shredded mozzarella, some torn-up fresh mozzarella, several thin slices of uncooked pancetta, and a generous sprinkling of 50/50 Parmigiano-Reggiano and Pecorino Romano over the dough. Bake as usual.

Blonde Blondies

- 6 ounces (170 g) unsalted butter, plus more for the baking dish
- 1¾ cups (210 g) whole wheat pastry flour
- 2 teaspoons baking powder
- 2 teaspoons kosher salt
- 1 cup firmly packed (200 g) dark brown sugar
- ½ cup (100 g) granulated sugar
- 2 large eggs, at room temperature
- 1 tablespoon pure vanilla extract
- 1 cup (240 g) butterscotch chips or blonde chocolate (broken or chopped into chip-size chunks)
- 1 cup (140 g) chopped salted roasted almonds or pecans
- 1 cup (125 g) crushed-up thin pretzels (not pretzel rods)

These are much more than your basic blondie, with salty notes from the pretzels and almonds adding to their allure. Basic butterscotch chips are totally fine, but you can upgrade by using one of the relatively new "blonde" chocolates on the market. These are white chocolates made using higher heat so the proteins and lactose in the milk solids turn brown and create caramelly flavor compounds. White chocolate has been redeemed! —**Makes twenty-four 2-inch (5 cm) squares**

Heat the oven to 350°F (175°C). Grease the sides and bottom of a 9 × 13-inch (23 × 33 cm) baking dish with butter. Line the dish with parchment so that the parchment extends beyond two sides (for easy lifting out of the treats) and then lightly grease the parchment.

Melt 3 ounces (85 g) of the butter in a small heavy-bottomed pot over medium heat. Cook, whisking the butter occasionally, until it starts to turn golden brown and then whisk constantly until it is amber brown and smells nutty and delicious. Remove from the heat, add the remaining 3 ounces (85 g) butter, and swirl the pan occasionally until all the butter is melted. Set aside.

Whisk together the whole wheat flour, baking powder, and salt in a medium bowl.

Whisk together the brown sugar and granulated sugar in a large bowl. When the butter has cooled enough that it's still warm but not hot enough to cook the eggs, whisk it into the sugars, then add the eggs and vanilla and whisk well.

Fold the flour mixture into the sugar-butter mixture. When the batter is almost blended, fold in the butterscotch chips, almonds, and pretzel pieces. Spread the batter into the prepared pan.

Bake until the blondies are dark golden around the edges and feel soft but not wet in the center, 18 to 23 minutes.

Cool in the pan for at least 20 minutes before removing from the pan and cutting. Store leftover blondies wrapped in plastic at room temperature for up to 4 days. They will get firmer and chewier as time goes on, but they'll still be delicious.

Variation

Amp up the gooey factor by drizzling the batter with ½ cup (120 ml) dulce de leche or other caramel sauce before baking.

Salted Caramel Double-Crust Apple Pie

Whole Wheat Flaky Pastry Dough (page 313)

FILLING

3 pounds (1.35 kg) apples, peeled, cored, and cut into ¼-inch-thick (6 mm) slices

½ cup (100 g) sugar

1 to 3 tablespoons cornstarch

½ teaspoon ground cinnamon

Egg wash: 1 large egg, beaten

CARAMEL SAUCE

¾ cup (150 g) sugar

⅓ cup (110 g) honey

¼ cup (60 ml) water

4 tablespoons (60 g) unsalted butter, cut into pieces

¾ cup (180 ml) heavy cream

FOR FINISHING

1 teaspoon flaky sea salt, or ½ teaspoon kosher salt

Note: The amount of cornstarch to use is hard to tell, as you don't really know how much juice your apples will give off, but you can get an idea by starting with 1 tablespoon. After the apples have sat for 15 minutes or so, check to see if a lot of liquid has accumulated. If so, toss with another tablespoon or so. You get tasty apples no matter what you do, but for a less juicy, more set filling, use more cornstarch.

This is a grand pie—deep-dish, double-crust, and topped with a layer of caramel with more served at the table. The crust is fairly thick—because pie is all about the crust, right?—so be sure to thoroughly bake the pie; it will take at least an hour. And leave another several hours for the finished pie to cool so the juicy apple filling thickens and develops just the right texture. This is true of every pie. If you want warm pie, bake it, cool it, then gently reheat the whole pie or a slice. Pie that's piping hot from the oven will leak out thin juices, fall apart, and never reach its full pie potential. —**Makes one 9- or 10-inch (23 or 25 cm) double-crust pie**

Make the dough as directed and divide into 2 disks, one slightly larger than the other. Wrap and refrigerate as directed. When ready to assemble and bake the pie, remove the pie dough from the refrigerator and let it warm up on the counter until it becomes more pliable, about 30 minutes.

MAKE THE FILLING: Toss the apples with the sugar, cornstarch, and cinnamon in a large bowl. Set aside.

Position an oven rack in the middle position, with plenty of room above it—the pie is tall. Heat the oven to 375°F (190°C). If you have a baking stone or heavy baking sheet, heat it also.

On a lightly floured surface, roll each of the disks of dough to a round about ¼ inch (6 mm) thick. Transfer the larger dough round to a 9- or 10-inch (23 or 25 cm) pie plate (you'll have plenty of dough for the larger size). Pile the apple filling into the bottom crust, along with any juices that have accumulated. Top with the smaller dough round. Let any extra dough hang over the sides of the plate.

Without stretching the dough, press the two layers of dough together to seal them and then trim off any extra dough, using kitchen scissors or a paring knife, to about ½ inch (1.25 cm) over the edge of the dish. Pinch the dough together and fold it under to make a thicker rim, then crimp by pressing with the tines of a fork or flute by pushing the dough toward the pie with the thumb and forefinger of one hand and away from the pie with the index finger of your other hand. Brush the whole surface of the pie with egg wash and cut a small hole in the top of the pie to allow steam to escape during baking.

Pictured on pages 284–85

Bake the pie, on the baking stone, if using, for about 30 minutes. Reduce the oven temperature to 350°F (175°C) and bake until the crust is dark golden brown, about 45 minutes more (a total of 1 hour 15 minutes). If the edges are getting too dark before the center is golden, wrap the edges in foil or use a pie crust shield.

MEANWHILE, MAKE THE CARAMEL: Put the sugar, honey, and water in a heavy-bottomed medium saucepan. The pan needs to be big enough for the mixture to bubble up to about four times its original volume, so err on the side of too large; you do not want a spillover.

Cook the mixture over medium heat, without stirring, until it starts to turn dark amber around the edges, about 5 minutes. Give the pan a swirl and cook until the mixture is a dark golden brown and smells like caramel, another 3 minutes or so. Remove from the heat and carefully stir in the

butter (watch out for bubbling up or spattering). When the butter is incorporated, add the cream and stir. Set aside to cool to room temperature or just barely warm.

Take the pie out of the oven (leave the oven on) and let cool for about 5 minutes. Set the pie on a sheet pan to catch any caramel that might bubble over and brush or spoon about ½ cup (120 ml) of the caramel over the top; reserve the rest of the caramel to serve at the table. Return the pie to the oven (on the sheet pan) and bake until the caramel is bubbling, 5 to 10 minutes. Sprinkle the top with the flaky sea salt.

Let the pie cool for about 3 hours before cutting into it. Resist the temptation to cut into the pie right away. The juices need to thicken before you dig in. Reheat the caramel sauce gently before serving.

Refrigerate any leftovers and reheat in a 375°F (190°C) oven for about 10 minutes before serving.

Whole Wheat Angel Food Cake, with Sprinkles!

1½ cups (300 g) sugar

1 cup (120 g) whole wheat pastry flour

12 large egg whites

1 teaspoon kosher salt

½ teaspoon cream of tartar

2 teaspoons pure vanilla extract

½ teaspoon pure almond extract

¼ cup plus 1 tablespoon (50 g) rainbow sprinkles

It's crazy to think that you can make this most ethereal of cakes with whole-grain flour . . . but you can. Whole wheat pastry flour is milled from softer wheat, meaning it has a lower protein content, which is ideal for tender cakes and pastries.

You can skip the sprinkles, but why would you? Be sure to use actual sprinkles, the long rainbow ones. Nonpareils will streak into the cake too much and the colors will get murky. Serve the cake simply, with a big spoonful of Malted Whipped Cream (page 308), or add some fresh berries, lemon curd, or a thick ribbon of warm chocolate sauce. —**Makes one 10-inch (25 cm) cake**

Position an oven rack in the middle and heat the oven to 350°F (175°C).

Sift ¾ cup (150 g) of the sugar with the flour into a bowl. Set aside.

In a stand mixer fitted with the whisk, combine the egg whites, salt, cream of tartar, vanilla, and almond extract. Whisk on medium speed until very frothy. Gradually add the remaining ¾ cup (150 g) sugar; it should take about a minute to add the sugar.

Increase the speed to medium-high and whisk until the mixture is glossy and at medium peak, almost as thick as shaving cream.

Transfer the meringue to a large bowl, sift about half of the sugar-flour mixture over the top, and fold to combine. Sift the other half of the sugar-flour mixture over, add the sprinkles, and fold to combine. Pile the batter into an ungreased 10-inch (25 cm) angel food cake pan.

Bake until the top feels firm and springs back when you press it lightly with your finger and the cake is an even light brown, about 35 minutes.

Cool the cake upside down (see Note). When the cake is completely cool, run a thin knife between the cake and the edge of the pan and lift the cake out. Run the knife under the bottom of the cake and around the center tube to separate it from the pan.

Transfer the cake to a large plate or cake stand. Store any leftover cake wrapped in plastic at room temperature for up to 2 days.

Note: A key step in making an angel food cake is turning the pan upside down as soon as you take it out of the oven, so that the delicate crumb structure can cool and set up without deflating from its own weight. Some angel food cake pans have tabs around the rim that serve as feet to stabilize the inverted pan. If yours doesn't, you can rest the pan on the neck of a soda bottle, but try to brace it somehow so it doesn't tip.

Creamy Mushroom, Potato, and Wild Rice Soup with
Paprika and Dill 292

Wild Rice Salad with Roasted Beets, Cucumbers,
and Dill 294

Butternut Squash Stuffed with Hazelnuts, Fontina,
and Italian Sausage 297

Wild Rice with Chicken, Broccoli, Bok Choy,
and Garlic-Chile Crunch 300

Baked Wild Rice with Salmon, Artichokes,
and Leeks 303

Wild Rice

Wild Rice

Zizania palustris

▸ GLUTEN-FREE ◂

•▷ ***Why I love it:*** As with my introduction to barley, I first tasted wild rice as a kid—as part of a boxed wild rice mix, complete with seasoning packet! Wild rice is expensive because it's labor- and water-intensive to grow and low-yielding per acre, so it makes sense that it would be sold blended with white rice.

As a cook now, I think wild rice's deep color and long, elegant kernels look gorgeous in any dish, especially salads. The flavor is more assertive than that of rice, making it a strong player in any dish.

•▷ ***What it tastes like:*** Emblematic of the upper Midwest of this country, true wild-grown wild rice can only be harvested by American Indians. Most use the traditional method of cruising the rice fields in canoes and knocking the rice heads with sticks, capturing the grains of rice in the canoes. The rice is then processed by parching it over an open fire to remove the outer hull. It's worth the high cost for its smoky, nutty flavor and distinctive chewy texture.

But I also love less expensive (though not cheap!) commercially grown wild rice, too. Grown mainly in California, cultivated wild rice ("tame" rice?), also known as "paddy rice," has dramatic black needle-like grains and a distinctive smoky flavor.

•▷ ***Common forms:*** Hand-harvested and commercially grown wild rices are available.

•▷ ***How to prepare it:*** My one caution is to be sure you fully cook your wild rice, to the point that the dark outer coating of the grain splits and the creamy center is revealed; that's how you'll get the wonderful chewy texture, and the open grain will drink up dressings and seasonings. Undercooking will produce crunchy rice—and not in a good way. I have more success when I use the boil-like-pasta method.

•▷ ***How it's good for you:*** Wild rice is fairly high in protein, as far as grain goes, and it may have up to thirty times the antioxidant properties of white rice.

Details

→ 1 cup uncooked wild rice weighs 6 ounces (170 g).

→ Use 1 part wild rice to 3 parts liquid as a rule of thumb for the absorption method, though I think the boil-like-pasta method works best, as commercial wild rice can take forever to cook properly.

→ Cook hand-harvested rice for 35 to 40 minutes; cook commercial wild rice for 1 hour.

→ 1 cup (170 g) uncooked wild rice yields 3 cups (425 g) cooked.

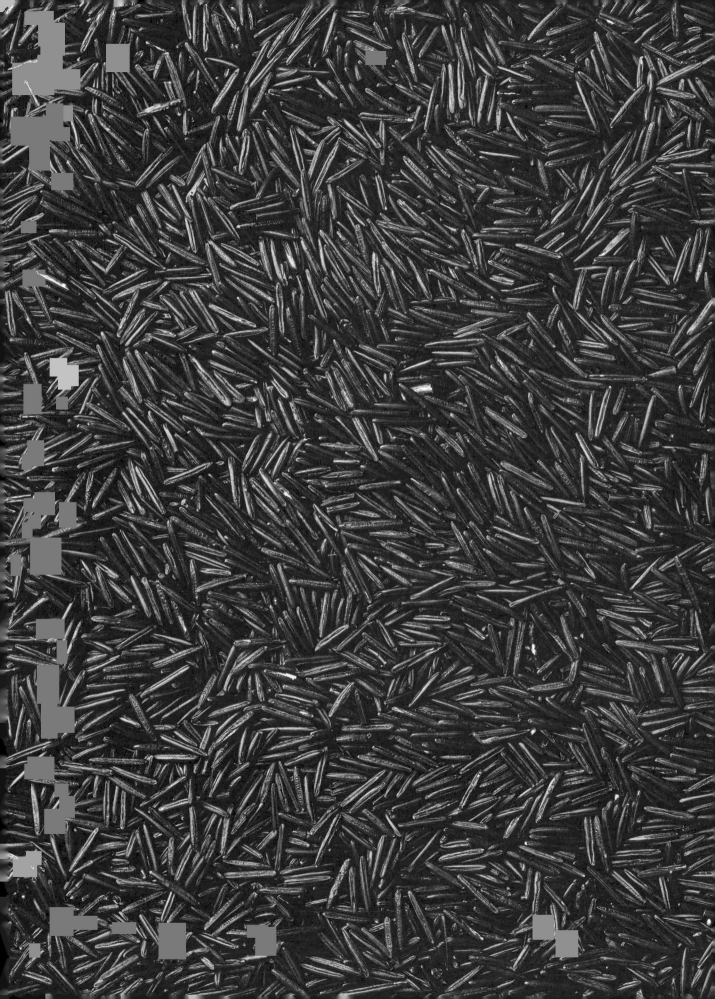

Creamy Mushroom, Potato, and Wild Rice Soup with Paprika and Dill

⅔ cup (110 g) uncooked
    wild rice

Kosher salt

Extra-virgin olive oil

1 pound (450 g) mixed fresh
    mushrooms of your choice,
    dry ends trimmed, thinly
    sliced

¼ teaspoon dried chile flakes

Freshly ground black pepper

4 tablespoons (60 g) unsalted
    butter

1 leek, white and light-green
    parts only, cut crosswise
    into ⅛-inch-thick slices
    (about 1½ cups/200 g)

3 garlic cloves, finely chopped

3 tablespoons tomato paste

1 tablespoon smoked paprika,
    sweet or hot

¼ teaspoon caraway seeds,
    slightly crushed

1 quart (1 liter) chicken
    broth or vegetable broth,
    homemade or low-sodium
    store-bought

1 medium Yukon Gold or other
    medium-starch potato,
    peeled and cut into ¼-inch
    (6 mm) dice

Small handful thyme sprigs

Two 4-inch (10 cm) sprigs
    rosemary

1 cup (240 ml) heavy cream or
    crème fraîche

¼ cup (7 g) chopped fresh dill

Gray day outside? Need something to lift your spirits? This will do it. While comforting and familiar—it's cream of mushroom soup, after all—this soup elevates the typical creamy bowl with intriguing herbal notes, a smokiness from the wild rice and smoked paprika, and a robust Eastern European flavor palette with caraway, paprika, and dill. As always, if you have access to a mix of wild mushrooms, use them, but basic creminis (which are baby portobellos, did ya know?) or white button mushrooms are totally fine. —**Makes 2 quarts (2 liters), serves 4 to 6**

Place the wild rice in a medium saucepan with 1 teaspoon salt and water to cover by about 3 inches (7.5 cm). Bring to a boil, reduce the heat to a lively simmer, cover, and cook until the wild rice is fully tender and most of the grains have opened up, about 45 minutes. Check occasionally to make sure the water hasn't cooked off. All the water may not be absorbed, so drain thoroughly. Set aside.

Pour a generous glug of olive oil into a large skillet or Dutch oven and set over medium-high heat. Add the mushrooms in an even layer and season with the chile flakes and a nice sprinkling of salt and pepper. (Cook the mushrooms in batches if your pan can't accommodate them all in one layer.) Don't disturb the mushrooms until they're nicely browned on one side, then flip them over and cook until all are browned and slightly crisp at the edges, about 10 minutes per batch. Depending on the mushrooms, they may give off

a lot of liquid; if so, just keep cooking until it has evaporated and the mushrooms will brown.

Scrape the mushrooms out of the pan into a bowl and set aside. Return the pan to the heat, reduce the heat to medium, add the butter and the leek, season lightly with salt and pepper, and cook until the leek slices are soft and fragrant, about 10 minutes; don't let them brown. Add the garlic and cook, stirring, for another minute or two, then add the tomato paste, smoked paprika, and caraway seeds.

Cook, stirring and scraping the pan bottom, until the tomato paste has darkened and thickened a bit, about 5 minutes.

Add the broth, potato, thyme, and rosemary. Bring to a simmer and cook until the potato pieces are tender and easily crushed with a fork (scoop a couple out to test), about 20 minutes.

Add the cream, drained wild rice, and cooked mushrooms and simmer gently until the soup has thickened a bit and the raw cream flavor has cooked off, another 15 minutes or so. If the soup is getting very thick, add a bit of broth or water. The soup should be rich and creamy but not gloppy.

Taste and adjust the seasoning with more salt, pepper, or chile flakes. If you can, fish out and discard the thyme and rosemary stems, then add the dill. Serve hot. The soup will be good in the refrigerator for up to 2 days; I don't recommend freezing this one, as the mushrooms can develop a weird texture.

Wild Rice Salad with Roasted Beets, Cucumbers, and Dill

1 cup (175 g) uncooked wild rice

Kosher salt

1½ pounds (675 g) beets, trimmed, peeled, and cut into 1-inch (2.5 cm) chunks

Extra-virgin olive oil

Freshly ground black pepper

1 tablespoon red wine vinegar

1 pound (450 g) cucumbers, preferably small Persian (mini) ones, peeled, seeded, and cut into ½-inch-thick (1.25 cm) slices

1 bunch scallions, trimmed (including ½ inch/1.5 cm off the green tops), sliced on a sharp angle, soaked in ice water for 20 minutes, and drained well

½ cup (120 ml) Yogo Ranch Dressing (page 313)

¼ cup lightly packed (7 g) roughly chopped fresh dill

½ cup (60 g) walnuts, lightly toasted and roughly chopped

4 ounces (115 g) feta cheese, broken into small chunks (Valbreso is a great brand)

I love the flavor profile of this dish, with wild rice providing a robust platform for earthy roasted beets and the husky flavor of walnuts. You could swap chunks of roasted carrot for the beets or use a combination of the two. Cucumber and feta are bright accents, along with garlicky-herby Yogo Ranch Dressing (page 313). If you don't have time to make that dressing, you can substitute your favorite store-bought ranch or season some plain yogurt with lemon juice, salt, and pepper to taste. —**Serves 4**

Place the wild rice in a medium saucepan with 1 teaspoon salt and water to cover by about 3 inches (7.5 cm). Bring to a boil, reduce the heat to a lively simmer, cover, and cook until the wild rice is fully tender and most of the grains have opened up, about 45 minutes. Check on occasion to make sure the water hasn't cooked off. All the water may not be absorbed, so drain thoroughly. Set aside.

Meanwhile, heat the oven to 375°F (190°C).

Toss the beets with 2 tablespoons olive oil, season generously with salt and pepper, and spread in an even single layer on a sheet pan (use two pans if necessary to avoid overcrowding the beets). Roast until the beets are tender and getting browned and slightly shriveled, 15 to 30 minutes, depending on the density of your beets. Transfer to a bowl, sprinkle with the vinegar, toss, and let cool.

Assemble the salad in a large, wide serving bowl: Spread the wild rice on the bottom of the bowl. Distribute the cucumbers and scallions over the rice, then drizzle about one-third of the ranch dressing over all. Arrange the beets in a layer on the cucumbers, distribute the dill and half the walnuts on the beets, then drizzle with another third of the dressing. Finish with the feta, the remaining walnuts, and the rest of the dressing.

Toss right before serving, making sure everyone gets bites of everything in their portion.

Butternut Squash Stuffed with Hazelnuts, Fontina, and Italian Sausage

1 cup (175 g) uncooked wild rice

Kosher salt

Extra-virgin olive oil

1 small butternut squash (about 1½ lb/675 g)

Freshly ground black pepper

3 tablespoons unsalted butter, at room temperature

8 ounces (225 g) bulk Italian sausage, sweet or hot, as you like

½ cup (75 g) hazelnuts, skin-on or blanched, lightly toasted and chopped

2 teaspoons red wine vinegar

1 teaspoon pure maple syrup

¼ teaspoon dried chile flakes

3 medium fresh sage leaves, thinly sliced

1 cup (120 g) lightly packed shredded Fontina cheese

This is basically a twice-baked butternut squash. The goal is to scoop out most of the roasted squash flesh—to be blended with other delicious elements—but to leave an even layer of flesh still attached to the squash skin, creating a container for the stuffing and some contrast in texture. I sometimes make this dish with delicata or sweet dumpling squashes, with a half squash being a perfect serving size. Feel free to experiment with other types of cheese, such as Gruyère or Comté, and while I love sausage, you could skip it and make this vegetarian. But do try your hand at popping the wild rice—it's easy and fun and brings great texture to the dish. —**Serves 2 or 3**

Place ¾ cup (135 g) of the wild rice in a medium saucepan with 1 teaspoon salt and water to cover by about 3 inches (7.5 cm). Bring to a boil, reduce the heat to a lively simmer, cover, and cook until the wild rice is fully tender and most of the grains have opened up, about 45 minutes. Check on occasion to make sure the water hasn't cooked off. All the water may not be absorbed, so drain thoroughly. Set aside.

Meanwhile, pop the remaining ¼ cup (40 g) wild rice: Arrange a couple of paper towels on a plate or tray. Heat 1 teaspoon olive oil in a heavy-bottomed medium saucepan with a lid over medium-high heat. Add 3 or 4 rice grains, cover, and wait until you hear a soft pop or two; you might have to lift the lid to check . . . wild rice is discreet!

Add the rest of the uncooked wild rice and cook, shaking the pan almost constantly, until almost all the grains have popped and puffed. It's okay if a few grains remain unpopped, because you don't want to risk burning the rice by keeping it too long on the burner. Pour the popped rice onto the paper towels and season lightly with salt. Set aside.

Heat the oven to 375°F (190°C).

Halve the squash lengthwise, scrape out the seeds and fibers, and poke the flesh all over with a fork. Rub 1 tablespoon of the butter on the flesh side and season it with salt and pepper.

Arrange the halves cut side down on a baking sheet and roast until almost fully tender but still with a bit of bite, 30 to 60 minutes, depending on the size and density of your squash. Remove the squash but leave the oven on.

Let the squash rest until cool enough to handle. Scrape out the flesh into a bowl, leaving about a ½-inch-thick (1.25 cm) layer of

Butternut Squash Stuffed
with Hazelnuts, Fontina,
and Italian Sausage,
continued

flesh on the skin, taking care not to rip the skin as you scrape.

Mash the squash flesh a bit, leaving it partly chunky. Add the cooked wild rice, raw sausage (pull it into bits so it blends better), and hazelnuts and stir gently to distribute the ingredients well. Season with the vinegar, maple syrup, chile flakes, 1 teaspoon salt, and several twists of black pepper. Stir again to mix.

Heat the remaining 2 tablespoons butter in a small skillet over medium heat and cook until the butter smells nutty and the milk solids are turning a deep golden brown. Drop in the sage leaves and fry them for a second to flavor the butter. Pour everything over the squash mixture and then fold in the Fontina.

Season the squash halves lightly with salt and black pepper.

Pile the stuffing back into the squash halves, mounding it up. Arrange them on a baking sheet and cover loosely with foil. Bake until the sausage is cooked and the stuffing is fully heated through, about 20 minutes. Remove the foil and bake until the top is nicely browned, another 10 minutes or so.

Cut into portions, shower with the popped wild rice, and serve hot.

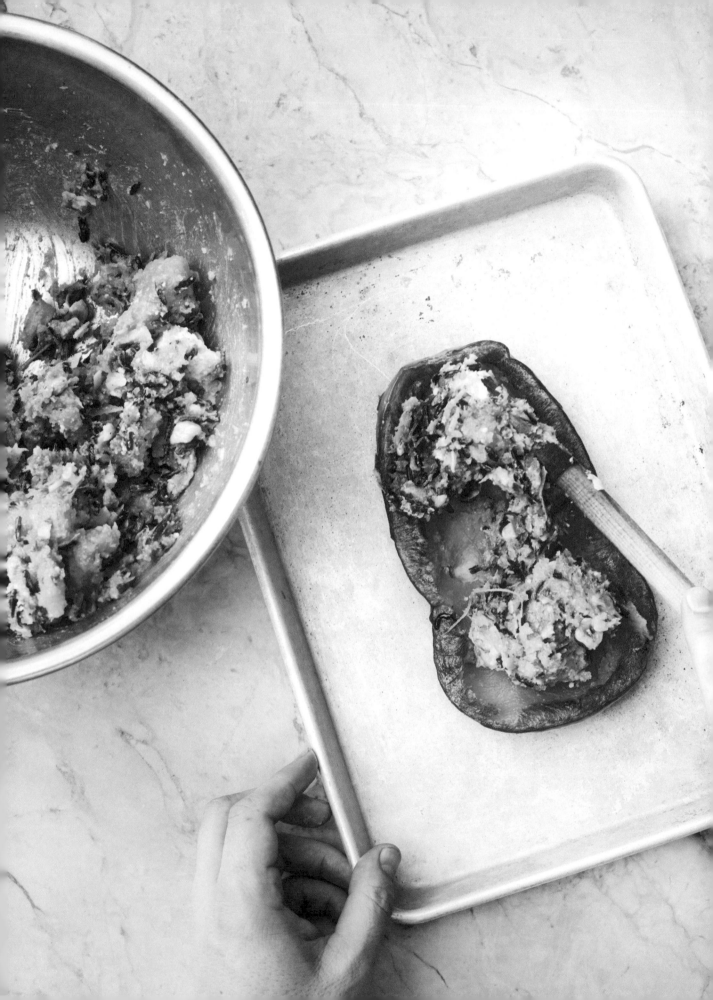

Wild Rice with Chicken, Broccoli, Bok Choy, and Garlic-Chile Crunch

Extra-virgin olive oil

1 pound (450 g) boneless, skinless chicken thighs, cut into 1½-inch (4 cm) pieces

Kosher salt and freshly ground black pepper

2 tablespoons finely chopped fresh ginger

4 garlic cloves, chopped

1 cup (175 g) uncooked wild rice

2½ cups (600 ml) chicken broth, homemade (page 311) or low-sodium store-bought

¼ cup (60 ml) soy sauce or tamari

2 tablespoons Garlic-Chile Crunch (page 306)

12 ounces (335 g) broccoli, stems trimmed and peeled, cut into long florets

1 small head bok choy, sliced lengthwise through the core to make long thin wedges

Finely grated zest of 1 lemon

1 tablespoon fresh lemon juice

Note: Because wild rice sometimes takes longer to cook than you expect, I prefer to use chicken thighs rather than breasts, as they are moister and more forgiving. (However, if you are a fan of white meat, you could sub in an equal weight of chicken breast.)

This highly satisfying dish has the bonus of being a one-pot meal (provided you have a large ovenproof skillet or Dutch oven), making it an excellent choice for midweek meals. The Garlic-Chile Crunch is truly delicious and brings an important flavor contrast, but if you don't have any, be sure to season the dish with your favorite hot sauce and use a bit more garlic. —Serves 4

Heat a glug of oil in a large ovenproof skillet with a lid or other wide heavy pot, such as a Dutch oven, over medium-high heat. Add the chicken pieces, season generously with salt and pepper, and brown all sides, about 4 minutes total (the chicken will get fully cooked later).

Transfer the chicken to a bowl and set aside. If the pan seems dry, add another few drops of olive oil and add the ginger and garlic. Cook, scraping up any browned bits from the chicken, just until soft and fragrant but not at all browned, about 1 minute.

Add the wild rice, chicken broth, and soy sauce. Adjust the heat to a lively simmer, cover, and cook for about 45 minutes. The rice won't be fully cooked yet, but it should be slightly tender when you bite a few kernels and you should see them starting to open; if the rice is still very hard, keep cooking until it becomes tender. Spoon on 2 teaspoons of the garlic-chile crunch and arrange the broccoli florets and bok choy wedges on the rice.

Cover and continue cooking until the rice is fully tender and most of the kernels are blown open and the vegetables are very tender. Check the liquid during this stage; if it looks dry, add another ¼ cup (60 ml) broth or water.

Return the chicken pieces to the pan, arranging them over the vegetables, cover the pan, and cook until the chicken is fully cooked but not so much that it dries out, another 5 minutes or so. The vegetables should be quite soft at this point.

Finish with the lemon zest, lemon juice, and remaining garlic-chile crunch over everything and serve right away, jumbling the rice, vegetables, and chicken together as you serve.

Baked Wild Rice with Salmon, Artichokes, and Leeks

1 cup (175 g) uncooked wild rice

Kosher salt

One 14.5-ounce (410 g) can artichoke hearts or bottoms, rinsed and drained, cut into bite-size pieces

1 pound (450 g) leeks (about 2 medium), top few inches of tough green trimmed off, white and light-green parts cut lengthwise into long strips ½ inch (1.25 cm) wide, washed, and well drained

1 cup lightly packed (120 g) finely and freshly grated Parmigiano-Reggiano cheese

½ cup (120 ml) heavy or whipping cream or crème fraîche

½ cup (120 ml) Italian salad dressing, homemade (page 318) or a simple store-bought brand, such as Newman's Own

Small handful torn fresh mint leaves

Small handful torn or roughly chopped fresh flat-leaf parsley leaves

Freshly ground black pepper

1 to 1½ pounds (450 to 675 g) skin-on salmon fillet (one whole piece or cut into portions)

Extra-virgin olive oil

1 lemon, cut into wedges

This dish is a stunner, and an excellent choice for a potluck or other group dinner—hooray for the casserole. You can make the rice and vegetable layer ahead of time, then do your final bake-off with the salmon on top just before you serve. —Serves 4

Place the wild rice in a medium saucepan with 1 teaspoon salt and water to cover by about 3 inches (7.5 cm). Bring to a boil, reduce the heat to a lively simmer, cover, and cook until the wild rice is fully tender and most of the grains have opened up, about 45 minutes. Check on occasion to make sure the water hasn't cooked off. All the water may not be absorbed, so drain thoroughly. Set aside.

Heat the oven to 350°F (175°C).

Put the cooked wild rice, artichokes, leeks, half the Parmigiano, half the cream, the salad dressing, and the mint and parsley in a large bowl and toss to blend all the ingredients. Season generously with salt and pepper and toss again (remember that the cheese and vinaigrette will be contributing some saltiness).

Pile the mixture into a casserole or gratin dish—something close to a 9 × 13-inch (23 × 33 cm) size works well. Bake until the leeks are tender, about 45 minutes. Take the dish from the oven and increase the oven temperature to 450°F (230°C).

While the casserole is baking, take the salmon from the fridge, pull out any large pin bones, wipe off any scales still on the skin, and season the flesh side generously with salt and pepper. Brush the skin side with some oil and season it with salt and pepper, too. Set aside so the salmon comes close to room temperature by cooking time.

When you've taken the casserole from the oven, distribute the remaining Parmigiano and cream over the top, and arrange the seasoned salmon on top, skin side up. Slide back into the oven and bake until the salmon is just cooked through, but still a bit pink in the center. (You'll have carryover cooking as the casserole rests, so stop short of done. Use the "10 minutes per inch of thickness" rule as a guide for timing. If you like your salmon "rare," cook it even less.) The casserole should be browned and bubbling around the edges by the time the salmon is cooked.

Let the dish rest for about 10 minutes, lightly tented with foil to keep the fish warm, and then serve right away, with the lemon wedges on the side.

Go-Tos

RECIPES TO USE MANY WAYS WITH GRAINS

Toasted Pumpkin Seeds

I recommend having a container of these in your pantry at all times, as they are excellent as a crunchy add-in to just about any salad or grain bowl, not to mention as a nutritious snack. Here I season them simply with salt, but you can add complexity with some Aleppo pepper, smoked paprika, ground cumin, or any combo of savory spices that you like. Just use some restraint, so you don't mask the distinctly nutty-but-green flavor of the seeds.

MAKES 1 CUP (140 G); EASILY DOUBLED OR TRIPLED

1 cup (140 g) raw pumpkin seeds

Extra-virgin olive oil

Kosher salt

Heat the oven to 350°F (175°C).

Toss the pumpkin seeds with about 1 teaspoon olive oil and ½ teaspoon salt. Spread on a baking sheet and toast until they go from green to tan, 8 to 10 minutes. They'll keep toasting a bit once they're out of the oven, so take care not to overtoast. Slide onto a plate and let cool. Store in an airtight container in the cupboard for up to 2 weeks.

Garlic-Chile Crunch

This zippy condiment lives on my counter by my stove in a little glass jar. I add it to vegetable dishes, fried grains, and eggs, and use it to finish many pasta sauces. I have yet to find something it doesn't taste good on.

You must have a nonstick pan for this, though I don't usually recommend nonstick pans due to their unfriendliness to the environment. (Plus, you rarely actually need a nonstick coating; if you heat your pan properly before adding your ingredients, your food won't stick!)

And yes, this is an enormous amount of garlic—you'll probably need 6 or 7 heads—but you'll have an excellent stash of this stuff to use whenever you want (you can also make a half recipe). Do NOT buy prepeeled garlic in a jar, which always tastes oxidized to me. I will be very disappointed if you do.

MAKES ABOUT 1½ CUPS (280 G)

1 pint (300 g) peeled garlic cloves, with the little nubs at the root end cut off

Extra-virgin olive oil

Dried chile flakes or crushed chile de árbol

Put the garlic in a food processor and pulse several times until the pieces are about the size of a grain of short-grain brown rice (they won't be evenly shaped like that, but you get the idea). Add about ¾ cup (180 ml) olive oil and pulse several more times until the garlic bits are more like peppercorn size and suspended in oil. The mixture is a paste but *not* a full-on puree. You want to see actual bits of garlic.

Scrape the mixture into a nonstick pan (a 10-inch/23 cm pan works well) on a cold burner. You should have just enough oil to cover the garlic; if not, add a few more drops to cover (this will depend on the size of your pan; it's important for the oil to cover the garlic so that it cooks slowly and evenly). Now turn on the heat to medium or medium-low. Cook the garlic slowly, stirring frequently with a silicone spatula and scraping any bits that stick to the pan, until the garlic is an even light brown. The goal is to reduce the moisture in the garlic without browning it too much, which would make it bitter. The process could take up to 45 minutes . . . but your patience will be rewarded!

As soon as you can tell that the garlic is evenly browned and getting crispy—listen as you scrape, you'll be able to hear when the garlic gets crispy . . . think potato chip crumbs—take the pan from the heat and stir in 1 to 2 teaspoons of the dried chile flakes, according to your heat tolerance. Scrape everything into a jar, cover tightly, and keep at room temperature for up to 1 month. Don't refrigerate it, or the garlic will soften again.

Variations

Add a tablespoon or two of finely chopped fresh ginger when you start cooking the garlic.

Add 8 to 10 finely chopped anchovies (oil-packed, not bocarones) about halfway through cooking the garlic.

Add a few big pinches of ground spice when you add the dried chiles, such as coriander, star anise, and/or black pepper.

Torn Croutons

I like the "torn" aspect of these croutons because the irregular edges catch and capture whatever juices and seasonings they encounter. Aim for croutons that are crisp on the outside but still with springy and chewy interiors. I love making croutons with leftover focaccia, especially homemade (page 266), as well as ciabatta. Any bread with lots of holes!

MAKES ABOUT 2 CUPS (80 G)

2 thick slices country loaf (cut from the middle)

2 tablespoons extra-virgin olive oil

Kosher salt and freshly ground black pepper

Heat the oven to 400°F (200°C).

Tear the bread, crust and all, into bite-size pieces. Toss the torn bread with the olive oil and a light sprinkling of salt and pepper.

Spread the croutons on a baking sheet in a single layer and bake until golden brown, checking every 4 to 5 minutes and moving the outside croutons to the center of the pan so they cook evenly. Don't let them get too hard; leave a little bit of chew in the center. The total baking time will depend on the type and density of your bread, but most likely will be 10 to 20 minutes.

Slide the croutons onto paper towels to absorb any extra oil and season again lightly with salt and pepper. Store the croutons in an airtight container for up to 3 days.

Brined and Roasted Almonds

This is the only technique I know of that actually seasons the interior of the almond, not just the surface. Even though they start out wet from the brine, the almonds end up toasty with a very light coating of fine salt, perfect for eating as a snack or chopping up and adding to a grain bowl, salad, pasta, or pilaf.

MAKES ABOUT 1½ CUPS (225 G)

1 cup (240 ml) water

⅓ cup (45 g) kosher salt

1½ cups (210 g) raw skin-on almonds

Bring the water to a boil in a saucepan. Add the salt and stir to dissolve. Add the almonds to the hot brine, remove from the heat, and soak for 30 minutes.

Heat the oven to 375°F (190°C).

Drain the almonds thoroughly and spread them evenly in a single layer on a baking sheet (use two sheets if you need to).

Roast until the almonds are lightly toasted and fragrant, about 12 minutes. Take one out to test by biting into it—the interior should be a light brown, almost the color of a paper bag. The nuts will still be soft at this stage, but once completely cooled they will be very crunchy and nicely salty. Store in an airtight container for up to 2 weeks.

Honey Butter with Bee Pollen

My aunt made this honey butter on her farm when I was young, and it's been a favorite of mine ever since. I add bee pollen to it for just a hint of magic, and of course plenty of salt for that sweet-salty thing I love so much.

MAKES ABOUT 1½ CUPS (370 G)

8 ounces (225 g) unsalted butter, slightly softened but not at all melted

¼ cup (60 ml) heavy or whipping cream

¼ cup (85 g) honey

⅛ teaspoon kosher salt

1 tablespoon bee pollen

In a stand mixer fitted with the paddle (or in a small bowl with a wooden spoon), beat the butter a few seconds to loosen it up (don't beat for long, though, or you risk separating it). As you beat, drizzle in the cream, then the honey, and finish with the salt and bee pollen. Stop beating as soon as the butter looks blended. Store in the refrigerator for up to 2 weeks. But it will never last that long, especially if there's any toast around . . .

Maple Butter

I look for maple syrup that has the strongest flavor. That used to be labeled "Grade B," but the maple industry has revised their grading system, so now all maple syrups are labeled Grade A plus a color and taste descriptor, such as "Grade A, Dark Color Robust Taste." Seems silly, but I guess everyone wanted to get an A on their report cards.

MAKES ABOUT 1½ CUPS (370 G)

8 ounces (225 g) unsalted butter, slightly softened but not at all melted

¼ cup (60 ml) heavy or whipping cream

¼ cup (60 ml) pure maple syrup, the darkest color/ flavor you can find

¼ teaspoon kosher salt

In a small bowl with a wooden spoon, or in a stand mixer with the paddle, beat the butter a few seconds to loosen it up (don't beat for long, though, or you risk separating it). As you beat, drizzle in the cream, then the maple syrup, and finish with the salt. Stop beating as soon as the butter looks blended. Store in the refrigerator for up to 2 weeks (see Honey Butter with Bee Pollen, above, for the likelihood of it lasting that long).

Malted Whipped Cream

I love this topping so much, especially on cakes that will absorb a bit of it, such as the Whole Wheat Angel Food Cake (page 286) or the Farro, Brown Butter, and Honey Cake (page 201). Or try it as a flourish on your Overnight Oat Parfaits (page 129) or a warm Tender Spelt Buttermilk Biscuit (page 218), or—you know I'm going to say it—just grab a spoon and eat a bowl of it like it's ice cream.

Note: Malted milk powder is usually sold near the dry milk, or possibly in the coffee and tea section of your grocery store. Ovaltine is chocolate-flavored malted milk powder and would be fine in this recipe, especially served with angel food cake (page 286).

MAKES ABOUT 2 CUPS (480 ML) WHIPPED CREAM

1 cup (240 ml) heavy or whipping cream, cold

2 teaspoons powdered sugar, plus more to taste

2 tablespoons malted milk powder

½ teaspoon pure vanilla extract

Generous pinch of kosher salt

In a bowl with an electric mixer (or by hand with a whisk), whip the cream until it is quite thick and almost holds a shape. Sprinkle on the sugar, malted milk powder, vanilla, and salt.

Continue whipping, making sure the new ingredients are well incorporated, until the cream holds soft peaks. Do not overwhip to the point where the cream is stiff, because it's likely to separate at that point.

Serve with the dessert of your choice right away. Leftovers will keep in the fridge for a day, though some liquid might weep out; just discard that.

Bacon, Scallion, and Black Pepper Cream Cheese

I love a thick slab of well-made bacon, but for this spread, I think a thinner bacon works best, because you want it to integrate into the cream cheese and not be too chewy.

MAKES 1 GENEROUS CUP (250 G)

8 ounces (225 g) cream cheese, at room temperature

3 slices bacon, cooked until crisp, drained on paper towels, and crumbled or chopped

3 or 4 scallions, white and light-green parts only, thinly sliced

Kosher salt and freshly ground black pepper

In a stand mixer fitted with the paddle (or in a bowl with a wooden spoon), mix the cream cheese for about 30 seconds until smooth. Add the bacon, scallions, a pinch of salt, and about 25 twists of black pepper, then blend again for about a minute to mash the bacon and scallions a bit so they give up some flavor. Taste and adjust with more salt or pepper. Keep in the refrigerator for up to 1 week.

Dill, Cucumber, and Celery Cream Cheese

This spread is best eaten within a day of making it, because the cucumbers will give off their juices and things can get a bit soggy.

MAKES ABOUT 1½ CUPS (300 G)

8 ounces (225 g) cream cheese, at room temperature

About ½ cup lightly packed (15 g) roughly chopped fresh dill fronds and tender sprigs

Kosher salt

½ medium cucumber, peeled, seeded, and cut into ¼-inch (6 mm) dice

1 or 2 celery stalks, preferably inner stalks with some leaves, chopped into ¼-inch (6 mm) pieces

In a stand mixer fitted with the paddle (or in a bowl with a wooden spoon), mix the cream cheese for about 30 seconds until smooth. Add the dill and a big pinch of salt and beat until the dill is incorporated and sort of mashed into the cream cheese. Add half the cucumber, beat for 30 seconds, then add all the celery and the remaining cucumbers. Spin for a few times, keeping the celery and some cucumber chunky. Taste and add more salt to taste. Keep in the refrigerator for up to 1 week.

Bacon, Scallion,
and Black Pepper
Cream Cheese

Dill, Cucumber,
and Celery
Cream Cheese

Beet, Smoked
Salmon, and Caper
Cream Cheese

Pickled Pepper
Cream Cheese

Beet, Smoked Salmon, and Caper Cream Cheese

Cook the beet any way that's convenient for you (steamed, boiled, roasted), but for the best flavor, salt the beet while cooking.

MAKES ABOUT 1½ CUPS (300 G)

8 ounces (225 g) cream cheese, at room temperature

1 small beet (red looks great, but any color will do), cooked until tender, peeled, and roughly chopped

2 ounces (55 g) hot-smoked salmon, skin and bones removed, in big flakes

2 tablespoons drained capers, roughly chopped

Kosher salt and freshly ground black pepper

Squeeze of lemon juice (optional)

In a stand mixer fitted with the paddle (or in a bowl with a wooden spoon), mix the cream cheese for about 30 seconds until smooth. Add the beet and beat until the beet (say that three times fast!) is smashed into the cream cheese . . . get ready for some color! Add the flaked salmon and capers, season lightly with salt and pepper, and spin a few more times. Taste and adjust the seasoning, adding a few drops of lemon juice if you like. Keep in the refrigerator for up to 1 week.

Pickled Pepper Cream Cheese

This comes into its full glory when you make it with two types of peppers, to get contrasting flavors, colors, and textures. I prefer peppers in brine, but peppers in oil can be delicious, too. You probably have something in the door of your refrigerator right now that will work here.

MAKES 1¼ CUPS (335 G)

8 ounces (225 g) cream cheese, at room temperature

½ cup (110 g) drained, chopped mixed peppers, such as pepperoncini or Mama Lil's brand

Kosher salt

In a stand mixer fitted with the paddle (or in a bowl with a wooden spoon), mix the cream cheese for about 30 seconds until smooth. Add the drained peppers and spin until well blended. Taste and add salt to your liking. Keep in the refrigerator for up to 1 week.

Best Chicken Broth

A rich, savory chicken broth is a magic elixir that you can use to make so many delicious and heart-warming soups and stews. The trick is to simmer the broth long enough to give it a deep, chicken-y flavor.

MAKE 2½ QUARTS (2.5 LITERS)

One 3½- to 4-pound (1.6 to 1.8 kg) chicken

1 large carrot (about 4 oz/115 g)

2 large stalks celery (about 4 oz/115 g total)

1 large onion (about 10 oz/280 g)

2 garlic cloves, smashed and peeled

1 bay leaf

10 black peppercorns

⅛ teaspoon dried chile flakes

1 small sprig thyme

Kosher salt

Pull the giblet pack out of the chicken (if it came with one). Put the chicken, heart, neck, and gizzard in a large pot (save the chicken liver for another treat). Leave the chicken whole unless it won't fit neatly; in that case, cut off the leg quarters so you can wedge everything into the pot.

Add water to cover the chicken by about 2 inches (5 cm)—about 5 quarts (5 liters). Drop in the carrot, celery, onion, garlic, bay leaf, peppercorns, chile flakes, and thyme. Season with 1 tablespoon kosher salt.

Bring to a strong simmer, reduce the heat so that the liquid simmers gently, and cook for about 1 hour 15 minutes—you want the chicken to be extremely tender, but not cooked so long that there's no flavor left in the meat. As any foam appears on the surface, scoop it off with a big spoon and discard it.

When the chicken is fully tender, cool slightly (so you don't scald yourself!), remove the chicken and set aside, then strain the broth and return it to the pot.

Pick the meat from the carcass and set aside to use in other dishes. (You can give the solids—bones and vegetables—a second boil in another pot, to make a lighter-bodied broth for other uses.)

Return the pot of broth to the stove and continue to simmer until the flavor is really deep and yummy, reducing by about half so that you end up with 10 cups (2.4 liters).

Season with more salt, and when the flavor is good, you're ready to make so many excellent soups. You can refrigerate this broth for up to 3 days or freeze for up to 3 months.

Whole Wheat Flaky Pastry Dough

This makes enough dough for a double-crust pie baked in a deep-dish pie plate, or for two shallow tart shells baked in 9-inch (23 cm) removable-bottom tart pans. Or anything in between!

Using vodka in pie dough is a trick I learned from *Cook's Illustrated* magazine; if you don't have vodka or neutral grain spirits (which are almost *all* alcohol), use only ice water, and increase the amount to ⅔ cup (160 ml).

You can freeze what you don't use; wrap well in a freezer bag and freeze for up to 3 months. The best way to thaw is overnight in the fridge, but a countertop thaw is fine, too, as long as the room isn't too warm. Turn little scraps of leftover dough into a snack: Roll them out, cut into pieces, sprinkle with cinnamon sugar and a few dots of butter, and pop them in the oven while you bake your pie.

MAKES ABOUT 2 POUNDS (900 G)

> **2 cups (240 g) whole wheat flour**
>
> **2 cups (240 g) unbleached all-purpose flour**
>
> **1 tablespoon sugar**
>
> **2 teaspoons kosher salt**
>
> **12 ounces (335 g) cold unsalted butter, cubed**
>
> **⅓ cup (80 ml) ice water**
>
> **⅓ cup (80 ml) cold vodka**

Put the whole wheat flour, ⅔ cup (80 g) of the all-purpose flour, the sugar, and the salt into a food processor and pulse a few times to blend.

Add the butter ● and pulse until the mixture resembles coarse sand with no lumps of butter. Take it a step further and continue pulsing until the dough just barely starts to clump together. It should look sandy with a few walnut-size clumps of dough ●; the dough may start to climb up the walls of the processor bowl, so knock those down every few pulses.

Dump the mixture into a large bowl and break up any large clumps of dough with your hands so that there are none bigger than a walnut half ●. Add the remaining 1⅓ cups (160 g) all-purpose flour and toss to combine ●.

Combine the water and vodka and drizzle evenly over the flour mixture, making sure to distribute it evenly. Gently toss everything together with a large flexible spatula or your hands, so the moisture gets absorbed by as much of the dough as possible ●.

As the mixture starts to form clumps, gently press and knead the dough together to form a cohesive but slightly shaggy log ●. Divide the dough in half for two tart shells or single-crust pies. For a double-crust pie, divide the dough into one portion that's a little bigger (bottom crust) and one that's a little smaller (top crust).

Flatten the dough portions into round disks ●, wrap in plastic, and refrigerate for at least 30 minutes before using. Freeze any dough you don't plan to use.

Variation

Whole Wheat Flaky Pastry Dough with Turmeric: Add 2 tablespoons ground turmeric to the dough along with the flour, sugar, and salt.

Yogo Ranch Dressing

I think everyone should indulge in as much ranch dressing as they want, whenever they want. Especially my version, which uses yogurt instead of mayonnaise, making it just a bit more healthful.

MAKES A SCANT 2 CUPS (450 ML)

> **1½ cups (335 g) plain whole-milk Greek yogurt**
>
> **2 tablespoons fresh lemon juice**
>
> **2 tablespoons finely chopped fresh chives**
>
> **2 garlic cloves, finely grated or minced**
>
> **2 teaspoons honey**
>
> **1 tablespoon onion powder**
>
> **1 teaspoon dried oregano**
>
> **½ teaspoon freshly ground black pepper**
>
> **½ teaspoon mustard powder**
>
> **2 teaspoons kosher salt**

Stir all the ingredients together, making sure the honey gets dissolved. Taste and adjust with more of any of the seasonings. For the best flavor, let the dressing sit for at least 30 minutes before using, so the ingredients can share their flavors with one another. Store in the fridge for up to 1 week.

Spicy Creamy Green Sauce

I love having this in my refrigerator at all times. It's a good all-around player, but I especially like it as an instant meal-maker when I spoon some into a bowl of cooked grains, like quinoa or farro, and then add a chopped tomato.

MAKES ABOUT 2 CUPS (480 ML)

½ cup (120 ml) extra-virgin olive oil

½ cup lightly packed (15 g) roughly chopped fresh flat-leaf parsley leaves and tender stems

½ cup lightly packed (15 g) roughly chopped fresh cilantro leaves and tender stems

1 small jalapeño, seeded and roughly chopped

5 garlic cloves, smashed and peeled

1 tablespoon fresh lemon juice

1 tablespoon ground coriander

2 teaspoons ground cumin

2 teaspoons kosher salt

1 cup (225 g) plain whole-milk Greek yogurt

Put the olive oil, parsley, cilantro, jalapeño, garlic, lemon juice, coriander, cumin, and salt in a food processor and blend well. Add the yogurt and buzz again until smooth but with bits of herb still visible. Store in the fridge for up to 1 week, giving it a good stir before serving.

Cilantro-Raisin Vinaigrette

This is my latest evolution of a dressing I've been making for years, which I learned from Australian chef Matt Wilkinson's cookbook *Mr. Wilkinson's Vegetables*. Sweet-tart is the key.

MAKES 1 CUP (240 ML)

⅓ cup (50 g) golden raisins

2 tablespoons plus 1 teaspoon balsamic vinegar

3 garlic cloves, smashed and peeled

3 tablespoons drained capers

One 2-ounce (55 g) can anchovy fillets in oil, drained

1 cup lightly packed (30 g) roughly chopped fresh cilantro leaves and tender stems

⅓ cup (80 ml) extra-virgin olive oil

Kosher salt (optional)

Put the raisins and vinegar in a small bowl and let sit for about 30 minutes, to plump up the raisins and give the dressing a better final texture (you can skip this step if you're in a hurry).

Put the garlic, capers, and anchovies in a food processor and pulse until finely chopped, scraping down the sides of the bowl as needed. Don't go all the way to a puree, however—you want some texture.

Add the raisins and vinegar and pulse until the mixture is blended but still slightly chunky. Add the cilantro and pulse again to break up the herbs.

Scrape the mixture into a bowl and whisk in the olive oil. Taste and add more salt if you like, though you've got some salinity with the capers and anchovies. Store in the fridge for up to 1 week, giving it a good stir before serving.

Ginger, Garlic, and Fish Sauce Dipping and Dunking Sauce

If you're new to fish sauce, this is a good way to get to know its incredible depth of savory flavor. You'll find various brands, from various countries in Asia, including Vietnam, Thailand, and the Philippines. My favorite brand is Red Boat, which is made in Vietnam by a company founded by an ex-Apple engineer who missed the purity of the fish sauce he remembered from his childhood in Saigon. Caramelizing the sugar is a technique that's used in Vietnamese cuisine (among others). I like this method because it adds sweetness, but with an edge.

MAKES ABOUT 2 CUPS (480 ML)

1 cup (200 g) sugar

¼ cup (60 ml) water

⅓ cup (80 ml) fish sauce (I like Red Boat brand)

¼ cup lightly packed (40 g) fresh ginger, peeled and finely minced

3 tablespoons minced garlic

1 ounce (30 g) fresh hot chiles, such as serrano or jalapeño, seeded and finely minced

1¼ cups (300 ml) fresh lime juice

Put the sugar and water in a heavy-bottomed medium saucepan over medium-high heat and bring to a boil, stirring just enough to get the sugar fully moistened. Let the mixture boil, without stirring but with an occasional swirl of the pan, until it is a light amber, 6 to 7 minutes. The syrup will be super hot at this point, so please be careful.

Remove the pan from the heat and let the syrup cool for about 1 minute, then whisk in the fish sauce, ginger, garlic, and chiles. The sugar might stiffen up, but don't worry, it will dissolve again once you add the lime juice.

Let the mixture cool completely and then whisk in the lime juice. Taste and adjust with more fish sauce (for saltiness) or lime juice. The sauce should be quite intense. Store in the refrigerator for up to 1 month, giving it a good shake before using.

Turmeric Mayo

This easy sauce shows that there's no need to make your own mayonnaise—good store-bought mayonnaise is an honorable and versatile ingredient. And by "good," I mean Duke's. Lest I get any Hellmann's fans upset, I like Hellmann's also. (Hellmann's is called Best Foods in some regions.)

MAKES 1½ CUPS (375 G)

> 1 tablespoon ground turmeric
>
> 2 teaspoons fresh lemon juice
>
> 1 teaspoon Dijon mustard
>
> 1 teaspoon onion powder
>
> ¼ teaspoon kosher salt
>
> 1½ cups (375 g) mayonnaise

Stir the turmeric, lemon juice, mustard, onion powder, and salt into the mayonnaise. Let sit for at least 30 minutes before using so the flavorings can mingle, then

taste and add more salt if you like. Store in the fridge for up to 1 week.

Creamy Nutritional Yeast Dressing

If you already know and love nutritional yeast, you or your parents probably lived through the seventies . . . or you're vegan! Nutritional yeast has made a comeback in recent years, due to the rise of vegan cooking, in which cheese, anchovies, fish sauce, and other animal-based savory additives aren't welcome. Made from de-activated yeast (meaning you can't leaven anything with it), nutritional yeast looks like yellow flakes and tastes sort of cheesy, in a good way. I love the stuff; think of it as your secret umami-boosting ingredient.

MAKES ABOUT 1¼ CUPS (325 G)

> ¾ cup (50 g) nutritional yeast
>
> ⅓ cup (80 ml) extra-virgin olive oil
>
> ¼ cup (60 ml) apple cider vinegar
>
> ¼ cup (60 ml) coconut aminos (optional)
>
> ¼ cup (60 ml) water (or ½ cup/120 ml if not using coconut aminos)
>
> 1 tablespoon sherry vinegar
>
> 3 garlic cloves, minced
>
> 1 teaspoon freshly cracked black pepper
>
> 1 teaspoon kosher salt

Put all the ingredients into a food processor and whiz until completely blended and slightly creamy. Store in the refrigerator for up to 2 weeks.

Romesco Sauce

This Spanish sauce is slightly sweet, slightly smoky, and super versatile, though you may find yourself simply eating it from the container. The base ingredient is a roasted red sweet pepper, and while you could roast and peel your own red bell pepper, red peppers from a jar are just fine for this. If you can find piquillo peppers, use them, as they are Spanish and delicious. Note that piquillos are smaller than a standard bell pepper, so you'll probably need a couple of them.

MAKES ABOUT 2½ CUPS (600 ML)

> 2 cups (280 g) raw skin-on almonds, lightly toasted
>
> 3 ounces (85 g) roasted red bell pepper from a jar
>
> 3 garlic cloves, smashed and peeled
>
> 6 tablespoons (90 g) tomato paste
>
> 2 tablespoons sherry vinegar
>
> 1 teaspoon smoked paprika
>
> ⅛ teaspoon cayenne pepper
>
> 1 teaspoon kosher salt
>
> ¼ teaspoon freshly ground black pepper
>
> ⅔ cup (160 ml) extra-virgin olive oil

Finely chop about one-third of the almonds and set aside. Put the remaining almonds, the red pepper, garlic, tomato paste, vinegar, smoked paprika, cayenne, salt, and black pepper in a food processor. Pulse until the almonds are very finely chopped and a slightly chunky sauce has come together.

Transfer to a bowl and whisk in the olive oil and reserved chopped almonds. Taste and adjust with more vinegar, paprika, cayenne, salt, or black pepper. Store in the refrigerator for up to 4 days.

Orange Garlic Confit Vin 8.18

Cilantro-Raisin Vin 8.14

Ginger Garlic Fish Sauce 8.15

Green Sauce

CREAMY — Nutritional Yeast 8.15

Spicy Green Sauce 8.17

Tzatziki 8.15

Salsa 8.21

Italian

"Date Shake" 8.16

·19

Tumeric Mayo
8·20

Cashew Vin
8.17

·17

Romesco
8.15

Yogo Ranch ☺
8·15

Hot Sauce 8.17

Cashew Dressing

Smooth and creamy, with all the good flavors—nutty, sweet, salty, tangy—this sauce is an adaptation of the peanut sauce found in some Asian cuisines. Warning: It's addictive.

MAKES 1½ CUPS (360 ML)

6 tablespoons (90 g) cashew butter

2 tablespoons soy sauce or tamari

2 tablespoons fresh lime juice

1½ tablespoons pure maple syrup

1 tablespoon minced fresh ginger

2 teaspoons toasted sesame oil

½ teaspoon kosher salt

⅓ cup (80 ml) water

Put the cashew butter, soy sauce, lime juice, maple syrup, ginger, sesame oil, and salt into a food processor and process until smooth. With the motor running, drizzle in the water to make a creamy, emulsified sauce. Store in the fridge for up to 1 week, stirring before using if the dressing looks separated.

Tzatziki, with Lots of Fresh Herbs

This sauce is almost like a salad in itself, given the large quantity of cucumber. It's so fresh, a perfect thing to pair with something fried, like Freekeh Falafel (page 211). The flavor is best after at least 2 hours, when the ingredients have had a chance to infuse their flavors into the yogurt. The sauce will get a

bit weepy after a couple of days, however, because of the cucumber; if that happens, just stir any juices back in.

MAKES ABOUT 2 CUPS (480 ML)

1 large cucumber, peeled

Kosher salt

1 cup (225 g) plain whole-milk Greek yogurt

Finely grated zest and juice of 1 lemon

3 tablespoons extra-virgin olive oil

2 garlic cloves, minced

½ bunch mint, chopped

½ bunch chives, thinly sliced

¼ cup (7 g) finely chopped fresh dill

Dash of hot sauce

Halve the cucumber lengthwise and scoop out the seeds with a small spoon. Grate the flesh on the large holes of a box grater.

Toss the grated cucumber with about ½ teaspoon salt and spread out in a large sieve. Let the cucumber drain for about 20 minutes, then squeeze gently with paper towels to remove as much liquid as possible.

Put the cucumber into a bowl and stir in the yogurt, lemon zest, lemon juice, olive oil, garlic, mint, chives, dill, and a couple of shakes of hot sauce. Taste and adjust with more salt, lemon, or hot sauce. For the best flavor, let the sauce rest for at least 30 minutes before using. Store in the fridge for up to 3 days.

Italian Salad Dressing

This is my upgrade to the Italian dressing that was always in my refrigerator when I was growing up. The key is having just a touch of sweetness, which I achieve by using a slightly sweet vinegar (from KATZ Farm; see page 332). If you are using regular white wine vinegar, add about ¼ teaspoon sugar.

MAKES 2 CUPS (480 ML)

¼ cup (60 ml) red wine vinegar

¼ cup (60 ml) late-harvest sauvignon blanc vinegar or other slightly sweet vinegar, such as white balsamic

1 tablespoon ground fennel

1½ teaspoons mustard powder

½ teaspoon dried basil

½ teaspoon dried oregano

½ teaspoon kosher salt

⅛ teaspoon freshly ground black pepper

¾ cup (180 ml) extra-virgin olive oil

½ cup (120 ml) grapeseed oil

Put the two vinegars, the ground fennel, mustard powder, basil, oregano, salt, and pepper in a blender or food processor and whiz to blend. With the machine running, drizzle in the olive oil and grapeseed oil. Taste and adjust the seasoning. Store in the refrigerator for up to 1 month.

Fresh Orange and Garlic Confit Vinaigrette

A basic navel orange works just fine in this dressing, but feel free to play with some of the other wonderful citrus varieties that are in season during the colder months. Cara Cara oranges are sweet and a beautiful blush pink, blood oranges will bring even more dramatic magenta color, and any sort of tangerine or satsuma is extra sweet and perfumey. You can adjust the amount of vinegar to match the sweetness or tartness of your fruit.

MAKES ABOUT 1 CUP (240 ML)

> 1 medium orange
>
> 1 tablespoon white wine vinegar
>
> 1 tablespoon honey
>
> 1 teaspoon kosher salt
>
> Freshly ground black pepper
>
> Garlic Confit (recipe follows)
>
> Extra-virgin olive oil (optional)

Using a rasp-style grater, zest the orange into a small bowl. Cut in half and squeeze out the juice; you want about ½ cup (120 ml). Fish out any seeds. Whisk in the vinegar, honey, salt, and a few twists of black pepper.

Pour the orange mixture into a food processor. Reserving the garlic oil, drain the garlic cloves and add them to the food processor. Process until smooth. Measure out ½ cup (120 ml) of the reserved garlic oil (if you don't have the full ½ cup, supplement with plain olive oil). With the machine running, pour in the oil. Taste and adjust with more vinegar, honey, salt, or pepper. The dressing should be fruity, lightly garlicky, and not too sharp. Store in the fridge for up to 2 weeks.

Garlic Confit

This method coaxes out all the seductive flavor from garlic by a method called "confiting" (pronounced con-FEE-ing)— meaning gently poaching in olive oil. The process produces tender, mellow garlic without any harsh notes. And oil-poaching is so much easier than roasting garlic—no need to fire up a whole oven for just a head of garlic; plus, you get a bonus of garlic-scented oil.

MAKES 10 TO 15 CONFITED GARLIC CLOVES AND ABOUT ½ CUP (120 ML) GARLIC OIL; INCREASE THE AMOUNTS AS MUCH AS YOU WANT

> 10 to 15 medium garlic cloves, peeled (about a heaping ¼ cup/30g)
>
> ½ cup (120 ml) extra-virgin olive oil, plus more if needed

Put the garlic and oil in a very small saucepan—the oil needs to cover the garlic so it softens evenly. If it's your smallest pan and the oil is still not covering, use more oil; you'll have plenty of lovely garlicky oil to use in all sorts of dishes.

Heat the oil over medium heat until you see little bubbles emerge from the garlic, then quickly reduce the heat to low; you don't want the garlic to brown. Cover the pan and cook the garlic slowly until it is completely soft, about 1 hour, depending on the size and freshness of your garlic. If you see the garlic darkening past golden brown, reduce the heat or pull the pan off the burner for a few minutes. Let cool. Store the garlic in its oil in the refrigerator for up to 1 week.

Updated Kale Sauce, for Pasta or Grains

This was one of the most popular recipes from my first book, *Six Seasons: A New Way with Vegetables*, and it's also one of the recipes I cook the most for myself. It's so versatile, I think of it as a "mother sauce," so I'm including it in this book along with several variations that show off its best virtues.

MAKES ENOUGH FOR 2 MAIN-DISH SERVINGS OR 4 FIRST-COURSE SERVINGS

> Kosher salt
>
> 2 garlic cloves, smashed and peeled
>
> Extra-virgin olive oil
>
> 1 pound (450 g) kale (any variety, though Tuscan, aka lacinato, is wonderful), thick midribs cut out and discarded
>
> Freshly ground black pepper
>
> ½ cup (60 g) freshly grated Parmigiano-Reggiano cheese

Bring a large pot of water to a boil and add enough salt so that it tastes like the ocean.

Put the garlic and oil into a small heavy pot or skillet over medium heat and cook until the garlic begins to sizzle. Reduce the heat to low and gently cook until the garlic is light golden, soft, and fragrant, 5 to 7 minutes. Pour the oil and garlic into a bowl so it can cool quickly.

When the water is boiling, add the kale leaves and boil until they are tender but not mushy or overcooked, about 5 minutes. Scoop out about a mugful of cooking water, then pull the kale leaves out with tongs or a slotted spoon and transfer them to a blender. It's fine if they are still wet.

Process the kale in the blender with the oil-garlic mixture, adding just a bit of cooking water to help the process along and to make a nice thick puree. Season with salt and pepper.

You can make the kale sauce up to 2 days ahead. Store in the refrigerator.

FOR SAUCED PASTA: Cook ½ pound (225 g) pasta of your choice until just al dente. Scoop out about a mugful of cooking water, then drain the pasta thoroughly. Return the drained pasta to the pot and pour in the kale sauce. Add half the Parmigiano and toss well. Add a touch more pasta water and toss until the pasta noodles have absorbed some of the sauce and cook a bit more until they are perfectly al dente and well coated with a bright green, creamy-textured sauce, another 1 to 2 minutes. Serve right away, with a big drizzle of olive oil and the rest of the cheese.

FOR BAKED PASTA: Cook ½ pound (225 g) short pasta noodles, such as penne, drain well, and fold together with the basic kale sauce or any of the variations that follow. Layer into a baking dish with lots of Parmigiano and maybe some sautéed vegetables and bake at 425°F (220°C) until bubbling around the edges; time will vary with the size of your dish, type of ingredients, etc.

FOR GRAINS: Fold the basic kale sauce or any of the following variations (except for the sausage version) into about 4 cups (about 700 g) cooked and cooled grain, such as farro, barley, or wheat berries, and serve warm as a side dish or let cool and serve as a grain salad.

Variations

Kale Sauce with Pistachios: I love the sweetness of pistachios, and of course their color works beautifully with the kale. If the nuts are not toasted, toast them gently when you toast the garlic in the oil. Add ½ cup (60 g) lightly toasted pistachios as you blend the kale.

Classic Basil Pesto: Try to find Genovese basil, which is the traditional variety used in pesto. It's super fragrant with big, tender leaves and a sweet-spicy flavor. Add 1 cup (120 g) gently toasted pine nuts and the leaves from 1 large bunch of basil as you process the kale.

Caper-Raisin Kale Sauce: I can't get enough of this sweet-salty flavor combo, which I think works so well with the hearty kale flavors. Add ⅓ cup (50 g) golden raisins that have been plumped in warm water for 20 minutes and drained, 3 tablespoons drained capers, and 2 tablespoons balsamic vinegar when you puree the kale.

Kale Sauce with Sausage and Cheese: This makes a gutsier, heartier version of the original kale sauce. (I would eat this on a camping trip; make the kale sauce at home and pop it in the cooler.) Crumble some mild or spicy sausage into a skillet, brown it gently over medium heat, and pour off excess grease. Puree the kale sauce as directed and stir in the sausage, maybe with some extra cheese.

Kale Sauce with Sautéed Shrimp: The sauce is excellent with some wild shrimp tossed in. I sauté them and then add the kale sauce and cheese (yes, cheese with seafood! I know many Italians will disapprove, but I love it), and finish the dish as described in the main recipe, adding a big squeeze of lemon as a final seasoning.

Kale Sauce with Fresh Tomatoes: Tomatoes are especially nice with the pistachio version of this sauce. Just before serving, add about 8 ounces (225 g) tomatoes (1 large tomato, sliced, or cherry tomatoes, halved) and a small handful of torn basil leaves to the pistachio kale sauce. If you like, garnish with more grated cheese, some crunchy breadcrumbs, and a sprinkling of chopped toasted pistachios.

Beef and Pork Ragù, for Pasta, Polenta, and Other Grains

Both of the meats in this recipe can be fatty, so I like to make this sauce at least one day ahead, chill overnight, and then spoon off the solid fat. Don't get me wrong, fat is great! That's where so much of the flavor is, but too much meat fat can feel heavy and too rich. I like to make this ragù with white wine, but red wine may be more traditional and tastes just as delicious.

I suggest you make a big batch of this ragù, divide it into portions, and freeze a few for almost-instant dinners. Serve the ragù on whole wheat pasta or the Whole Wheat and Ricotta Cavatelli (page 260), or on polenta, or for a less traditional pairing, spoon some over a big bowl of brown rice or farro. It's all good.

MAKES 2 QUARTS (2 LITERS)

Note: If you have time, salt your beef up to a day ahead, which enhances the beefy flavor. Sprinkle it generously with kosher salt and spread the beef onto a large tray, ideally on a rack set over the tray. Let sit at room temperature for up to 2 hours; if you're going to "age" it longer, put it in the fridge. When ready to cook, blot off any moisture from the surface and proceed with the recipe, bearing in mind that you've already salted the meat so you don't need to add too much more during cooking.

2 pounds (900 g) boneless chuck roast, big pockets of fat and any silver skin or gristle removed, cut into 2-inch (5 cm) chunks

Kosher salt and freshly ground black pepper

Extra-virgin olive oil

1 pound (450 g) ground pork

2 cups (300 g) finely chopped onion

½ cup (80 g) finely diced or chopped carrot

½ cup (85 g) finely diced or celery

4 garlic cloves, finely chopped

Four 4-inch (10 cm) sprigs thyme

4 medium fresh sage leaves

Three 4-inch (10 cm) sprigs rosemary

3 tablespoons unsalted butter

1 cup (240 ml) dry white wine

One 28-ounce (785 g) can whole peeled tomatoes, undrained

Season the beef with salt and pepper (a day ahead if possible, see Note).

Heat a glug of olive oil in a very large deep skillet or Dutch oven over medium-high heat. Blot the beef chunks with paper towels so they are nice and dry and add to the pan in an even layer with plenty of room between the chunks. You'll probably need to do this in batches, or use two pans.

Cook until all sides of the chunks are nicely browned, about 15 minutes for the whole batch. Take your time to develop some nice browning, which will add so much flavor to the ragù; reduce the heat if your juices are starting to blacken in the pan. You do NOT want that to happen. Transfer the browned beef to a tray and set aside.

Break the ground pork into a couple of large chunks, add to the pan, and cook all surfaces well so they get deeply browned and slightly crusty, 5 to 10 minutes. Once the pork has browned, break it into smaller bits.

Add the onion, carrot, and celery and cook, stirring to dissolve the cooked-on meat juices in the pan, until the vegetables are soft and fragrant, about 5 minutes. Add the garlic and cook for another minute, then add the thyme, sage, and rosemary.

Return the beef and any accumulated juices to the pan, then add the butter. Cook, stirring everything around, until the butter has melted and is starting to brown a bit, then add the wine. Simmer until the wine has reduced by about half, 2 to 3 minutes. Add the tomatoes and their juices. Break up the whole tomatoes with your spatula or wooden spoon.

Reduce the heat so the ragù simmers merrily but not hard when covered. (Letting the sauce actually boil will toughen the beef, which is not what we want.) Cover and simmer, stirring every 20 minutes or so, until the sauce has reduced and has a nice slick of oil on top and, most important, the beef is completely tender; you should be able to shred the chunks with a fork. This can take between 1 and 3 hours, depending on your beef. It's critical to leave yourself enough time to cook the ragù until the beef gets to this point; otherwise, you'll have chewy beef, which just won't be succulent, even if you cut it into smaller pieces.

Taste and adjust the final flavoring with more salt or pepper. If time allows, chill the ragù for several hours so the fat solidifies, then remove and discard it. Keep in the fridge for up to 5 days or in the freezer for up to 3 months.

Larder

Basics You Should Always Have on Hand

▶▶ *Seasonings*

SALT

Good food requires two things: high-quality ingredients and proper seasoning. And when I say seasoning, I mean salt. The point of salt is not to make food taste salty, but to make it taste more of itself. Whether it's a tomato, a slice of ripe melon, a bowl of buttered noodles, or a steak, your dish wants salt, to dial in the natural flavors, heightening their best qualities, muting the more acerbic ones, and making the whole thing taste better.

You could spend a small fortune—and valuable cabinet space—collecting the many types of salt on the market. There are pink salts from the Himalayas and black ones from Hawaii and countless other colors from regions around the world. While it's fun to try them all, you really just need two—kosher salt for cooking with and a flaky finishing salt for a final bit of flavor and crunch just before serving.

Despite the range of colors and places of origin, the main differences in salt varieties are the shape of the crystals. Those shapes affect the density, which means that volume measures of salt are wildly variable. For instance, ½ cup (145 g) of Morton's table salt weighs about the same as 1 cup (135 g) of Diamond Crystal kosher salt.

The dramatic differences aren't just between table salt and kosher salt. The variation among kosher salts is crazy! We measured four brands of kosher salt: Diamond Crystal, Morton, La Baleine, and David's. Diamond Crystal weighs 8 grams per tablespoon, but all the others weighed 17 grams—twice as much salt per tablespoon!—so it's important to know that for the recipes in this book, we tested with Diamond Crystal kosher salt. Of course, if you weigh your salt, you can use whatever type you like, but if you're measuring by volume, you'll need to make some calculations.

Once I've finished cooking a dish, I take a final taste and adjust the seasoning. More often than not, I'll sprinkle on some coarse flakes of what's known as finishing salt. In addition to a last layer of flavor, these flaky salts add a bit of crunch that's delightful to bite into. My favorite is the pure flake salt that Jacobsen Salt Co. collects from the Oregon coast. Maldon also makes an excellent coarse salt.

Salt has no expiration date. Just make sure to keep it dry and it will last forever. Keep it near the stove in a bowl that you can reach your fingers into, and use it early and often as you cook.

BLACK PEPPER

My peppercorn of choice is Tellicherry. These large, mature peppercorns have a more developed flavor than many other varieties and a nice kick of a finish. I find that just a small amount can really elevate a dish.

Always buy whole peppercorns and grind them just as you need them. That fresh-cracked flavor only lasts a few minutes and you want to take full advantage of it. Storing peppercorns in an airtight jar and keeping them away from light and heat will help preserve their flavor. Preground and precracked pepper are a waste of your good money.

SPICES AND DRIED HERBS

My way of cooking relies more on fresh herbs than dried spices, but there are a few spices that I reach for often, such as cumin and coriander. I recommend you buy whole spices rather than ground ones, which are never as fresh. Buy spices in small quantities and store them in glass jars. To use, toast them gently in a dry pan to maximize their flavor, then grind in a spice mill or crush with a mortar and pestle. If you're pressed for time, preground spices are fine, as long as they are fresh. You should "overhaul" your spice cabinet at least once a year.

▶▶ *Oil and Vinegar*

EXTRA-VIRGIN OLIVE OIL

Olive oil is hands down my favorite cooking fat. I really don't think I could cook without it. When shopping for oil, keep in mind that it's an agricultural product and its quality depends a lot on where it was grown and how it was processed. Olive oil is essentially fruit juice and its flavor changes over time, so you need to learn to read the labels. You want to pay particular attention to expiration and harvest dates. Look for an oil that tells you when the olives were harvested, usually in the fall or winter, after which they may be left in tanks for a few months so the sediment settles, hence the harvest year should be the year prior to the current year. If the harvest date is two years prior to when you're buying the oil, pass.

Many oils don't list harvest date and simply say "best by," which is a turn-off to me. That date could be two or three years after harvest, and while the oil may not actually go bad in that time, it won't be as delicious, nor as healthful. The many antioxidants in olive oil diminish over time.

I like to support small farmers and use oils produced by my friend Albert Katz at his ranch in California, but there are many other excellent olive oil producers. Taste as many as you can to educate your palate and see which ones you like best. California Olive Ranch is a good, modestly priced, and widely available oil that lists a harvest date.

Keep your oil away from the stove and don't set the bottle on a windowsill, no matter how pretty it looks. Heat and light are the enemies of its flavors.

VINEGAR

Acid is an essential component of cooking. Without it, food can taste flat and bland, but when acid is well balanced in a dish, the flavors are forthright and focused, not necessarily sharp, but bright, clear, and taut. My taste in vinegar skews slightly sweet. I find the flavors more complex and gentler, which pairs well with my style of cooking. The word "agrodolce" (Italian) or "agridulce" (Spanish) on a label indicates a sweet-sour vinegar.

Along with their olive oils, I really like the vinegars from KATZ Farm (see page 332). They are made with great care, mostly from late-harvest (sweet) grapes, and are beautifully balanced. Unio's agridulce vinegars from Spain are quite good, too, and an excellent value.

Vinegar lasts a long, long time and often improves with age. Just protect it from heat and light and keep it in its original bottle.

NUTS

For adding texture and flavor to a dish, nothing beats a nut. Roasted salted nuts are great for snacking, but when purchasing nuts for cooking with, you want to buy them raw and toast them yourself.

Freshness is especially critical when it comes to nuts. Because of their high oil content, they can easily go rancid. Buy them from a busy market with a high turnover. Choose walnut or pecan halves over pieces. Hazelnuts, which grow locally in Oregon, are a favorite of mine. They're sold out of their shells but covered in a thin papery brown skin. Some people boil or toast the nuts in order to remove the skins, but I don't bother. Most will fall away once you toast and chop the nuts, and hey, they're natural and probably highly nutritious.

Pistachios, another favorite nut, are sold both shelled and in the shell. They're relatively easy to shell, though you occasionally come upon a stubborn one. Shelled pistachios come at a premium, often three times the price of those in the shell.

Toasting nuts does wonders to coax out their flavor, and it's a step I urge you not to skip. Use a gentle heat—about 325°F (160°C) is good—stir them occasionally, and keep an eye on them. Nuts can go from browned to burnt in the time it takes to check your Instagram.

Nuts are high in oil content, which means they're more perishable than they look. Store them in the freezer and use within six months.

DRIED FRUIT

Sweetness is an underrated quality in savory food—just a little bit of it, particularly combined with an acid such as vinegar, can bring some unexpected deliciousness to a dish. Dried fruit like apricot and figs, dates, raisins, dried cherries, and cranberries are wonderful additions to a stew, salad, or braise.

Dried fruits have a long shelf life, so I buy them in bulk and store them in airtight jars. Rehydrating them before using is always a good idea. Warm them in a small pan with a bit of vinegar, wine, or water and let them steep until plump and tender.

CANNED TOMATOES

For acidity, body, umami, and straight-up flavor, canned tomatoes are an essential part of my pantry. I use them in pasta sauce (obviously), in soups, on pizzas, and as a liquid for braising vegetables and meats. At my restaurant, we use Stanislaus brand whole peeled tomatoes. They're grown in California and have a fantastic flavor and consistency. Because Stanislaus caters to the food-service industry, its products are rarely found in grocery stores, but they are available online. One caveat is that they come in 6.7-pound (2.92 kg) cans. But you can just use what you need right away and then freeze the rest in zip-top bags to have on hand for later. Two more readily available brands I like are Muir Glen Organic and Bianco DiNapoli. Canned tomato products will last in your pantry a good long time.

Tomato paste is the other canned (or tubed, or jarred) tomato product I recommend you keep on hand. It brings a rich, concentrated pure tomato taste without the additional liquid that comes with canned tomatoes. The trick to getting the most flavor out of tomato paste is to caramelize it first. Add it to a hot pan with olive oil and let it sizzle until it begins to darken and stick to the pan. After a few minutes, add a little water, wine, or stock to deglaze the pan.

Whenever you buy tomato products, pay attention to the labels, and skip over any that come with herbs or added seasonings. Pure tomato is all you want.

PRESERVED FISH

We are living in a golden age of canned fish. Check the shelves of your local specialty grocery and you're likely to find a range of wonderful products—pickled mussels, smoked oysters, octopus, and mackerel. Some of the best canned fish comes from Spain. Look for the José Gourmet brand with their whimsically illustrated boxes. I also like Ortiz tuna, as well as sardines from Matiz. I like to support Wild Planet and American Tuna, brands that are dedicated to sustainable tuna fishing.

Many canned fish also happen to be wildly nutritious—packed with healthful omega-3s!—and are quite often made with some of the most sustainable fish in the ocean, such as sardines and anchovies. They all make delicious, elegant additions to a salad or appetizer plate.

Anchovies are indispensable to me, as they are a flavor powerhouse. Their fishy aroma tends to disappear when added to a sauce, leaving behind only their delicious umami, so that even people who profess to hate anchovies often love dishes that are flavored with them. Oil-packed anchovy fillets are the easiest to use. Just blot them dry and you're good to go. Drape them over a salad or wrap one around a pickled pepper or green bean to serve with cocktails. Salt-packed whole anchovies require a little more effort. They need to have their spines removed and then get rinsed and soaked. Be sure to cover any salt-packed anchovies left in the tin with more salt so they don't dry out, and store them in the refrigerator.

FISH SAUCE

Not long ago, fish sauce was rarely used outside of Southeast Asian kitchens, but by now cooks of every stripe have discovered the magic of this powerful elixir. Made from fermented fish, it's essentially umami in a bottle. I add it to marinades and dressings and use it to season vegetables and meats. I find Red Boat brand to be nicely balanced. Three Crabs is another good brand.

An unopened bottle of fish sauce will last a couple of years. Open bottles should be stored in the refrigerator and used within one year.

PICKLES, OLIVES, AND CAPERS

Thanks to the iconic *Portlandia* skit, pickles and Portland (where I live) will forever be linked. I can live with that. The truth is that I'm unabashed in my love of just about anything fermented or brined.

I'm also always on the hunt for something salty, bright, and briny to season a dish with, and olives and capers provide just that. I like them in salads and pastas, or smashed and used in sauces to garnish grilled meats.

Pickles

Thanks to the popularity of artisan pickles, there are many wonderful brands to choose from. I like the whole kosher dills from Sonoma Brinery, the spicy pickled green beans from Rick's Picks, and the pickled curried cauliflower from McVicker Pickles.

Though they are pretty much a perfect snack, pickles also make a great ingredient for salads. Add a few pickled green beans to a leafy green salad and use some of the brine to make a vinaigrette. Pickled cauliflower tossed with boiled Yukon Golds and a few hard-cooked eggs makes a great potato salad.

Store open jars in the refrigerator.

Olives

The advent of the supermarket olive bar is in my view one of the best grocery innovations of the twentieth century. I've learned a lot about olives by browsing there. And though there are many kinds of olives to love, I tend to stick with these four:

Castelvetrano. You'll recognize these Sicilian olives by their shocking green color. They're meaty and buttery, and a great snacking olive.

Cerignola. These big green olives from Italy's Puglia region are mellow and sweet.

Taggiasca. Similar to Niçoise olives, these black olives from Liguria, Italy, are dense and delicious with a beautifully balanced taste.

Kalamata. This widely available black olive from Greece has a meaty texture and smoky, fruity flavor. It's a classic choice for tapenade and it goes especially well with brassicas like broccoli and cauliflower.

Store open containers in the refrigerator, where they will last a long time.

Capers

Considering their size, capers pack a whole lot of flavor. They're salty, yes, but vegetal, too, and a little bit sour. I find the flavor of salt-packed capers preferable to brined, but they do require soaking first to remove the excess salt. Kept in the refrigerator, they'll last for a long, long time.

CHILES: DRIED, PICKLED, AND PRESERVED

I'm a sucker for chiles, and I have a hard time resisting adding them to a dish. It's not just their heat, though I admit to being a spicy food fan. Chiles are fruity and floral, too, and I love the dimensions they bring to a dish. Today, we can buy chiles from all over the world: gochujang chile powder from Korea, Aleppo chiles from Syria, and Marash chiles from Turkey, in addition to wonderful products from Mexico, South America, China, and Italy, each one with its own character and unique flavors.

I find chiles de árbol to be the most versatile. The small red dried chiles are hot but not fiery and pair well with pretty much everything. I also find myself reaching for dried red chile flakes. If they're going in a cooked dish, I usually bloom them in warm oil at the start of cooking to bring out their flavor and soften them slightly. For salads and other cold dishes, I just sprinkle them on and find that the flavor blooms once I add an acid like vinegar or lemon juice.

I like the tang of pickled chiles like pepperoncini in salads and sandwiches. Oil-packed Calabrian chiles are another staple in my kitchen. I like to add them to red sauces, both hot and cold, chop them up as a garnish for pasta, and puree them into marinades and salad dressings.

Refrigerate any opened jars of pickled and preserved chiles. Dried chiles can be stored in your pantry or frozen for even longer storage.

CHEESE

There are few ingredients as versatile as cheese. More than just a great snack, cheese is a primary seasoning. I use cheese to balance salt, boost umami, and add rich, fatty flavor to a dish.

There was a time when most great cheeses came from Europe, but the boon in artisan cheese making in the United States over the past twenty years means that we now have many excellent cheeses made close to home. My best advice for buying cheese is to find a great cheese shop and make friends with the people behind the counter. A good cheesemonger will take their time to learn your preferences, offer tastes, and explain how and where the cheese was made and the best way to use and store it.

All cheeses live somewhere on the spectrum from hard to soft, with lots of variation along the way. Hard cheeses have a lower moisture content and undergo aging that gives them characteristic sharper, saltier flavors. Soft cheeses run the gamut from milky and mild to quite intense and stinky (hello, Époisses!).

For cooking, I rely most often on a handful of aged hard cheeses, and a few soft fresh ones.

Aged Cheeses

To store aged cheeses, wrap them in waxed paper; this allows them to breathe. If you only have plastic wrap on hand, use fresh wrap each time you rewrap it. Give it a dedicated spot in your refrigerator such as a drawer or its own plastic container where it won't absorb flavors from other strong-scented foods.

Parmigiano-Reggiano. Twelve months is just about the perfect age for this Italian icon, made from cow's milk. The flavors are balanced between sweet and salty, the texture is still a bit moist but grates beautifully. Older Parmesans are still delicious, but I like them best for snacking or as part of a cheese plate, rather than for grating over my pasta and shaving into salads. Save the rinds (you can collect them in a bag in the freezer) for adding deep umami to broths and soups.

SarVecchio Parmesan. This Wisconsin-made cow's-milk parmesan comes very close in flavor to the Italian-made cheese. It's less pricey than the import.

Pecorino Romano. When I want a cheese that's less sweet than Parmigiano, with a saltier, tangier punch, I pull out the Romano, a lightly aged sheep's-milk cheese. I especially love the way that it pairs with vegetable dishes and in salads.

Provolone. This Southern Italian cow's-milk cheese comes in two forms. Provolone dolce is aged for just two to three months. It has a sweet flavor and a pale yellow color. I prefer provolone picante, which is aged longer and has a sharper, spicier taste. It's a classic pizza cheese, but I like to use it in salads, too.

Fresh Cheeses

Milky, sweet fresh cheeses are pure luxury, and they're an easy way to add richness to a dish. I particularly love the way they pair with sweet-tart ingredients like tomatoes, fresh melon, and stone fruits. All fresh cheeses are at their best shortly after they're made. Plan on using them the day that you buy them, if possible. Keep them cold in the refrigerator in the liquid in the original containers.

Mozzarella. Mozzarella and ricotta (below) are the products of a single process. Mozzarella is made from heated fresh milk, while ricotta is formed from cooking the leftover whey (*ricotta* means "twice cooked"). Fresh mozzarella is wonderful in salads, and I love the way it melts into pasta and baked dishes, though too much heat can turn fresh mozzarella rubbery. To mitigate that, drain fresh mozzarella on paper towels for about an hour before using it.

Ricotta. I use fine-curd ricotta primarily in cooked dishes, layering it into lasagna and other baked pasta. It's also lovely spread on a thick layer of toast and topped with jam or honey. Draining it in a paper coffee filter or a colander lined with cheesecloth will help concentrate the flavor.

Burrata. Creamy, delicate burrata is mozzarella's rich cousin. This highly perishable, tender cheese is essentially mozzarella filled with cream and soft curds.

BUTTER

Good butter starts with good cream. It should be sweet-smelling and -tasting with a smooth texture. European-style butter has less water and more fat, as much as 86 percent butterfat, compared to 80 percent butterfat in American-style butter, and is ideal for pastry-making.

Cultured butter has a wonderful tangy, almost cheese-like flavor, the product of lactic acids that are produced when the cream is inoculated with live bacteria. Cultured butter is delicious when spread on a biscuit or used to finish a sauce, but it is not the best choice of butter for baking.

I prefer unsalted butter, but if salted butter is what you have on hand, use it and just adjust the amount of salt you use for seasoning the recipe.

It's okay to keep a day or two's worth of butter on the counter so that you're not trying to spread cold butter on your toast. Its high fat and low water content mean that butter is less attractive to bacteria than other dairy products. But beyond a day or two, keep butter in the refrigerator to keep it from going rancid. Butter also freezes well for up to six months.

CREAM

The amount of butterfat contained in cream determines how well it will whip and how stable it will be. Higher-fat cream has a better flavor, has a richer texture, and doesn't curdle as easily when used in cooking. Cream must be at least 18 percent butterfat but can go as high as 40 percent. In comparison, whole milk is just 3.25 percent butterfat.

Ultra-pasteurized cream is heated at a higher temperature for a shorter amount of time than regular pasteurized cream. More bacteria are killed off, allowing for a longer shelf life, but ultra-pasteurizing makes cream harder to whip and producers sometimes add an emulsifier to help stabilize it. It also has a "cooked" flavor that I don't love. Look for simply pasteurized heavy cream, sometimes labeled "whipping cream." Keep in the refrigerator and use within a week. Half-and-half is for coffee. Don't use it as a substitute for cream.

CRÈME FRAÎCHE

True crème fraîche is made from unpasteurized cream that thickens naturally from the bacteria it contains. What we call crème fraîche is actually pasteurized cream that's lightly fermented to help it thicken and give it a wonderful tangy, nutty flavor. It's easy to make a version of crème fraîche at home by adding a bit of buttermilk to fresh cream and letting it stand at room temperature for about twelve hours. Once it's thickened, it should be stored in the refrigerator.

YOGURT

When it comes to yogurt, I keep it simple—plain whole-milk Greek yogurt is all I need, though "non-Greek" is versatile as well. Use it for dips, as a marinade, or to stir into sauces; just make sure it doesn't come to a boil or it will curdle. Yogurt will keep in the refrigerator for about two weeks.

Sources

Alnd to share some whole-grain love . . . This list represents some of the key growers and producers who make my cooking good and my life happy. Look for farmers, millers, and other local producers in your own area to get the freshest grains, grown as close to your table as possible, and then support them!

Anson Mills
ansonmills.com

Arrowhead Mills
arrowheadmills.com

Blue Bird Grain Farms
bluebirdgrainfarms.com

Camas Country Mill
camascountrymill.com

Central Milling
centralmilling.com

Hayden Flour Mills
haydenflourmills.com

Lonesome Stone Milling
lonesomestonemilling.com

Organic Grains
organicgrains.com

Small's Family Farm
smallsfamilyfarm.com

Sunrise Flour Mill
sunriseflourmill.com

Weatherbury Farm
weatherburyfarm.com

Wild Hive Farm
wildhivefarm.com

BOB'S RED MILL (WWW.BOBSREDMILL.COM)

I also admire Bob's Red Mill, founded in Oregon by Bob Moore and now owned by its employees. They produce and/or sell a head-spinning array of whole grains and whole-grain flours (along with seeds, herbs, and a few more items). Bob's does mail order, but their products are quite widely available at grocery stores in the United States.

OTHER PRODUCTS

These aren't grains, but they're good products. I love these condiments and other essentials of a well-stocked pantry. Not all these companies sell direct to consumers, but you may find them in your local grocery store or, with a bit of sleuthing, for sale online through third-party vendors.

Duke's mayonnaise
dukesmayo.com

Gina Marie cream cheese
sierranevadacheese.com

Jacobsen Salt Co.
jacobsensalt.com

KATZ Farm
Olive oils and vinegars (and more)
katzfarm.com

Mama Lil's
pickled peppers
mamalils.com

Martin's Famous Pastry
Shoppe, Inc.
For the best potato rolls to use
for your Super Grain and
Veggie Burgers (page 43)
potatorolls.com

Stanislaus
Alta Cucina whole peeled plum
tomatoes, the best canned
tomatoes for pizza sauce
stanislaus.com

Acknowledgments

I want to thank Martha Holmberg for making this book possible. Ashley Marti, for doing what she does best and adding layers on top of that. AJ Meeker for all the laughs and photos. David Alvarado for flying in an airplane to get shots of grain fields. To everyone at Artisan and Workman Publishing, especially Lia Ronnen, Judy Pray, and Allison McGeehon, for putting up with me and so much more.

I would like to thank Lucinda Scala Quinn, because I forgot to thank her in my first book and our brief meeting changed my life. I want to thank Nora Mace for making the world taste better and helping out with so many recipes in this book. I want to thank Daniel Green for his laughter and knowledge of bread making and so much more. To JoMarie Pitino for changing the pasta game at Ava Gene's and in the city of Portland.

I want to thank the entire Submarine crew for eating all the foods and putting up with a mountain of grains and flours everywhere. I want to thank pizza because life without pizza would not be life. **—Joshua McFadden**

Thanks, first, to Joshua McFadden for inviting me on another fun, crazy, delicious ride. I'm always honored to be your partner.

To Lia Ronnen, Judy Pray, Allison McGeehon, and all the other cool and talented people at Artisan, thank you for making me feel like I'm part of the Artisan family, and thank you for producing another gorgeous book for us.

Thanks to my good friend and talented cook Helen Baldus for her excellent recipe testing, always complete with questions and insights that make the recipes better.

And everlasting thanks to John D'Anna, for cooking through this book with me, focusing his laser palate on the recipes, supporting me in all the ways I need, and for keeping us happy and healthy with nonstop batches of Muesli with Buckwheat, Dried Fruit, Coconut, and Turmeric (page 132). **—Martha Holmberg**

Index

Note: Page references in *italics* indicate photographs. "INS" refers to the four foldout sections.

Recipe Index

P.S.
Eat more grains, keep them whole.

About the Authors

Joshua McFadden

Joshua McFadden is the founder of Submarine Hospitality in Portland, Oregon. He owns and manages Ava Gene's, Cicoria, and Tusk restaurants. In between running the restaurants, he is bringing new life to Berny Farm, a historic fifty-acre farm in Springdale, Oregon, with the goal of creating an agricultural complex that will host collaborations between farming, food, and design. His first book, *Six Seasons: A New Way with Vegetables*, also written with Martha Holmberg, won a James Beard Award in 2018.

Martha Holmberg

Martha Holmberg is a food writer who cowrote, with Joshua McFadden, *Six Seasons: A New Way with Vegetables*—a 2018 recipient of the James Beard Award. Holmberg studied cooking in Paris at École de Cuisine La Varenne and stayed in that wonderful city for a few years to work as a private chef. She was the editor in chief of *Fine Cooking* magazine for a decade, followed by five years as the food editor of the *Oregonian* newspaper in Portland, Oregon. Holmberg has authored or coauthored nine books, including *The Bar Book*, with Jeffrey Morgenthaler, and her own books *Puff, Crepes, Plums,* and *Modern Sauces*. She is an avid though undisciplined tomato grower and, in between testing whole-grain recipes, is working on a tomato cookbook.